STORIES
OF
TRADITIONAL
NAVAJO
LIFE
AND
CULTURE

AŁK'IDÁÁ'
YÉ̜E̜K'EHGO
DINÉ
KÉÉDAHAT'ÍNÉ̜E̜
BAA
NAHANE'

Ałk'idą́ą́' yę́ę́k'ehgo Diné Kéédahat'inę́ę́ Baa Nahane'

Hastói dóó Sáanii Naadiin Naaki Yilt'éego Hane' Ádayiilaa

Editor
BRODERICK H. JOHNSON, Tempe and Tsaile, Arizona
(Director, Navajo Community College Press)

Illustrators
RAYMOND JOHNSON and HOKE DENETSOSIE
Artists on the staff of Navajo Community College

Composition, Design, Layout
NAVAJO COMMUNITY COLLEGE PRESS, Tempe and Tsaile, Arizona

Printing
IMPERIAL LITHO/GRAPHICS, INC., Phoenix, Arizona

Binding
ROSWELL BOOKBINDING, Phoenix, Arizona

Stories
of
Traditional Navajo Life and Culture

by
Twenty-two
Navajo Men and Women

Publication of this book was made possible by a grant from the Bureau of Indian Affairs, Contract No. N00-C-1420-7155. The volume is part of a series of tribally-controlled studies, some of which are developed under contract with the Bureau.

Published
by
NAVAJO COMMUNITY COLLEGE PRESS
Tsaile, Navajo Nation, Arizona 86556
1977

LIBRARY OF CONGRESS CATALOGING IN PUBLICATION DATA

Main entry under title:

Stories of traditional Navajo life and culture.

1. Navajo Indians—Biography. 2. Navajo Indians—Social
life and customs. I. Johnson, Broderick H.
E99.N3S84   940'.004'97   77-22484
ISBN 0-912586-23-0

International Standard Book Number 0-912586-23-0
Library of Congress Catalog Card Number 77-22484

FIRST EDITION
Printed in the United States of America

With parts of a corn stalk and some yucca tied together the Navajos made brushes for writing on the walls of the canyons.

In This Book...

THE REGENTS OF NAVAJO COMMUNITY COLLEGE

TO THE NAVAJO PEOPLE —
AND ESPECIALLY TO THE MANY
WHO REVERE THEIR TRADITIONS,
FAITH, LIFE AND CULTURE. . .

This Book is Dedicated

Foreword

THIS VOLUME CONTAINS PERSONAL, *true accounts by 22 elderly Navajo men and women, most of whom tell in detail about their training, from earliest years to adulthood, in hogans scattered over various parts of their Reservation which, the size of West Virginia, is by far the largest in the United States. The stories focus upon traditional life and culture and education, going back, as one 96-year-old narrator does, more than nine decades. The youngest interviewee was born 56 years ago.*

The accounts, which vary in nature and substance, also discuss legends, philosophy and some history—in most cases bringing the action and comments up to today.

The life stories and expressions of opinion were recorded in the Navajo language and then translated into English—a laborious task. Thus, the true Navajo thinking and "flavor" were preserved and the Navajo viewpoint was retained. In other words, insights and narrative matter are published here the way that the Navajos believe and tell. The result naturally is not pure and specific history. On the other hand, it is authentic autobiographical material—not stories heard, interpreted, published and presented by non-Indian sociologists, anthropologists, educators, researchers and historians.

A highly important point is that the volume is one of many publications developed by the Navajo Community College Press in accordance with the desire of the College's Board of Regents that books—and other materials—be produced about, for and by the Navajo Indians.

Another compelling reason for developing this publication is that, as far as can be determined, no other work has covered the subject of TRADITIONAL Navajo culture and education—that is, from the purely Navajo point of view. And it should be borne in mind that traditional patterns even today have a significant place in the life of many Navajo families on the Reservation, especially those not living in the more centralized communities. Times are changing, however. Modes of living have been altered by "progress," and many members of the younger generation have lost, or are turning away from, the old and respected life ways, a trend which is deplored by the older Navajos.

A number of the 22 stories express concern regarding the habits, inclinations, attitudes and actions of many young members of the Tribe. Elders feel that undesirable traits have been acquired through contact with the dominant society and through television, modern literature, the generally low quality of the cinema, the nation-wide deterioration of family life (which is affecting the Navajos) and the growing lack of respect for parental guidance, as well as other factors which are the opposite of the traditional Navajo regard for their basic culture and their close family, outfit and clan relationships. Several narrators fear that many Navajos, and other Indians, are losing their identity.

Navajo Community College and its Press are proud to add another "first" to a series of major publications, most of which, thus far, are truly Navajo. The word "first" means the first time that much of the material has been put into print AS THE NAVAJOS TELL IT. The College considers it highly important that the thinking of the older generation be recorded so that, as time goes by, traditional life styles, education and culture will not be lost.

B.H.J.

May, 1977

Acknowledgments

MORE THAN FOUR YEARS HAVE PASSED *since plans for this book were initiated, and many persons—a greater number than can be named here—have worked at various times in the numerous stages between preliminary discussions, interviewing elderly Navajos, recording their "stories" in the Navajo language and the final step—delivery of the volumes from the bindery. For a lengthy period in the middle of the four-year span it was necessary to put the project aside, and no progress was made; but its completion was considered highly desirable as one of a series of books published by the Navajo Community College Press which authentically depict Navajo life, culture, legends, traditions, tragedies, history, education and hopes for the future.*

In attempting to acknowledge the parts played in making the volume possible, great credit must be given to the Bureau of Indian Affairs for its interest and especially for a substantial grant without which the publication would not have been possible, and the desire of the Navajo Tribe to have another book about, for and by its own people could not have been fulfilled.

Heartfelt thanks also are extended to the 22 elderly Navajos—men and women—who spent considerable time and thought in taping their contributions, ranging from seven to 78 typewritten pages (after translation). Their names appear in the Table of Contents, as well as at the beginning of each account.

Among the Navajo-speaking interviewers were Kee Jackson, Nia Francisco, Leonard Begay and Hoke Denetsosie, the last of whom also recounted his life story (pages

73 through 104) and was one of the book's two artists. The interviewers traveled in good and bad weather, over paved roads and over narrow sandy, rocky and muddy ones, sometimes to remote areas of the 16,000-square-mile Reservation.

Casey Allison, Kee Jackson, Dolly Tabaha and Henry Brown translated the 22 recorded accounts.

Typing, from original handwritten translations through the final manuscripts, was done by a number of persons, including Miss Allison, Laura Begay, Claudia Roanhorse, Susie Yazzie, Karen Jones, JoAnn Hicks and Marsha Deem.

Mrs. Deem and Miss Hicks also did the typesetting (composition). Then, the latter assisted the editor-director with design-layout of the book, and the former prepared the camera-ready pages.

Two Navajos to whom we are especially grateful, and who contributed immensely, are Ray Johnson and Mr. Denetsosie—the artists who produced all of the beautiful and appropriate illustrations. Their work is significant, indeed, adding immeasurably to the value of the book. The photographs were taken by Mr. Denetsosie and a fellow Navajo, Melvin McKenzie.

Our deep gratitude also goes to members of the College's Navajo Board of Regents and Administration who favored the concept of the book and continued to support it—through many problems—to fruition.

Finally—sincere thanks to all others who encouraged or shared in the labor of love in making this volume possible.

B.H.J.

NAVAJO EDUCATIONAL GOALS

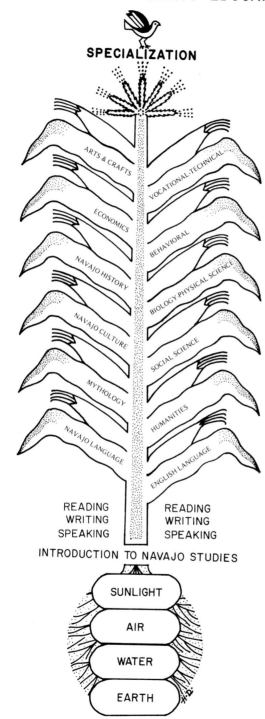

SPECIALIZATION

ARTS & CRAFTS

VOCATIONAL-TECHNICAL

ECONOMICS

BEHAVIORAL

NAVAJO HISTORY

BIOLOGY-PHYSICAL SCIENCE

NAVAJO CULTURE

SOCIAL SCIENCE

MYTHOLOGY

HUMANITIES

NAVAJO LANGUAGE

ENGLISH LANGUAGE

READING
WRITING
SPEAKING

READING
WRITING
SPEAKING

INTRODUCTION TO NAVAJO STUDIES

SUNLIGHT

AIR

WATER

EARTH

A complete total Navajo understands the brotherhood of man and can cope with both cultures—thus being able to use his skills and his understanding for the benefit of his people. . .

SPECIALIZATION

Master Craftsmen
Professional Reputation
Art
Professional Skill
Technical Skill
Individual career

PLANNING

Implementation
Deliberation
Habits
Practical Wisdom
Civic Virtue
Career Planning
Self-Diagnosis

REASONING

Career Thinking
Wisdom
Insight
Research
Inquiry
Independent Judgment

FOUNDATION

Roots
Support
Self-Establishment
Motivation
Attitude
Self-Respect
Self-Identity

Other Major Publications of Recent Years by the
Navajo Community College Press Include:

PAPERS ON NAVAJO CULTURE AND LIFE
NAVAJO HISTORY, Vol. 1
NAVAJO STUDIES AT NAVAJO COMMUNITY COLLEGE
NAVAJO STORIES OF THE LONG WALK PERIOD
NAVAJO LIVESTOCK REDUCTION: A NATIONAL DISGRACE
THE NAVAJOS' LONG WALK FOR EDUCATION
OUR FRIENDS—THE NAVAJOS
(Revised edition of "Papers on Navajo Culture and Life")

_____

To be published in 1977. . .
A POLITICAL HISTORY OF THE NAVAJO TRIBE

To be published in 1978. . .
BITTER ROOTS
(A history of Indian education)

Shiprock Peak, as seen from the southeast.

Max Hanley

FROM SHIPROCK, NEW MEXICO, toward the west is a place called Red Rock Trading Post; then, farther to the west is a spot called Cove, Arizona; and, from there to the northwest is an area known as Line of Cottonwoods. At that place there is water flowing from Carizzo Mountain; also, at Rocks Struck Apart, there is another stream, and, right at the point where the waters meet, is Line of Cottonwoods. The place is covered mostly by sagebrush, with red cliffs around. I had relatives who resided there. They lived right on the state line. On one side was New Mexico, and on the other was Arizona.

Once, near Shiprock, a Yei-be-chai dance was planned. It was in the fall. Everybody from the house left for the ceremonial, except an aunt of mine who still is living, and my mother. They were the only ones at home taking care of the sheep. I had a grandfather named Mr. Brady who arrived at our place in the evening. He lived at Round Rock, Arizona. He was on his way to the Yei-be-chai and was planning to spend the night at our place. It was in 1898.

That night I was born. They had a sheepskin prepared for me. My aunt later told me, "You were born right on the state line." Then I asked her, "Which side did my head rest on—and my feet?" And she answered, "Your head was in Arizona while your feet were in New Mexico." So, having my head in Arizona was the reason why to this day I have lived mostly in Arizona. After I was born I was wrapped in the sheepskin and placed on the west side of the fire in the center of the hogan, with my head toward the flames because they wanted warmth on my head. They used to do that; also, they made sure that the baby's head would not be out of shape. My mother must have overheated my brains because I'm not a fast thinker today, and I blame her for it. But most Navajos don't do that anymore. I did not eat for three or four days; but, instead, I drank the juice of the white part of the juniper bast (inner bark), also corn pollen and water. After four days I could drink milk.

My clan is Red Running Into Water *(Táchíí nii*—on my mother's side), born FOR the Cove of the Mountain clan *(Dziłtł' ahnii*—on my father's side). However, the Sleeping Rock clan *(Tsénahabiłnii)* and the Red Bottom clan *(Tł'aashchi'i)* have been close to me and very helpful and kind. I am many years of age—born in the year 1898.

I was told that, when I was four months old, one day during the winter I was being held outside in the warm sun when the sheep were brought home. I was looking at two little billy goats. They were rearing up, with their horns clashing, when suddenly I laughed my first laugh. Right away my family said, "Let's have a little feast for him." (The reason why there is a dinner at the time of a child's first laugh is because in the future he or she will not be selfish.) My parents butchered a goat; then cut it into portions and gave much to the neighbors who had heard the news. I was helped in passing out the mutton and some salt to the people, with my mother holding things together by pressing my hands. Right away the people built fires and started charcoaling the meat. It all was done for me.

Later, when I reached the age of four years, there was a place called Lying Horizontal on Top of One Another which is west of where I was born, and I realized that we were living there. (East Sheepskin Point, in the cove of Where the Water Splashes Out is the place where we spent the winter. This I remember.)

One time, when we still were living there during the spring, my mother, young sister and I were sleeping in the hogan. We had a mean black dog with a white collar. He slept across from us, and something came in the hogan during the night. At that time, there were no doors on hogans—just blankets that covered the doorways. Later, we found that it was a Skin Walker; I don't know whether the skin, which covered a man, was of a coyote or a wolf. But when the Skin Walker came in the black dog heard him and jumped him. Then the dog started howling while fighting. The neighbors' dogs heard the noise, and a whole bunch of them came and attacked the Skin Walker. They all howled very loudly. My mother and I wakened, and I sprang up. She was at the door, holding the blanket under the moonlight. The dogs howled for quite a while, but by that time the noise was down in an arroyo close by. Then my mother took down the blanket, threw some things on it, wrapped them, and we took off over the hill to where my grandmother lived.

There were two hogans. Between our hogan and my grandmother's there was a sheep corral. When we arrived at the place people were having a shoe game. There were many of them. Right away my mother told the reason for coming over, and we stayed there for the night. Early the next morning my uncles and cousins and many others, who also were spending the winter at that location, started to track down the Skin Walker. They started from the hogan where the dogs attacked. From there they went to the edge of the cliff of the arroyo and to the canyon where the dogs had left him. They continued down to Line of Rugged Rocks. Then they went to Many Ghosts Area and on to Streak of Pointed White Ashes where there were a lot of fallen rocks. Through this place our people tried to follow the tracks of the Skin Walker, but they could not do it.

19

That is how it was told, and I remember the incident.

The following year when I was at a place called Ugly Canyon, near Sweetwater, Arizona, there was a stream coming out of Ugly Canyon Arroyo, and I took notice of where the Navajos used to plant crops. That summer I lived there, and my mother told me, "Now you are five years old and have some knowledge; from here on start counting your own years of age and see how far you can count."

I said, "Okay." Also, she said, "I want you to herd the sheep up the mountain and return them home just when the sun is setting." I said "Okay" again, and I began to take the sheep out. I herded them up a low mountainside. There was a clear area with little hills here and there, and at those places I walked around while the sheep were grazing quietly. I kept watching the sun until it was close to sunset; then I started herding them back. All of a sudden I saw something moving behind a hill—something dark. I thought, "What is trying to steal from me?" Then I got behind a bush, from where I tried to observe, and when the figure came out in the open—I saw that it was my mother. The reason she had come was because she wanted to know what I would do. By that time the sun had almost set, and we both took the sheep home. From then on, beginning at the age of five, I always was sent with the sheep.

I was not brought up in the middle of riches, except for sheep, horses and cattle. It was my grandfather, Mr. Brady, whom we visited when I was young, at the place called Line of Rugged Rocks, where he lived. He had some pigs, down in a hollow, where they were running back and forth. That was the first time I saw pigs. I was six or seven years old.

Time went along, and we were living again where we usually spent the winter. The weather was warmer there, and I was seven or eight years old. I was herding sheep one day with my mother because the flocks were large. My mother was a distance from me. I had a dog named Fuzzy Face with a rope around its neck, while the other end was around my waist. The reason I did it was because I was afraid of coyotes. Sometimes, all of a sudden, a coyote would be chasing a sheep, and, if the sheep ran into difficulty of some kind, he would be dragged off. That was why I was scared.

At this particular time, I was sitting on a point under a shady juniper tree, and the dog was next to me. My mother was quite a distance away, with the sheep that were grazing in her area. Just then I heard a noise and the dog jumped up. I looked down into a rocky area where a sheep was running. A coyote was biting it while running along by its side. The dog saw it and took off, with me right behind him. We ran down the hill leaving clouds of dust. Fuzzy Face ran quite a distance with me until I fell under a small juniper. The dog turned back, I untied the rope from my waist and the dog took off after the coyote again while I sat spitting out dirt. I guess all this time my mother had been watching me. She told me later there was a cloud of dust around me.

Another year went by, and, one day, an uncle, whose name was Mr. Yellowman, and I were herding the sheep. It was in the spring at the place called Lying Horizontal on Top of One Another, in the mountains. There were quite a few cattle there which belonged to my mother. Some of the cattle had calves, one of which was sleeping under a tree when I came across it. Its white face was cute. I looked around, but there were no other animals. Just over the hill, though, others must have been lying in the shade. I knelt down and patted the calf's nose and forehead because it looked like it was sleeping. Then it bawled real loud, which scared me; and it started running after me, still bellowing. So I raced ahead of the calf toward an arroyo. I guess the mother and others heard it, but I had run quite a distance when I heard sounds from the mother cow from the other side of the hill. I looked back and saw her running after me, bellowing. Then I really took off and ran like a jack rabbit. I saw a bunch of bushes, but it turned out that two bulls were behind them.

20

One bull was lying just behind the bush that I threw myself into and I almost bumped him. The bull jumped up. I almost fainted, but, instead, I fell into a rocky ditch where I stayed for a little while. The calf just passed on ahead. Then I ran in the ditch until I came to a ledge which I crawled under. All I could hear were dogs barking on top. Then I cautiously came out, and, when I looked for the cattle, they were 'way across on the other side of the field.

After another year or two had passed and I was 10 or 11 years old, I was herding sheep one day with my younger sister who was mature by that time. It was in the spring, and we came across an eagle's nest in a canyon. The eagles were there every spring to hatch and feed their young. I would herd the sheep back to the place and observe. From the top of a ledge I would try to catch an adult, but with no success. They would fly back and forth across the canyon. Then, when I herded the sheep down into the canyon, they would fly around above me. When I would try to catch one from on top, they would fly down into the canyon.

One hot day, as we herded the sheep, I had a long rope which I tied to a tree trunk. I told my sister to hold onto it because I planned to swing down over the canyon edge, with a bunch of tin cans tied together. I expected to shake them and make the young eagles come out of their nest while they were not yet strong enough to fly. The eagle mother and eagle father were not around, but soon one of them came flying back, and started bothering us by charging rapidly past. Our folks had said that an eagle is dangerous once it starts doing that. I knew it myself, because when an eagle saw a rabbit it would circle around for quite a while. Then it would go into a nose dive, and I would think, "I wonder what happened to the rabbit." When it would take aim at the rabbit sounds from the attack sometimes could be heard. Then it would circle around for a while again. If it flew off, I would run over to where it had made the attack, and the rabbit would be lying there with blood coming out of its nose or ears, and it would still be kicking.

When an eagle acts like that you are not supposed to bother it, I had been told; so I usually didn't touch the rabbit, but just looked at it. Now I knew that what I was doing was dangerous, but, mostly, I was interested in getting a young eagle for a pet. One of the adults really started attacking us; and, to stop its charging, we picked branches off a piñon tree and threw them at the bird. That caused it to fly higher and not get close to us; so we gathered a pile of sticks

21

for our protection. The rope had been tied to the tree, and my sister was holding it as I tied the other end around my waist. The only problem was that the eagle kept charging; but one of us always would throw a stick at it. Pretty soon, though, there were two eagles, which caused a big problem for us. Every time I tried to climb down my sister would yell, "Here comes one again." So I never did go down; but, from the top of the canyon, we just shook the tin cans— but the young eagles never came out. I think there were two or three of them. We just gave up.

The sheep had wandered off while we were busy with the eagles; and, because it was hot, we were real thirsty. We set off looking for the sheep, and we found them quite a distance away under some trees. We were so thirsty that we started taking the sheep back to the corral, and we herded them to the water in the arroyo at home by late afternoon.

We knew that owls had a nest in the arroyo; so we turned the sheep in that direction. Two young owls had gotton out of the nest, and we started bothering them. We caught one just as the mother and father started charging at us, making clacking sounds with their beaks as they passed. Because I had a bow and arrow along, I was wearing a bow guard made of leather. The young owl had sharp claws. I picked it up by the neck and set it on my bow guard, which it grasped tightly with its claws. It's a good thing it did not grasp my bare arm because it would have caused an injury. I tried to let it loose from my arm, but I couldn't do it. Pretty soon its claws started to go through the leather—those claws were really strong. My sister and I got a stick and tried to lift its claws, but we couldn't do it. Then we both started to be scared. If the owl's claws had been on my flesh I would have been hurt pretty badly.

I started to think, "How will I get free?" Suddenly, I remembered an incident that happened to me when I was very young. We were taking a herd to a sheep dipping when we came upon a pond. A small prairie dog was swimming in it. Without a second thought I reached for the animal, and I caught it; but it bit my finger. It was hanging on to my flesh so hard that each time I tried to get loose by pulling, it made my flesh pull with it. Without thinking, I hit its head, then pulled its jaws apart and got my hand free. It was this incident that I remembered. I think it had been two or three years since it had happened. So, I picked up a stick and hit the owl on the head. It lost consciousness, but still had its claws in my arm.

We started putting sticks under the claws until I could be free of its clutching. Meanwhile, the mother and father owls still kept bothering us. We hit him (the little owl) to death. Then I said, "Boy, it's dangerous! Besides, his feathers are still small and tender and can't be used for feathers on my arrows."

Two more years went by (maybe I was 12 or 13); and, at that time, there were wild donkeys in the desert-like areas. They would be

The setting of the Teec Nos Pos boarding school in Arizona, with Carrizo Mountain forming the background to the southwest.

23

rounded up and roped. Wild horses were common, too. A gray donkey with a white face was roped for me; he must have been about two years old. The donkey was just like a horse—frisky. He was saddled and ridden until he was well-trained, and pretty soon I rode him while herding sheep. He became very gentle. When he was three years old he was quite big, and I would pinch him on the shoulder to make him start to buck. I thought that I would train him in bucking. This I did, and soon I mastered riding him while he was bucking. I would whittle a twig to use on him, poking between his shoulders. He would jump and start to buck, at first, maybe just two times; then he would buck maybe three or even four times. I could handle him well and would not fall off.

Sometimes, when I brought the sheep back at noon there would be a number of ladies at the hogan because the season was summer or fall when the crops were ripe. They (the women) would be grinding corn for corn bread. I would be a little distance off, watching them. I could hear laughter, but I didn't know what they were talking about. One time I got the idea of showing off in front of them by making my donkey buck. Just when they were putting the bread in the pit and laughter rose up again, I poked the donkey, and it started bucking. The women all ran into a brush shelter—one of the ladies fell into the corn meal. I let the animal buck with me a little way off; then, acting big, I jumped off easily and tied him to a post. Some of the ladies were shouting at me because they were upset. Others were just laughing—especially about the one who had fallen into the corn meal. After a while I went behind the hogan and sat there laughing.

Having a bucking donkey, I showed off quite a bit, especially whenever children would visit me. The animal had started to become a little mean once it started bucking; so, whenever the children would see me riding the donkey, they would be scared. I was the oldest and tallest of a number of children who belonged to aunts and uncles of mine.

A few more years went by, maybe two (and I was probably 15), when we moved up to Carrizo Mountain. We lived against the mountain at a place called Arrival of Navajo Man. At that location the weather was cool and beautiful. It was in the forest; the grass was nice and green, with lots of pretty flowers.

One of my aunts and I were herding sheep one day when we came upon a beehive. The honeycomb was in one of the old dried-up trees. It was real noticeable. The only reason we killed bees was for their honey. Sometimes we just barely got a teardrop from a honeycomb, or, maybe a part of it. This we would eat. About the one we came across this time, we wondered, "How shall we get the honey?" Then we picked some jimson weed and started hitting the bees with it. We said, "Let's hit all of them away; then we can get some honey." At first, there were only a few flying around, which we were hitting. Then I guess we got them all mad, and the ones that we had knocked down were getting up again. Pretty soon there were a lot. One of them flew at an upper eyelid and stung me. It was in the late afternoon. I didn't think it had stung me that much until the eye swelled and looked like a red puffball. All this time we tried to get the honeycomb but finally had to give up because of the bees guarding it.

By that time my eye was swollen shut. We brought the sheep home by evening, and my relatives asked, "What happened to you?"

I said, "Nothing is wrong with me."

They went on, "Where's your eye? What happened to your eye?"

"It's under my skin," I replied.

I guess I had a bad habit of speaking out in any way I wanted to, ever since I was young. And people used to tell me, "You said it that way."

This time I didn't notice how I spoke; it seemed to me like I had talked perfectly. It was then that my aunt said, "We were bothering bees at a place and one stung him when they swarmed around us."

"I'll bet you were disturbing the beehive," someone said.

"Yes," was my reply, "because we saw a lot of honey in an old dried-up tree, and we wanted to get it."

They started laughing at us, and one said, "You two would do it."

After a while my mother examined the eye closely, and she found the bee's stinger still sticking in my upper lid. She tried to take it out, and that wasn't tough, but it was half broken off. From it my face was all swollen. It had a glossy look. Ever since then I have been afraid of bees. Whenever I see one flying by, I avoid it by a far distance.

25

At that time, how was I dressed? Did I wear shoes? No, I had none. Sometimes my family would make moccasins for me from buckskin. Cowhide was used for the bottoms, after it was tanned. But they never lasted long on me. They would get ripped very quickly. Maybe they would last as long as a month or more. My aunts were the ones who made the moccasins, but my mother also knew how to make them. The tops were of deerskin, dyed. The sole was the cowhide. So deerskin and cowhide, sewed together, made my footwear. Many times I would go barefooted, and the bottoms of my feet were like leather. They were rough and hard. When I wanted to build a campfire, I would strike a match on the heel of my foot; the match would make a striking sound and light up. I'll bet the soles of my feet were like sandpaper.

In those days there were hardly any fabrics for clothes. From flour sacks I would ask that shirts be made for me. The crisscross design of wheat would be on the back. These I really liked, and I wore them while herding sheep. Other sacks were made into jeans, with slits up the sides. These I wore during the summer while herding. It was during the winter that heavier blue jeans usually were better. They were bought for me. Also, when I was very cold, I wore something warm as underwear. There were no coats. Instead, blankets were used. Lambskins or sheepskins were sewed together, just the right size for me, and I wore the garment under the blanket, which was really warm. That way I herded sheep.

My hair was long, and my bun in the back was big. Whenever I washed my hair, the length of it was down below my waist. My late aunt (the youngest then) was the one who generally took care of my hair. It often would come untied; and she was the one who usually mended my moccasins. My late grandmother also mended my moccasins and combed my hair.

I also had pierced ears; and my earrings were of turquoise, about the size of one's thumb. I don't know how or when I received them, but I already was wearing them when I was young. That's why I have earrings. A red cloth was used for a headband to prevent hair from straggling behind my ears.

One of those years, a man came to visit us from Lukachukai. I herded sheep with him in the winter. At that time the rams were not separated from the ewes. Every year, lambing season was in the summer and also in the winter. The number of sheep never would go down; it always would be about the same. I had five uncles, and every time one or two of them would come to visit, my late grandma would butcher one or maybe two sheep for them. Or, if three or more came, three sheep might be butchered. The sheep's head always would be given to me, along with the breast part and the feet. They always would be saved for me; and, because of this, I was not too stingy with having the sheep butchered.

Herding sheep was my main chore. Sometimes I herded with my younger sister; at other times it would be with one of my uncles—the youngest one. Otherwise, it would be with my grandmother. Whenever I herded with my grandmother, she would teach me songs—like

My mother used flour sacks to make shirts and jeans for me, and the pretty designs showed in various places on my clothes.

26

the sheep song or the donkey song. I thought I was a fast runner, and I would ask her to race with me. At first, she would outrun me. I guess I was quite young then. Later, I would outrun her by quite a distance because she was getting older and I was growing bigger and stronger.

Flour was brought from somewhere, but it was not like the flour of today. It was yellow. The sacks had a design of crosswise wheat stems, which I thought was pretty. The flour was not brought often, maybe just every month. Corn was the main food I grew up on. From it were made corn meal, tortillas, kiki (paper bread), *kineesh bizhii* (dumplings), blue bread and corn cooked underground; also Navajo cakes. There were *nanoo yeshii* (pumpkins), too.

When it became cold in the late fall, the first snow never would be forgotten because it was the thing that young people had to roll in. The exercise always was stressed to me by my uncles, as it was to my relatives who were children of my aunts and uncles. The first snowfall sometimes would be as deep as one foot because in those days it used to snow a lot. (In the summertime there was much rain.) We were told, "Be sure and roll in the snow," whenever it would snow during the night. At the break of dawn, a fire was made; then we would be herded outside, with no clothes on, to roll in the snow. Once we did this, we ran back inside; and we had to do it four times. I had grown uncles and others who were my grandfathers; and it was with these men that we did it. Each one would throw snow on himself, too. After returning into the hogan and warming up, then going back into the snow—that was when it really stung, especially when shaking snow on oneself from a tree. I used to cry. It was really painful; it felt like being spanked, or it seemed like being hit all over by objects which burned. While I was growing up I always cried when doing it.

I never slept past dawn. I had grandparents who seldom had to speak twice to their grandchildren about doing something. If they did speak twice, the rope came. A child would be spanked until he or she would get up and run out at dawn.

But I got used to the cold because during winter nights lambs often would be born, and I always would be sent out to them. In those days there were no flashlights. The only light was from crushed-up juniper bark, with yucca tied on. These were ready at hand to be lit, and they were our "flashlights." The new-born lamb would be brought inside with its mother and put into a corner where

27

it would be dried. At times it would start sucking milk, but if it failed to do so some milk would be warmed and put into its mouth. When it got up and was dry, the lamb and its mother would be taken out again. Maybe two, or sometimes three, lambs would be born in one night, and it was quite a difficult job. When my younger sister grew older I would go with her to the sheep. Sometimes she would cry while putting on her shoes or moccasins.

That was how we grew up.

I had an uncle, Mr. Bad Canyon, who was real strict. He was small in stature, but he could handle horses really well. In the fall, after it got cold, he used to chase us out when the water froze on the pond. He would set pieces of ice aside and then herd us into the water. The ones who were afraid he would grab by the necks and dunk them into the icy water. It would bring results of crying while racing back to the hogan.

We were told to bring ice back, but that was almost impossible because we never could carry it. It would freeze and stick to the fingers. Holding it with something was the only way. One time I really tried to carry it, but it stuck to me, and, when I jerked it away, the skin came off with it. After that, it scared me. The problem was having it stuck to you. Doing this type of thing made experiences to remember.

All year long, when it just became dawn, we would be wakened and told to race toward the east, shouting while running. All of these things we did in the past. I think it was real good for us. I never slept when it became sunrise. I was never lazy.

Over in Shiprock, New Mexico, was a school, and there were quite a few pupils, including one person who lived among us. He passed away when an epidemic came around more than 50 years ago; also his younger and older brother—three of them—passed away. So only one kept on going to school. He was the oldest; we called him Haskeh (Anger). He ran away from school many times. Once, I guess before he reached home, the policeman caught him, gave him a beating with a stick and took him back to the place. I don't know the last grade he completed. It must have been high, maybe sixth or seventh grade, because it's said that he could really write.

I came along after he was quite mature. Anger's mother was a Ute who limped. They called her The Lady Who Limps.

One of my grandfathers was named Mr. One who Hammers. It's said that some Utes brought a baby all wrapped up to him. It

28

The town of Shiprock, N. M., looking toward the southwest with the BIA boarding school at upper center, right.

wasn't far from where we lived to the Ute country. I guess they were in need of food when they exchanged the baby for a sackful of corn. It was a girl. After some years went by, one day the Utes started to complain about the matter, and they came to our place quite a few times. By then the little girl was tall. She would be put at a place where nobody could find her, and she never was discovered by the Utes. My grandfather (Mr. One Who Hammers) and the little girl went to Lukachukai, where she grew up.

My grandmother's older sister, who could not have children, was given a child—one of my grandmother's own children. This child was the oldest and an uncle to me. She took care of him while he was growing.

Also, I had a grandfather whose name was Mr. Mustache. His clan was Within His Cover (*Bit'ahnii*). His wife (The Lady Who Limps)—was called *Baa* and was the one who had been given away when she was a baby. She had not started walking until the age of two and one-half years. By the time she could run fast and started understanding certain things she could ride a horse excellently. I don't know at what age she married my grandfather. The clan she married into was Within His Cover, and she started having children who became quite a few. It was one of her oldest children that went to school. While the boy was getting an education was when I came into being.

I was told that he had a habit of running away. When he ran away from Shiprock he came to our place, even though he knew that the police would catch him. Once, at a time they were having a Yei-be-chai dance, he ran away along with some other boys. It was about that date that I was born, he later told me. He said I was born on September 25; so, ever since then, I always have remembered that date.

At that time school plans were being made for me. One of my youngest uncles said, "Go to school, Nephew. It will be good for you. Life will be different once you learn the white man's language. The boys who are going to school at Shiprock are riding stallions with red saddles. So, once you learn the white man's way, you will be like them; or you will get a job and work in Shiprock like the other boys—and you will be paid money by the white man."

That was the way he made plans for me, and I mentioned it to my grandmother who exclaimed, "Oh, no! What are you saying, my grandson? People like you are not put in school. It's only for those who don't have homes and just roam around, the ones who are not well-mannered—they are the ones who are put in school. What would you do over there? You have livestock here—sheep that we depend on, wool that we depend on. We sell the lambs in the fall, we eat mutton; and if you go to school who's going to feed you mutton? So what you are thinking is useless."

That's about what she would say whenever I brought up the subject.

So, at those times the matter would be dropped. But I came back to it all the time, until, I guess it was going on three years, when a man named Mr. Tall Boss left the school. A big white man took his position whose name was Mr. Eaststep. He was short but huskily built. The news was that pupils were needed.

At home something was going on. As I remember, it was a sing because there were many people. In the evening the men were having an arrow-shooting contest. I, too, had a bow and arrows, which I used. They somehow would measure with their arms, but I don't know how the winning was ruled.

It was on that evening plans were made for school. Someone said, "Who is going to go to school from here? The one that's sitting in the doorway sure wants to go—the one with the earrings."

It was I whom they meant. Another person said, "He wants to go, and, because he wants to go, that is good for him. Our brother, whom we call Angry, ran away many times, and that was the reason he received mistreatment from the police. If it's like that, then 'No'."

That was the way they talked. I heard it myself. It was then that they suggested, "Well, let it be he from our area."

30

That's when I became real excited; it was during the summer. When I herded sheep I would think, "I wonder how I'll be talking English? What will I be saying?" Even at nights, when I woke, I would be thinking about it. "I wonder if they'll cut my hair? Will I still have my earrings? What will they do to me? The school children's clothes and shoes are nice. That I know I'll have."

The days went on and on, and it was the only year that summer seemed real long. When the time to leave finally was near (I think in another month the crops would have been ripe, like watermelons), the school people said, "Come on." At a place around Sweetwater speeches were made about school, and I knew many of the boys and girls. A man would say, "So and so's children will be going over there to school. You will not be going alone."

When the day came, my father hitched the horses to the wagon. He was not my real father—just an uncle, but he called me his son. My mother, along with one of my uncle's children, left with me in the morning; and we arrived in the late afternoon at Shiprock. There were a lot of big houses. I had been there only once before, when I was about 12 years old. It was when my grandparents took some piñon nuts to be sold. I remembered what it was like, with lots of cottonwood trees. Along the streets everything was green, with water running.

We arrived at the school, and my hair was cut short. My earrings were cut off and given back to me, and I put them in my pocket. My queue was given to my mother, plus the hairstring, and she took them back home. Then my head was shaved, which made it look like melted lard, and I was told to take a bath in a white bath tub. There was something that looked like black lard that made a ring in the tub. I must have been real dirty. I was given some clothes that smelled with a nice aroma. They were blue; and I received some underclothes, too. The shoes were black, and the soles were hard and felt like boards. I thought, "Boy, the things I wanted have been given to me."

I was 18 years old—and happy about starting to school!

The next day I began to mingle among other students, and pretty soon I got used to the place. Many of them were from my general home area, including the ones who were there a year ago. I did not understand the white man's language then—not one word.

It was close to winter. I was told to work, milking cows. They were big, black and white spotted, the ones that are called Holsteins.

31

There also were horses, pigs, chickens and sheep in the corrals. Every morning several of us would get up at 4 o'clock, bring the cows in, wash their udders and milk them with our bare hands. Nowadays, it's all done by a machine, with electricity, but, at that time, there was no such thing.

Many months went by working in that way. Then we were switched around, and I was placed in the blacksmith shop where wagons were made and horses were shod. I hammered metals. And I was growing tall.

As I said before, I was 18 years old when I started to school, but nobody over 16 was wanted; so two years were taken from my

32

At school I was real happy about the new clothes that were given to me. They smelled good, and the shoes had hard soles.

age. That was my mother's doings. They wrote "16 years old" for me.

I spent a whole winter there, and I had a good time. Running away never occurred to me. There were pupils who did run away; some of them suffered frostbitten ears and feet. Others froze to death. As for me, I didn't want to leave.

Those of us who had arrived recently at the school were told that no teacher was available. Instead, we just worked until past Christmas, when a teacher came. It was a white man, short in stature, with gray hair. We became his students.

Two or three months went by. Whenever the English language was used, I would pay close attention, and soon I had learned certain words. "Yes" and "no" were the first two. Whenever white persons spoke to me, and if I didn't know what they were talking about, all I would say was "yes." Then they would say "all right" or "okay." Those were other words that I learned. I always would hang around where white people would be carrying on conversations, and I would be wondering what they were saying. Pretty soon, I began to pick up the language. By then the season was toward spring. It would snow; then the sun would shine; then it would snow again.

33

One day the white person we were working for said, "The sun is shining." Then I started thinking about it—"The sun is shining, the sun is shining," along with pronouncing it; and I asked one of the boys who understood English, "What does it mean?" He explained it to me in Navajo. He also wrote it on paper for me. I practiced and practiced writing it. "The sun is shining" was the first thing I learned to write.

I guess by then we had classes for four months. One day the teacher said, "Write something that you have learned on the blackboard." One by one our names were called and we walked up to the front of the room. We were given a piece of chalk. Right away, I wrote "The sun is shining" because I already had learned that, and, by now, I knew how to write it. I was real proud. Some just stood there, while others wrote "I see a cup" or "I see a horse." Mine was the only one that was different, and the teacher was proud of me. That incident I always have remembered.

School continued like that until it was time to go home. I wondered, "How will I go home?" But a man I knew happened to be around. Over at Teec Nos Pos, Arizona, there was to be a sheep dipping, and he had to drive his wagon over there with the equipment. He said, "Get in. From Teec Nos Pos to your home is just a little way." Upon our arrival I set off on foot. At Stream Running Out was the place where we were living. I guess plans had been made to come after me, but I had returned.

Early in the fall, members of my family took me back to school, and once again I learned. It was the year 1916 that I first was placed in school. Now it had turned 1917, and I had learned a lot.

Another year went by. In the blacksmith shop I had spent a year and a half, and I could do perfect work. There was a man (he was short and his name was Harvey Dickson) who also went to school there, although he already was educated. It was him that we worked for in the blacksmith shop. I could make horseshoes; and, when the white men brought their horses around, I would shoe them. In return, they would pay me. I fixed wagon wheels, too. There were few automobiles. Just once in a while a car would be seen. Its headlights could be turned on by something—not by electricity, just by kerosene, maybe. That was how lights were on those old cars when I first noticed them.

I had mastered blacksmithing really well; so they put me in the dairy department again where I worked for many months. About five or six months would go by before I would be changed to another job. In that way the students learned various jobs, including planting, hoeing and harvesting corn and cutting hay. The man in charge of the cornfields raised crops like watermelons. Also, there was sap or juice from the trees that we would gather. The liquid would be boiled; then the syrup would be put into wooden barrels and transported to different schools like those at Crownpoint, Ignacio, Towac, Toadlena and Tohatchi. We would make syrup for our own use, too, and, in the winter, the girls would use it to make taffy candy.

Then, after our country got into World War I, hunger was felt by everyone, and we didn't eat as much. Those of us who worked on the farm fed the animals and gathered the eggs from the chickens. School was out for the day at 4 o'clock. Not far away was a grove of trees where some boys lived. We would go over there, and they would scramble eggs with bacon. The grease would be saved. Corn would be cooked; and, every day, those boys would have corn in their pockets to eat. That was how we continued our schooling, being constantly hungry. The hunger and hardship were the reasons why many pupils ran away at that time.

Later, in 1918, it was in the fall during piñon-picking season and when people were gathering the nuts, that sickness came around. At other areas, some people died from the epidemic. It was a real bad flu. We who were in school were told to go to bed. Some of the students had bad headaches. I myself had some headache but not much. Still I went to bed. The work that we usually did was put aside. Several policemen had to keep the fires going and bring in coal.

We had to stay in bed for two weeks until most of us got well again. Three persons died. One was a Navajo girl—a daughter of an uncle of mine. Another one passed away, but I don't know the race she was. She looked like a black person, for she had dark skin. She could not talk, and, at the same time, she was deaf. Then another Navajo, who was a former student, died. He had worked for the Agency.

After our recovery, we started to attend school again. Day after day it was classes and hard work until 4 o'clock.

In 1919 I was put into the blacksmith shop again; and, when summer came close, I played on a baseball team. In front of the blacksmith shop there was a stream of water which was well taken care of with boards along the bank. I drank from it, I think two times. It was perhaps six days before a rodeo was to start. Then I noticed that about every two days my head would ache, the pain just coming and going. The evening before the rodeo my head started hurting badly; so I lay down. Sometime during the night I awoke and found that I didn't feel right. I was very hot. I didn't go to breakfast; and, when the boys' dorm aid, Mr. Roundhoe, came in and took my temperature, he said, "You're sick. Go to the hospital." When I arrived there they put me to bed.

It had been not too long before when it was announced, "Those who want to volunteer for the military service sign your names." And there must have been 12 of the tall, bigger boys who signed up. Even though World War I already had been fought, there was still tension in the world. We were told there would be training at Fort Bliss, Texas. That was the place where we were supposed to go, but, instead, I was in the hospital when the departure date came around. The other boys came to see me, and we all shook hands. Then they left.

It was July 4 that I entered the hospital because I noticed that the flags were raised. The days I stayed must have totaled three or four weeks, or more, because I got worse for a while. I started to have dreams. I dreamed that I was walking among a multitude of people, all going toward the west, dressed up. They all had brand new Navajo blankets. I didn't know where we were heading; I was just walking among them. I looked sideways and saw many people around me. We were in a green pasture with rolling hills. I didn't know how long I dreamed that. I guess the hospital people weren't expecting me to recover. I must have been sort of on a balance, like

35

a scale—to live or to die. I learned later that for two nights and a day I was not expected to make it. Then I had the same dream again, walking among the people; and I didn't know how long it lasted.

I was given some shots, however, and I woke up. I heard someone calling my name, sounding very far away, just like a prairie dog sounds when deep underground. My name was being called—"MAX!" The voice kept getting closer and closer, like someone coming nearer. When it sounded right close, I opened my eyes, and I saw doctors and nurses around my bed. I just glanced at them without moving my head. They were talking to me. I guess by that time my temperature had started going down.

I must have stayed in the hospital for about a month. My food was kept to a certain limit and certain kind, which was just a glass of egg yolk and milk, four times a day. My temperature went down until I was getting strong again. I was told to sit up for 30 minutes a day; then I would have to lie back down. Soon I was told to walk at least 30 minutes a day, which I did for a week and a half. Then I was asked to run an errand to the boys' dormitory.

Soon I moved back there, and I stayed for a month and a half, after which time a white man came from California. It was said he was a superintendent. He was short in height, and his name was Mr. Consent. He brought some forms which could be filled out if we wanted to go to school there. Right away I signed my name for Sherman Institute, Riverside, California.

The time came to go. It was in October that 35 of us (boys and girls) left from Shiprock. We were hauled in big Army trucks. The driver of my truck was Mr. Tanner. At a big wash just before Naschitti, New Mexico, we got stuck in the mud because it had been raining, and it took quite a while before we got the trucks out. In those days the roads were bad; mostly they were just wagon trails. Finally, we got to the Naschitti Trading Post where we spent the night. We used Navajo rugs as mattresses and blankets. Boys and girls slept in the same room.

The next day, early in the morning, we were told that we would have breakfast in Tohatchi, which we did. There more boys and girls joined us, so we were a lot. We arrived in Gallup, New Mexico, before noon. Just west of the Indian ceremonial grounds there was some housing, with a big building which we used as a place to wash up. Then we were hauled downtown. It was almost noon. It must have been the time for the big Gallup Indian Ceremonial because there were lots of people. Airplanes were flying around, too. That was when I first saw a plane. We walked around town for a while. Soon after noon a train was supposed to arrive. When the time came it did arrive, and we all got on board. Our driver from Shiprock had brought some lunch for us, which he had in baskets. Our clothes were dark blue; so we all were dressed something like soldiers.

Then we were off toward the west. There were a lot of boys and girls from Shiprock, Toadlena and Tohatchi—all in New Mexico. With the three schools put together, there were 305 of us. Some girls, even the older ones, cried. I wondered, "Why are they crying?" For myself, I was excited. We traveled through Holbrook, Arizona. At Winslow we stopped for a few minutes; then on to Flagstaff, where we saw the sunset through the pine trees. Another stop was made where there were some Indians, but this place I don't remember. As we went along and made the stops there were a lot of Anglos and Blacks. Sometime during the night we reached Barstow in California. Then we traveled on and on, and we crossed what looked like a river in the darkness. As we went farther into California it became dawn; then the sun came up. As we were heading for San Bernardino, I got turned around. The sun came up from the west, instead of the east. I wondered what had happened! Finally, I mentioned it to some boys who were sitting with me. I said, "We're not heading the right way; we're heading back toward the east." But some of them said, "We're heading toward the west." At San Bernardino we stopped, and the white people went to eat breakfast for 30 minutes. Then we were off again; and, just before noontime, we arrived at Riverside.

Some big trucks were waiting. Our luggage was put into them, and we students walked into town, where we saw some red street cars which ran by electricity. We all got into the cars, and they took off. I guess it was several miles to Sherman Institute, but we got there at noontime because the students were in line for lunch, looking like military people. They would move along one step at a time. The girls were separate, on the other side. After we had washed up, we were led into the dining room which was big in size. One of the new boys among us was Woodrow Nelson from Shiprock. He and I were toward the back of the line. Clanging of tableware was loud. About halfway down the line, as we moved along, I guess some students who had entered last year (boys and girls) from Shiprock recognized us, for our names were called several times.

37

A table was set aside for the group I was in, and we all sat down and ate for quite a while. When the regular students finished, most of them took off outside, but we continued to eat, and soon some of them came over to us. There were many who knew individuals among us. Those students of the past year were the first Navajos to be at Sherman, and we were the second group. We shook hands with a lot of them.

In two or three days the Riverside Fair would begin, and the students were really polishing their shoes and getting ready for it. When the day came, we left in the morning, all riding in the street cars—the whole school. We got there and mingled with the crowd. There were many Anglos, mixed with Spanish, Blacks, Chinese and members of various tribes of Indians. We Navajos numbered quite a few. We saw the various events, and it wasn't until evening that we returned to the school. It was the first fair that I ever had seen, and I studied many of the exhibits.

About a week after the fair I was told to work in the laundry room. Woodrow Nelson worked there, too. He was the one who advised me to work there with him. The washing machines were run by big leather straps. I knew how to work with leather because my grandfather had sewed saddles; so, just by observing him, I could master leather work quite well. This had included making leather ropes, which, at the tips, would be tied and braided. I had learned all of this from him. So, there at school, my leather braiding came in handy. Whenever one of the straps broke that made the washing machines run, I always was the one who fixed it by sewing it back together.

I was in the laundry for a whole winter. On Saturdays we worked for a lady named Mrs. Long, who was tall and strong. She set up things for us to do among the Anglos in town—like cleaning out a chicken coop or raking the yard around a home. Even at her own house we would work. I sometimes got $2.00 or $2.50 from her. At that time earnings were in small amounts. Because I knew how to work real well and was willing to do almost anything, the Anglos would ask me to work for them again. So, throughout the winter, I had money.

Another year went by. West of our school, maybe about five or six miles, there was another school. It had a dairy farm. The milking cows were black and white. It was called the Indian Farm. I was among those who went there to study. I attended school at that place another year, along with milking the cows. When summer came, I was placed to work for a white man. I was supposed to be with him throughout the summer. I worked in the fields, baling hay and tying the bales, for two months, and, when classes started again, I returned to Sherman.

The money that I had earned had been sent to the school for me, and just a little at a time was given to me for spending. It was that way as time went on. I had been about a year at the Indian Farm; and, when I returned to the Riverside School, I was placed in the blacksmith shop. I worked there for I don't remember how many weeks. A boy had to go through all the various jobs that were offered for males at the school. The girls did the same, only in different kinds of work. Then, when he or she had finished a certain amount of time, the question was asked, "Which job did you like the best?" That was when the boy or girl chose the job he or she liked, and that was why each student had to go through various jobs that were offered. I experienced this, and I liked the shoe shop, the leather shop, the sewing shop, as well as others.

39

I had left in 1919 for Riverside; and it was not until 1923 that I returned home. By that time, a student had to pay his own way; so I paid my railroad fare. I took a vacation and spent the summer at home on the Reservation. It was arranged that when fall came and school was ready to start again I already had a ticket for the train that I would return on. It was called a "round-trip ticket."

I had left on a trip with my father during that summer, and we passed through Dennehotso, Kayenta and Narrow Canyon. In those places sheep and cattle were being sold. We had five big Ute horses that we took along. We also had two brand new saddles. For these (horses and saddles), sheep and cattle were traded to us. When we were in Narrow Canyon, however, my head started hurting, and I became ill. We spent three days there, and a lady gave me some medicine which was an herb that was real bitter. This I drank, and I became better. Then we herded the livestock back home.

At that time we were living at Walker Creek, near Chinle, Arizona. When we reached there it was time for me to depart for school; but, by that time, my train ticket no longer was valid. So I was taken to Shiprock. A man by the name of Jack Morgan was in charge of the school there at that time. He also was a music teacher. I told him my situation. He said, "At Sherman, where you went to school, it is said students are needed. So there are students from here whom I want you to go down with." I wasn't expecting that.

"You can go back for free," was what they said, and I was thankful. But that same night a phone call came from Sherman in which someone said, "There's not enough room here; we are crowded now. A lot of students from elsewhere have enrolled."

That's when Mr. Morgan said, "My grandchild, go to school in West Virginia." He had received his education there. He added, "Anglos and Blacks and even some Indians were going to school there when I attended. You will learn a lot; so go that way. I will make a phone call. Now, what do you think?"

I said, "It's all right."

40 After that I don't know what happened, but from a school in Ganado, on the Reservation in Arizona, a phone call was received. A person said, "We have enough room for four more students. Do you have any available? Hurry up!"

That was the day after the plan for West Virginia had been made; and I was told, "Go over there, instead, because it's just a little way from your home." Again, I agreed.

Two girls and myself and another boy were taken to Ganado. Our driver, as before, was Mr. Tanner. The weather was cold. We took the turn toward Window Rock, Arizona, which was not far from Gallup. We traveled past Window Rock and St. Michaels, and, when it became evening, it started to snow. By nightfall we arrived at Ganado, and it still was snowing.

At the school there were many boys and girls from Shiprock whom we knew. I spent the winter there—the year of 1923-1924, and I learned how to read in Navajo. Also, I learned to sing. And I got to know a lot of young people besides those who lived in the vicinity. To this day, many still are around. They now have white hair. Some have passed on.

During the next summer, over at San Francisco Peak (near Flagstaff, Arizona), there was a white man who was building a house. We were told that at least four of us would go there. I was among them. One was Andrew P. Johnson, who was from Alaska. Also, Luke Peshlakai, who has passed away, and Francis Peshlakai (I don't know whether he's still living), along with myself. We were taken to the San Francisco Peak area. Today the place is called the Northwest Conference Ground, and it is where members of the Catholic Church gather. The foundation of cement and rocks was just being laid when

The San Francisco Peaks, camera facing due south from Highway 89.

we arrived. We worked on it until it was finished. We then painted the building, cleared the landscape and made it a nice place.

In August we had a big gathering. There were members of many different tribes of Indians and many Anglos. I was a spectator. After the conference was over, I left for Riverside by train. Two of the boys I worked with (the Peshlakais) left for Ganado, and Andy Johnson, the one from Alaska, left on foot. He bought himself a knapsack and food and took some water. He was leaving just as I departed for Riverside. That was in 1924.

When I started classes again I was told, "You are too old for going to school now; you are a grown man." But I kept pleading to let me attend. I wanted to learn a good career, and they finally agreed. It was because I wanted an education that I spent a lot of years in school.

While working in the blacksmith shop I learned a lot, including welding metals together and fixing wagons. I worked in the shoe shop, too, and in the bakery. Between the blacksmith shop and the bakery I guess I worked for four years. Besides, I worked in the dairy and cornfields. I realized the importance of getting along with the white people. Three jobs I mastered quite well. In the white man's words, "I specialized"; and certificates were filled out for me which identified what I could do best.

In 1927, about three weeks after school started, fire broke out on a mountain near San Bernardino and east of it. They called it Arrowhead. A siren was heard, for whenever a house or something was on fire a siren went off. We were in school, but we evacuated the buildings and went to the outside where we all lined up.

"The older boys will help fight the fire. We need at least 40," we were told. The names of those to help were called.

I was among those who had been instructed before in class about fire prevention and fighting; so I think that was the reason why my name was called. Only the young men who knew about fires were to go. We were loaded into two big trucks, with our coats, hats and gloves. We were hauled on and on; then, toward evening, we arrived at the mountain. It was rugged, and the fire was burning with huge clouds of smoke. Already a big area was burned. There were a lot of Mexicans and Anglos preparing to fight it.

At the spot where we made camp we had a place to cook. It was north of where the fire was burning. The area was made up of big arroyos and rugged ground. The fire was burning on the western side of the mountain. A fellow named Herbert Cash—a Hopi—was my roommate. He was my partner, and we were glad about being together because we knew each other.

After we had finished eating it was evening, and we started moving along into an arroyo, across a wash and over a mountain—a distance of about two and a half miles. Already some men were there fighting the fire.

Animals like deer, mountain lions and wolves were running from the fire. It was dark, except for the light from the blaze. We started making something like a road for putting out the fire. Big trees were chopped down so the fire could not go on to other trees. Somewhere along about midnight other men brought lunch and water for us. Each carried a lantern, and the lunches were passed out to us. We were all very hungry. I still worked with Herbert Cash, side by side, while the other boys from Sherman were scattered here and there. Some of the boys were getting a little sleep so that when it was our turn to rest they would take over in our place.

As we were eating our lunches, deer would run out of the forest. We were told not to shout. Right among us they would run. Sometimes, as one started past, a fellow would kick dirt, which would cause the deer to prance high, or it would jump back. When we were doing that, one deer almost ran over a guy. But, instead, it jumped over him and landed in a bunch of bushes where his antlers got caught. For a while he tried to get lose, and he finally succeeded. Coyotes and mountain lions also ran out from nowhere. It was sort of scary, but if a fellow stood still they would just pass by.

We continued working very hard until morning. We then returned to camp after being relieved by the other boys, and we all went to sleep. Our group was assigned to work only at night. That evening some boys were told to stay and make food for others. I guess they knew I had experience in cooking, and my name was called, along with my partner (Herbert Cash); so we stayed and helped the cooks. We slept until noon, and, late that afternoon, we started to work again with the cooks until the sun went down. Then, after dark, we fixed the sack lunches and water and started on foot, carrying our lanterns. We went to where we already had put out the fire. That was along about midnight, maybe later.

Herbert and I were the first to turn back when we noticed that a strip of fire had started behind us, because it was windy in that direction. Suddenly things did not seem right. "What a big fire!" we said. So we headed toward the east, where there was a ridge. We knew that going back would not be easy because the fire was close behind us. The fire had jumped across the place where we had dug the fire lane. On the front rolling edge the wind would blow the fire, causing a big noise like thunder. It moved like a whirlwind, and was frightening. In the mountains echos could be heard from it. We kept going the opposite way from the fire. We had been instructed about the ridges and mountains of that area; so we knew that over a big hill south from it, maybe about four miles, there was a road, and on that side of the mountain was a lake. It was in that direction we started, and we were hurrying. We kept on going, and, when we came to a hill, we could see quite a distance by moonlight. Once, from the top of a hill, we saw that we were not far from the lake because the road was near. "That way we will go," we said.

I guess a fire had started close to the camp. We were walking between two mountains when we saw a stream of water, and we hurried that way. Herbert was walking in front of me, and I was carrying the lantern. I guess I must have tripped over a root because I took a fall. The lantern went flying and broke, but it did not start a fire. I guess I scared my partner so much that he jumped behind a tree. Then he said, "I sure thought a wolf or a mountain lion had jumped on you." I said, "No, I just tripped." Then we laughed.

So we went on, crossing an arroyo toward the south and the lake. While we were walking, it became morning. We were very tired. Whenever we looked back we saw flares of light which, once in a while, would flame up higher here and there. The sun rose, and we saw that we were a long way from the fire. When we arrived at the lake we decided that if the fire ever caught up with us we could go in the lake; so we lay down under a tree and went to sleep. It was almost noon when we woke. Then we walked up a hill, and, from on top, we looked back to where we had come from the fire.

We were still far from the camp, and we started toward the north, toward Arrowhead. Late in the afternoon we came to a road, and we took it. It must have been at least eight miles to where we were going because, just before the sun went down, we returned, arriving in camp the opposite way from which we had left it.

The others had noticed our absence, and word was: "We think two boys burned to death last night."

Already phone calls had been made, and newspapers read, "Two boys from Sherman burned to death last night, we think, for they have disappeared." I guess we were big news. The others were eating when we arrived in late evening, and they were real happy to see us.

44

That same night a Mexican was killed by a big boulder which crushed him. When a boulder is supported by a tree and the tree is burned from under it, the boulder gets loose, and it rolls down a hillside. Sometimes just one boulder would be loosed, but it would cause a whole lot of others to start down the hill. That is what caused the accident. Altogether, three lives were lost fighting the fire.

The other firefighters in our group were glad to see us return safely. They had thought that we had been burned to death, and we even became big news in the papers.

It took a long time, but finally we stopped it. Still, we stayed there another week. Even we two who were once lost were kept there, just in case the fire would start again. The last six of us finally returned to school.

Another year went by attending Sherman. Then, just before school let out, my eyesight got poor. I was doing some welding and the plastic glasses that one is supposed to use were cracked. I thought "It won't hurt to just wear them for a while." But, pretty soon, I started having pain like something was sticking into my eyes. I guess we weren't allowed to wear defective glasses, so it was all my fault. The condition got worse, and I could not read a paper too well. I did not go to school for quite a while; I just worked outdoors.

South of Riverside was a place called Marshfield, and, close by, was another named Hammond. At Marshfield a group of Indians lived, and a hospital was being built there for them. Seven students went there. I could have continued in school, but my eyesight kept me from it. The seven of us helped build the hospital, working under the supervision of a white man. We mixed cement, painted and did other jobs. So I got experience in painting, along with electrical wiring, pipe lining, metal lapping and wood lapping. We worked all through the summer and winter. Then, when summer had come again, near the place where we built the hospital, at Hammond, a motel was being built. It was going to be a two-story building. Our supervisor was offered a job there, and we went with him. We worked with him all summer.

45

Close to Christmas, a white man whom we used to work for in the cornfields (I don't know how he found out where we were) came to visit us. "Why don't you work for me?" he asked. "It will last longer." Three of us said, "Okay. We'll stay here for one more month and then work for you." We agreed on it; and, when one month was over, we left the place, even though the men there wanted us to stay. We returned to Sherman Institute and then went on to a town between Corona and Ontario. It was a big farm. I was assigned to the blacksmith shop where I fixed broken machines, while the others worked in the fields plowing, fixing fences and irrigating. We all worked there for a whole winter and a summer. Then, when winter came again, two of us said we wanted to go home for a while. So another fellow, William Scott, and I started back. That was in 1929. It was almost Christmas. From Corona we caught a train to Gallup. Finally, we reached Shiprock; and I went to Sweetwater and my home. William also went home, and we spent Christmas in Navajoland.

On January 5, 1930, I went to Shiprock because I planned to go to work; also, if possible, to go back to school. In Shiprock I was told that the school superintendent wanted to see me. He asked, "The students that you made the trip to Sherman with, do you ever see them?"

"Yes," I answered. "Some are working in Los Angeles, while others are still going to school." Names and whereabouts were written down, and I was told, "Whenever you see them again tell them their parents would like for them to write."

While I was sitting in the office with him the phone rang and he talked a while. Then, after discussing the other matter (the students in California) again, he asked, "What did you learn at Sherman?"

I told him what I had learned, and he made a list which became long.

He asked me, "Do you really know these trades?" And I replied that I had mastered three of them quite well.

"Over in Ignacio, Colorado, the school cook left and has not returned," he said. "There's nobody to bake for the children; so go over there. From here to there it's not far; also, your home is not far. You would be able to see your mother, father and the ones you grew up with quite often."

That was the way he started making plans for me, and I agreed. I was told that a man would drive me to Ignacio the next morning.

It seemed like it would start snowing because it was cloudy, and that certain chill was in the air. I was told to be in the superintendent's office at a certain time. I was there, and my ride arrived— a driver named Steve Barton. He drove me through Farmington, Aztec and Durango. Then we headed east, and it wasn't far until we arrived in Ignacio. The snow was deep, and it still was coming down. The town was in mountainous country. It was then that I really came back to the snow, for I had not seen much of it for many years.

The house that I was to stay in was within walking distance of the school. I unloaded my belongings, and the next day I went to where I would be working. I was instructed as to where things belonged and how to run the place. I walked about and observed; and I was told to start work the following day, which I did. The oven that was used for baking bread had to be heated by firewood; so one of the first things I did was go out and chop wood.

The San Juan River—at a spot south of Shiprock.

That was the way I started my new job. I worked there all through the winter. In the spring, when the students were let out of school, I began to have problems with my health. The trouble was caused by lifting 100-pound flour sacks and 100-pound bags of sugar. My helpers were only little boys. Even when I had arrived at Ignacio I had a physical problem. At Sherman, I had been on the football team. I was on it for two years. At the beginning of the third year was when the trouble started. One day I got tackled. Several fellows were on top of me, and the cleats of one of their shoes almost punctured my stomach. It seemed to be only a little wound, but sometimes it would swell up. That was when our coach, Mr. Pierce, told me that I had ruptured my stomach.

"You can't play anymore," he said. "You will have to go to the hospital sometime and have surgery and stitches."

So I had to quit football. The injury caused only a little problem mostly, but whenever I carried something heavy my stomach would swell.

It was after arriving in Ignacio and starting to carry heavy loads that it became a serious problem. I told the doctor about it, and he said, "You have a pretty bad rupture. It is best you resign from your job and go to the hospital. Go back with the boys when they are returning to Shiprock, and then go to Albuquerque." I said, "Okay." So, after school was out, I returned with the students to Shiprock.

47

I stayed around there for almost a month. The doctor who would perform the surgery in Albuquerque was away, I was told. It was not until the fairs were over that I was taken to Albuquerque where I was operated on. There were three of us—a lady, a Hopi man and me. I didn't know how they got ruptured; so I asked the man, and he said it was from carrying heavy rocks around. I did not ask the lady, so I don't know what had happened to her. We all had our surgery and were made well again. I walked around the hospital, and I cut the hair of the ladies who worked there. I also polished their shoes, and, by doing things like that, I became quite popular.

I was told not to carry heavy loads for seven months. After that time was up, I started to carry heavy objects and found that I couldn't. My stomach would hurt. So I was instructed not to carry anything even slightly heavy for at least a year. After that, the ruptured place was better, but I still didn't carry real heavy things.

One day a white man came to see me in Shiprock. I knew him from when I went to school. He had been a band leader. We shook hands and exchanged our greetings. He then started asking me questions, which took several hours. I guess that, while I still was in the hospital, he had spoken to the superintendent, for, during the summer, I was told that the superintendent wanted to see me. I went to his office.

He said to me, "You did not finish your schooling; how come?" So I told him the reasons why I had not finished school. And I explained, "I intended to go back to school but you asked me to be a bakery man in Ignacio, and they hauled me over there."

He replied, "Well, then, go back to school in the fall. I will send for your records, and they will be available here." I agreed, and he did as he said.

In less than two weeks I was called in again, and I found that everything had been sent. He said, "All your papers over there are just fine."

Then he advised me to go to school in Albuquerque. Again, I agreed. I signed my name, and, early in the fall, I entered school. I started with the 11th grade because at Sherman I had just begun the 12th. So, I spent two years in the Albuquerque Indian School.

I continued my education until I had completed it. During those last two years in Albuquerque, I was placed in different organizations like playing in the school band and being in the drama group.

48

I went to many places where other Indian tribes lived, especially those in New Mexico. Taos was one, along with the small villages near Albuquerque.

I was in the Albuquerque band, too. In Gallup, during the fall, an Inter-Tribal Ceremonial was held annually. We played there two years. We were named the "State Band," which meant we were the main band for those years. Whenever different tribes of Indians held events we would be advertised, and we often would play for them. We even went down to the Mescalero Apache Reservation. We also played for the Laguna and various other Pueblo tribes during the two years that I attended school.

I also was a member of the Albuquerque National Guard for two and a half years. Twice we traveled to Las Vegas, New Mexico. These activities really helped me money-wise during my school years.

In the summer I did not go anywhere. I just worked in the bakery at the school. Whenever our boss would go somewhere, like on a vacation, I would be in charge. I worked in the dairy, too, milking cows—going back and forth between the two jobs.

There was a white man in Window Rock, and also a lady, who wrote letters to me. Once, the lady wrote, "When you finish your schooling, help your own people. While you were in school at Sherman Institute you said you would. In one of your classes (English) your teacher asked what you were going to do after you finished school, and she said you answered, 'I'd like to go back to my own Reservation among my own people and be able to help them.' That also was written on one of your papers; so we need your help now here on the Reservation."

Then I remembered I had said that. When school was out for the day at 4 o'clock, she (the English teacher) would tell me to wait, and she started asking me questions like, "When you finish school what are you going to do?" I would answer, "I don't know what I'm going to do, maybe work somewhere, or go back to Navajoland. Then she would try to do all she could for me. So, the things I'd said had caught up with me. I don't know why, but in Albuquerque I really got interested in the armed services, wanting to go overseas.

That's why letters were sent to me from Window Rock by this gentleman and lady. They also advised me that I should get married so that my wife could work at a school by being a housekeeper. At that time I had not even thought of a wife. I asked myself, "What shall I do?" And I told my friends about it. They told me, "It's okay.

There are plenty of girls around here. Pick a good one who can work with you."

They made three or four suggestions, but not one did I know. This went on for a while. Then, at last a certain girl seemed to be the right one; but, as soon as school was out for the summer, the news came that she had got married. Maybe it's a good thing it happened that way. For, as I think about it, if I had married that girl, in later years there might have been problems.

After that happened, time went by until, one day, another one was selected who still was in school. I was working in the dairy. She graduated in 1935, while I had graduated in 1932. It was not until then (1935) that, with help from other girls who worked, along with advice from some of the teachers that I had, we were married in a church. I found that the ceremony was a lot of work. When it was accomplished, however, we left the church together. She had a job at the school, while I still milked cows. Because there was plenty of milk, I drank a lot of it. In the fall we were told that a phone call would be coming through soon; so be prepared for it. I think it came on October 4. Then an old Army truck arrived for us; so we loaded our belongings and left with it. The driver took us to Gallup, New Mexico, and on to Fort Defiance, Arizona, which we reached by evening. We spent the night there. The next day we continued to Ganado and to Steamboat. We were told, "You two will be working in Steamboat." I thought we would be working at a good place, but I would not speak of it. I just wondered, "What's so scary at Steamboat? Maybe it's hunger or poverty."

The place was sort of in a big wash, with plains south and west. Thus, it was in 1935 that we moved back to the Navajo Reservation. We started to work. My wife was a cook and dorm aide, while I was a bus driver. We worked hard there for two and a half years. During the second year we had a big snowstorm. The roads were very bad, which caused much sticky mud. Many were not yet paved, and vehicles would break down. During that time I really had hardship on my job. While living at Steamboat our oldest son, Max Hanley, Jr., was born. So we became three in the family. Soon he grew to where he could walk. He stayed inside mostly and never was taken anywhere.

Then we moved again, this time to Lower Greasewood, where we stayed another two years. I was still a bus driver. Soon it was recommended that we should go to a larger school. That was at Crystal, New Mexico, in the mountains of the Reservation. We went there; and, just as we moved, we had a lot of bad snowstorms. We never set foot on the dirt of the roads for I guess about three months. We stayed there for three years, and we had another son, Wallace. So we were four. Time went by, and, just before two years came up, we had another son, Benjamin. He went to school in Phoenix.*

From Crystal we moved to Lukachukai, back in Arizona, where we spent two and a half years. I still was a bus driver. In those various places where we lived we got to know a great many people.

After spending two and a half years at Lukachukai we moved to Shiprock; and, while living there, we finally had a daughter. There I was in the bakery department, for the man who had held that position had been called into the armed forces. I worked in Shiprock for two and a half years; then, when the former baker returned, I left the position and was sent to Tuba City. We went there, but, in five months, we were moved again—this time to Chinle, where I was the baker for five months. Then we were sent back to Tuba City. That was 26 years ago. The students were many in number. I was their baker and also helped the cooks.

51

In 1949 we had an especially big snowstorm which caused us much hardship. Much of the bread that I made was hauled to Navajo Mountain, Kayenta, Chilchinbito and Shonto. The remainder was kept in Tuba City. I always worked hard, but the snowstorm caused me to labor until midnight every day.

I don't know how many years went by before I received word that there would be no more bread-baking. Ready-made bread would be brought from Flagstaff, and the only things I made were the pastries. My past job had become my name—One Who Makes Bread. Often when people saw me they said, "Here comes the One Who Makes Bread. Where's some flour. Let him make some bread for us." And I answered, "Bring all the ingredients here, along with the baking pans." Usually there would be nothing to mix it in. They would tease me like that, and they made my name quite well known. But, as I said, for some years I have quit making bread.

---

*When this volume went to press—May, 1977—Benjamin Hanley was serving his third two-year term as a member of the House of Representatives (serving as Democratic Whip) in the Arizona State Legislature. He is a graduate of the Arizona State University College of Law, class of 1971.

After beginning as a sheepherder I had got an education, and I was good at several trades; but finally my name came from my last job—"One Who Makes Bread."

One day at a big gathering I was asked to speak. I think it was during a Yei-be-chai dance. I talked for a while. One man asked, "Since you don't bake bread anymore, what do you do now?" I explained, "I still work at the same place making sweet pastries for the students." Then the people said, "Your name will be Mr. Sweetman."

Year after year went by in their different seasons until, in 1962, I was told to retire from the Bureau of Indian Affairs service. I did it, and papers were filled out for my retirement. They were sent off and returned, and I was told to rest, which I did, just staying at home. But I was not comfortable. I would dream of my past job. I was used to getting up early every morning. At times I would jump out of bed thinking, "Oh, I hope I did not oversleep!" Then I would remember, "Oh, I forgot—I don't work these days." And I would lie down again. Many times I dreamed that I was making bread, and one time I dreamed that the boys who used to help me make bread by hand were slapping dough together—when, actually, I was slapping my leg when I awoke. I thought, "Where am I?" Then I realized I was just dreaming. This happens, I guess, to people who have worked for many years. It happened to me for about six months. I slowly overcame it, though, until it passed out of my mind.

I worked for 32 years, four months and seven days after my schooling. Then I finally finished.

After two years of retirement I certainly was rested, and that was when I started to plan the house that we are living in. I traveled to Window Rock and back many times to inquire about it, or else went to Flagstaff, where we knew some white men, and I would ask them to build a house for us. I continued this traveling and talking for two years, when, finally, work began. There were three of us who had houses built.

53

After moving in, I had a visitor from the University of Michigan whose name was Dr. Gotman. He asked me to help him in interviewing elderly Navajo men and women. I said that I would. Along with him were two young men who went to school there (at the university). I worked with them for three months that summer. The Navajo elders were asked questions like: "Why is it that it takes the Navajos a long time for them to become of old age?" This was because they had observed that when Navajos are 80 or 90 years old they still are riding horses, or the man might be doing some kind of heavy work. "What does he eat?" was another question. I helped as an interpreter, and I liked it. The reason for the research, I discovered, was that, in Mexico, it had been learned that some Indians live in low areas, while others live in the highlands, and they also were researched that way. The questions were such as, "What is the reason for the vigorous old age? What do they eat? How do they live?" That was why research was done in Mexico, too. Even the Anglos around Kansas City, Missouri, had the same kind of research study. Altogether, three groups of people were studied—Anglos, Mexican Indians and Navajos.

A year went by; and, when summer came around, these same people visited me again. We did the same research as we had done the summer before, except with different people.

After that, something occurred which was good for our people. Money was provided by the Office of Navajo Economic Opportunity to help the Navajos. Interested people began to think that the older men and women who knew the stories of long ago were passing away. They said, "Before all of them are gone, let's interview them about their knowledge, legends and history." I worked with this project for a year among the people of the western Navajo region. There were five of us. We gathered many stories, taped in the Navajo language on recorders, and we went to Fort Defiance with them. The information that we gathered was to be translated into English and published in books. Plans also were made to publish some of the material in the Navajo language. Younger men and women helped us. Some of the translators were older men and women who really knew both languages. These people listened to the tapes and wrote the material on paper. Then it was transcribed on typewriters.

This we did for another year. But money became low, even though we got more funds from other sources. Finally the funding ran out, and we had to quit the project. Maybe sometime there will be money available again so that the project can be finished. I hear this is going to happen, and I hope it is true because it is very important to get our history, legends, traditions and culture printed in books.

The stories that the elderly people tell begin with a place called the "First World" and come up to the present time. The stories are good, and I hear that a number of books already have been published from our material—some by persons at the Rough Rock Demonstration School and five or six by the new Navajo Community College and its Press. Some stories are of long ago; some are biographies of important Navajos (in history and still living); others are about the Long Walk, livestock reduction, education and modern subjects.

We gathered songs, too. The material that we taped for the ONEO really will make a whole set of books if money can be found to publish them. Once that is accomplished the books will be useful to Navajo young people in their schooling. In fact, that is what has been happening already, and we are striving for more. Maybe, sometime when an Anglo comes up to a person and asks, "Are you a Navajo?"—if the answer is "Yes," he will say, " Okay, then, let me hear you sing a song." If that Navajo sings a song, then the Anglo will say, "You're right, you are a Navajo." On the other hand, if the Navajo says, "I can't sing a song," the answer will be, "You're not a Navajo."

That's why our young people who are going to high school and college should know about our culture, our history, our mythology and our traditions. That's why the recordings and transcribings are being made. We should remember that. It's the main reason why I worked hard on the project.

Today, I am becoming quite old. I can tell because whenever I get up my knee joints crack. I think that it is because, when I was small, I sometimes rode a billy goat.

55

Navajo Mountain, in Arizona, from the south.

Myrtle Begay

CANYON DE CHELLY WAS MY BIRTHPLACE, at a spot called Parallel Trail, on March 15, 1912. My clan is the Salt People (*Áshįįhí*— my mother's side), and I was born for the Bitter Water People (*Tódích'íí'nii*—my father's family). My related clans on my mother's side are the Coyote Pass People *(Mą'ii deeshgíízhinii)*, the Honey Comb Rock People *(Tsénjíkiní)*, the Black Sheep People *(Dibéłizhin í)* and the Yucca Fruits Strung in a Line People *(Hashk'ąą hadzohí)*. Both of my parents are deceased.

My father's name was Man With Words. He died when I was six years old, but I remember him well. He was a medicine man, and he loved me very much. When my father placed me in a boarding school in 1918 it was because he wanted me to get an education. My mother's name was Stout Woman. She died February 10, 1940. She had lived a long life. I was very happy with my father and mother because they loved me.

After my father died my mother was left alone to take over all the responsibilities of raising the children. She preached to us about the good ways of life. I am very grateful to her that I learned many things. Of course, my father also lectured to us until he died. I still remember all of my mother's teachings. I often think about what she said. I also think of my father's words. I feel very fortunate to have had such good parents and I still miss them deeply. That is why I am proud of them. Now I can say that my parents brought me up in the right way. Parents should begin to teach their children at an early age which is as soon as the children become aware of what is going on around them.

Times were different during the period in which my parents gave me lessons on traditional education. Food was scarce. The trading post had only a few of the items which the people really needed to buy. Today, we have supermarkets full of varieties of produce, canned foods, sweets and many other things. We can shop and choose what we need.

When I was a girl the people raised their own crops. The womenfolk ground the corn and prepared it in various ways. There were corn breads, meal gruels and mush—which I learned to prepare. The younger Navajo girls began grinding the corn very early in the morning before breakfast, and the mother prepared the meal, with the help of the older girls. That was all part of the routine of family living. Everyone was kept busy all day. There never was a dull moment. The corn was the main source of food. People raised abundant crops.

57

Keeping the yard clear of trash was part of our duties as children, too. We did not live in houses then. Our home was a typical round-shaped hogan. Some Navajos lived in the conical-type (forked) hogans. There were no such things as brooms like we see today. The people made primitive brooms from rabbit brush tied together at the stems, and we used them to sweep the yard and clean our hogan. My grandmother used to say, "Visitors will talk about your being lazy if they see a dirty hogan and a messy yard."

People who had sheep took good care of them. They moved about with their herds to greener pastures and to where there was water. In our family we had a few head of sheep. My older brother and I took care of them. I remember herding them into a nice box canyon where there was plenty of foliage to graze on. We would play at the gate-like entrance so the sheep could not wander away. The people who lived in Canyon de Chelly at that time had only small herds of sheep. Now we see larger flocks in the canyon.

Learning to be a good housekeeper was among my lessons at home. After everyone got up in the morning, I took all the sheepskins outside, shook them hard and then aired them on a long pole that extended between two posts. We took good care of our sheepskin bedding, even though some was getting ragged. Fetching drinking water was no problem for us. We lived near a waterbed, with a shallow well dug where we got plenty of drinking water. We washed our clothes in water from the same well.

One of my chores was to take the sheepskins outside, shake them hard and then hang them over a long pole for airing.

Mother used to tell us she wouldn't be around all our lives; so we would have to learn to do the things that had to be done and not depend on her too much. She urged us to be independent. For instance, she taught us how to weave rugs. For a beginner's course, she made a small loom and I practiced on it until she knew I could weave as well as she could. "This will be a good provider for you. You will be able to support a family in the future, if necessary, by making good rugs," she would say to encourage we girls.

My mother discussed with me the facts of family life which a lady should know. She said, "When you mature, a young man will come into your life. But first you will have to really know him. You cannot marry on love at first sight. Young people should judge a man or woman by character and actions—whether he or she is an ambitious type or one who wants leisure. So, select a man you can depend on to be a good husband."

These were my mother's words. Long ago, in the making of traditional marriages, the parents chose their daughter's husband-to-be. They looked for a reliable man who could make a good living for their daughter. They then would go to the man's home to propose for their daughter.

58

All that my parents taught has done a lot for me, and I am grateful to them.

I was placed in a boarding school when I was five years old. This was a new start in my life. After my father passed away, life changed in our family. My mother was strong, and she took upon herself all the responsibilities of running a household to the best of her ability.

About my father, he told us stories of events that had happened many years ago. He told us how the people took snow baths naked. This usually was done when the first big snow fell. It was said that the first snow of the year fell along with all the good things in life, such as precious possessions and precious sacred stones. After a person rolled in the new snow several times, he or she ran inside the hogan, where the snow thawed from his body. Then, still dripping wet, the person ran back outside and got under a tree that had a lot of snow on it. This he shook to make the snow in the branches come down upon him. My father said that felt colder than rolling in it. Another thing the people did was to race to the lake or a large pond and break the ice, no matter how thick it was. Some washed themselves in the ice water, while others just plunged in naked. Then, a person would pick up a good-sized chunk of ice and run home with it. Often it would stick (freeze) to our fingers, and that was very painful. It was all done very early in the morning when the air was extremely cold.

My mother told us a story about her mother. She and her older brother, whose name was Yellow Mustache, raced out at dawn to the pond to break the ice. My grandmother broke the ice quickly and washed. Then she grabbed a chunk of ice and ran home with it. Just before she got to the hogan doorway, she dropped it. Then she saw her brother running home dry and empty-handed. He did that several times. "Later," my grandmother said, "my brother had many sheep and cattle and was well off. Why was that? They told us that if we did our physical exercises at dawn and carried ice to the hogan we would be gifted with wealth. But, the one who seldom took ice-water baths had more wealth than we had. We suffered with half-frozen bodies for nothing."

Our parents were patient with us. They taught us to care for the sheep. During lambing season, we took extra care of the little lambs. We fed the orphan ones from bottles every morning and evening. It was a lot of fun playing with them. In those days the people had

59

only a few cows. Today, some Navajos have become cattle raisers, and we can see large herds grazing in many places.

The elders did much more lecturing to the young people—and training—when I was young than they do now.

My grandmother's name was Salt People Woman and I knew her well because she was very old and my mother made me take care of her. She preferred to live alone, in spite of her age. There was a hogan in the field where she stayed. When she wanted to visit my mother I walked beside her in case she stumbled so that I could help her. She was a nice old lady, and she kept up a strong resistance until she finally got ill and passed away. My mother said she died from natural causes. I was in school when it happened.

60   All traditional education came to us through actions and lectures. My mother talked to me about how when I got married I should have a home of my own and never live with my in-laws. She warned me that in-laws often were unkind and very critical. She added, "They will make you miserable by talking behind your back. If your children beg for something to eat when they are hungry, your in-laws will scold them, and this will hurt you and cause problems. Children's crying will annoy them, and you will never be happy and be able to do the things you want."

My mother advised me never to allow my children to beg for any kind of sweets. "If you buy candy for them every time someone goes to the store, they will expect this all the time and cry if they want it. It is a bad habit. Sweets are not good for the growing child, and begging is very bad. Your children will not be hungry if you feed them well. You have hands to cook with and to make things to support your children."

How true her words were; and I listened to her. Today, I do exactly what she taught me. With a mother like that, it is hard to forget her teachings. The elders used to say that words of wisdom never die; they go on and on forever. That is true. I remember all that my mother said to me. Many times I would sit and ponder what she preached about. I have not once taken my children to a neighbor's home to beg. Nor did I make a retreat to my relatives when times were poor.

My husband and I built our own home. His name is Tall Edge of the Water Clan's Son. He is from Chinle, Arizona. We lived in Canyon de Chelly until my mother died.

We had only one horse when we moved out of the canyon. I was on horseback with one child sitting behind me and with the baby in my arms. My husband had our other child with him, walking by our side. We had a few sheepskins, with a coffee pot and some cooking untensils tied to the horse. These were our only worthwhile possessions. It happened over 30 years ago. We simply left our home in the Canyon to make another home in the Chinle Valley. We found a good site where we set up camp. We put together a crude shelter in the midst of a greasewood wilderness. I had some large sewed-together flour sacks which I spread over some taller greasewood bushes as a temporary shelter.

My husband went into the forest daily to chop logs for our new home. In a short time he built a nice, cozy small hogan. After that he began the long struggle of clearing the land for our farm. After he had fenced the farm he cultivated the land and planted the corn and other produce which we lived on. When we were settled we had all that we needed.

61

A scene in Canyon de Chelly. The striped effect on the rock wall is caused by minerals which have been dissolved by the rain.

My husband then decided to look for some kind of employment. He went off the Reservation to work on the railroad away from home, but he would spend the winter months with us. In the spring, he planted and then left again. The children and I took care of the farm. We watered the vegetables and weeded the corn. My children were good and helped me a lot while their father was away. We raised abundant melons, vegetables and a large field of corn. Many people came around to buy melons, fresh corn, potatoes and other vegetables. Some traded their sheep, and that was how we began our first herd. First, we had only two or three, but they began to increase yearly, and soon we had a good-sized herd.

In the fall, when my husband returned from his summer work, we steam-cooked the late corn in a deep, hot pit; then we dried most of the cooked corn for winter use. After we harvested the corn, pumpkins and potatoes and dried the beans, we stored them in an underground cellar for our winter food. Our children were well trained. They never asked for sweets or fruits. They ate what we produced on the farm and were satisfied. I have felt fortunate to have a fine husband; he has loved us very much. My mother was right when she said to choose a good man to care for the children and me. I have lived with my beloved husband for over 40 years. We are both old, however.

When my children all were old enough I got a job as a housekeeper, and I worked about 16 years. I also worked for the government at the Bureau of Indian Affairs boarding school in Chinle. My husband is working for a construction company, and he still is supporting us.

I have told you briefly about my education. My father encouraged me to learn to speak English. He said, "You might work for white people someday. Whatever you learn in school will benefit you in your job." When my father first took me to enroll we went in a two-horse buggy or buckboard. That was in 1918. My father told me to go to the Roman Catholic Church while in school because the missionaries there instructed the children to be good Christians. Even though I was a small child, I knew what my father was talking about.

I stayed in school there for five years. At first, everything was strange to me. I do not remember what I learned that first year, except that I recall playing with clay. We made all kinds of silly figurines. We also had crayons with which we drew odd pictures in many colors. The following year we began to learn to read and write. First, we learned our A B C's. Then we read short sentences like, "I see a cat," "I see a dog," and so on. I learned more year after year. However, in those days, the school did not have all the instructional aids in the dormitories like today's schools have. We had only one matron who looked after all the girls in one dormitory. Strict discipline was practiced then. When a girl was naughty she got a spanking with a ruler or a strap.

I will tell you a story about an awful experience in school. One day all the girls took a long walk into Canyon de Chelly. It was on a Sunday afternoon. We walked and walked until we came to an apple orchard. The apples on the trees were still small and green. Among the girls I had some friends with whom I always chummed around. We were walking together. Then, one of the girls said, "Hey, let's stay behind and hide."

After the other girls had walked back toward the school for a while we got out of our hiding place and picked some of the apples. It was getting late in the evening. We always had a few things with us in small terry-cloth bags that we had made ourselves. We filled the bags with sour apples and ran back to the school as fast as we could. When we arrived at the dormitory the girls had eaten their supper and the dorm doors had been locked. We banged on the doors until the girls' matron heard us. She unlocked the door without a word. Then we stayed around for a while in the playroom. When it was time, we all went to our beds. Then, everything suddenly became quiet when the matron came in and called our names. She told us to pull our blankets down and lie on our stomachs. She had a wide strap in her hand. She began whipping us one by one, and we screamed with agony. We had broken one of the school's rules. We all deserved the punishment. Our mothers and fathers did not say anything to the matron for strapping us. They all knew we were wrong. It was a good lesson. Thereafter, I learned the rules of the school. I never backtalked to my teachers or the girls' matron, and I learned not to be led into temptation by others.

In our classroom we learned to keep our desks clean and to be polite to others. I am grateful to all of my teachers who worked hard to educate me. Discipline was strict. We hustled at each command. Hesitation meant punishment. That was how we were treated at the time. Our parents wanted us to get an eduction, and we learned the hard way. When one of the students got naughty or stubborn in the

63

classroom he or she sat as the "dunce" in a corner for hours. When one of us got caught chewing gum the teacher made the student put the gum on the tip of his nose and stand facing the class all day until school was dismissed. All of the government boarding schools were run the same way.

In 1923 I was transferred to the Fort Apache Boarding School. I was in the fifth grade. We went to Gallup, New Mexico, in a big truck. From there we boarded a train. It was my first train ride. The trip seemed almost eternal before we reached our final destination. Come to think of it, though, we traveled only 96 miles by rail to Holbrook, Arizona; and, from Holbrook we were taken to Fort Apache in trucks. We arrived at the school late in the evening. The Fort Apache school had been an old Army post. I think that all the places in the West with the word "Fort" were once Army headquarters. It was dark; so we were taken to our dormitories and straight to bed, without a meal. The next morning was our first chance to look over the place. To me it seemed like a desert. I felt very lonely. I had never been that far from home. Everything was strange. That evening all the girls I came with gathered together. We sat talking about our homes and wept all evening.

The school had many activities, but we were not interested at first. Students still were coming in, and classes hadn't begun yet; so we had idle hours for several days, which made us homesick. After classes began our loneliness disappeared. I was so involved in my lessons that I did not have time to be lonely. Often, in the evenings, though, I thought about my family and home.

64

Spider Rock in Canyon de Chelly, as it appears from the south rim.

The school did not furnish our clothes. When we left Chinle we had packed only two changes; so we had to wash our clothes every evening to have clean ones to wear the following day. We had high-topped tennis shoes and long black stockings. Washing our clothes too much wore them out rapidly. Soon they were practically all rags. Finally, the school sewed us some new clothing.

In those days, we washed our clothes by hand. There were no washing machines or dryers in the dorm. There was a laundry where the school linens were laundered, but we were made to wash our own clothes. At Fort Apache we had two girls' matrons who worked in shifts. Today, a larger number of adults work with the children in the schools. I was taken to Fort Apache in 1923, and in 1927 (after four years) I decided to go home for the summer vacation. Then, the following summer, I chose to work for a family in the neighborhood as a housekeeper. We called this type of work "outing." That was how we learned to work, earn our own money and spend it. The wage we received was five dollars weekly. It was a lot of money to me; so I was tickled and could not wait for each payday. I enjoyed my work very much. Thereafter, I stayed at Fort Apache and earned enough money by working so that I could buy what I needed and have spending money during the school year. I did not return home until 1931—four more years.

I learned a lot while in school. I was in the band, and we went on trips with the sports teams and gave concerts in many places. It took me a while to learn my instrument, but I got the hang of it. My bandmaster was Mr. Howard W. Gorman who became a well known Navajo. He is now a retired Navajo Councilman from Ganado, Arizona. After Mr. Gorman left, our new bandmaster was Mr. Tafoya, a Pueblo Indian from New Mexico. When a music student learned to play one instrument really well, the bandmaster gave that student another instrument. Thus, some of us learned how to play pretty nearly all the instruments we had in school. That was very good because if a student was sick he could be replaced easily.

I worked in the school laundry, too, where we learned how to iron shirts really well. We washed for the school employees who were mostly teachers. They paid us 10 cents each for dresses and shirts, which was another way we could earn spending money.

I dropped out of Fort Apache before I had finished high school. I don't know why I never went back. I just stayed around home and worked for some families in Chinle. Then I worked in the home of the school superintendent at Fort Defiance for three years. His name was John G. Hunter. I enjoyed working for his family. They were very good to me.

My opinion is that traditional education and Anglo education are similar in many ways. Both teach a student to be independent, to have self-respect, to know the facts of life and so on. Getting involved in home activities gives a young person knowledge of Navajo family life. Then, in school, he must be involved in all the activities to learn, advance and constantly be a better student.

I have said that I learned many things in school because I got myself involved by being detailed to various departments. For example, learning to be a good housekeeper began in the dormitory with cleaning and making beds neatly. In the laundry, we learned to wash, iron and fold clothes nicely. In the dining room we learned to set the tables and serve plates. In the kitchen we learned how to cook, make menus and wash the dishes. In the bakery we made bread and pastries. In the sewing department we learned to cut out patterns and make dresses, shirts and many other things. In the classrooms we learned to write, read and speak English, as well as many other academic subjects as we advanced through the grades. All of that was education and was very important to us. That is why we now put our children in school.

While I was a student I also learned to work with small children, teaching them good behavior and how to get along together.

We elders, who are called traditional educators, have an important job. We try to teach our children what we know and have it passed on to their children. In some cases the sequence is broken, and family cultures die out. But my husband and I wanted our children to know themselves—who they really are and how not to be an imitation character. We also wanted them to be educated; so they were placed in school as soon as they reached the proper age. We knew that their education would benefit them in the future.

We have three girls and four boys. They all are grown now. The oldest girl is married and has seven children. Our next girl is married, but she does not have any youngsters. Then we have a boy (a man) who is married and has two children. Next, there is another young man, married with three children—two boys and one girl. Another, a young woman, is married and has three girls and a boy. Our sixth child is a young man with three children—two girls and one boy. Finally, our youngest son, unmarried, is a senior at Northern Arizona University in Flagstaff, as I tell this story.

I am deeply thankful for all of my wonderful children and my grandchildren. The children worked very hard to get good educations, and we, as parents, did our best to help them. Now, all of them who have families also have their own homes and are taking good care of themselves, their spouses and children.

All of my preaching and lecturing was not in vain; and I still continue to lecture to my grandchildren. Our older people long ago taught us never to laugh or mock at our elders, and never to gossip or spread untrue rumors because it created trouble. When a person laughs about, or at, an old man or woman, someday the person who laughs will become worse than the people he is making fun of— even while still young. I have watched my children closely as they were growing up, and I never have seen or heard them joke or laugh at their seniors. Perhaps they did when I was not with them. I don't know. However, as long as they practice what I have taught them, I will be well satisfied and content. And I love them all for it.

67

My husband also has done his duty as a father. When a child got out of hand, he used strict punishment on him or her by using his belt to keep the son or daughter under control. I always knew it was necessary; so I never interfered by shielding them.

Our children have showed their appreciation by telling us how grateful they are for their upbringing. They have all the respect in the world toward us. Many times they recall their experiences about how their father punished them, and they will say, "Thank you, Dad, for the correction." This gives us such an emotional feeling, and we love them that much more. Now my children are all adults, and my husband and I are very proud of ourselves for bringing up our family. We feel that we have done our part well. I hesitate to say it, but I do not know any parents today who lecture to their children, and I wish they would do it.

Our Navajo children need to have good manners and self-respect, as well as respect for others. Parents must reason with their children so that they will understand that father and mother have the upper hand. Parents must not shy away and let their children tell them what to do. Even today, when we have a family get-together that is when my husband and I do most of our counseling. All our children and grandchildren come to the dinner table; and, when we discuss things, we make our plans and decisions in the proper understanding manner.

*I used the dinner table as a good place and time to lecture my family
about how to live proper lives and be credits to the Navajo people.*

Today, many schools have classes in Navajo and other Indian studies. The students are taught the Navajo language and Indian culture, a field that never was thought of when I was in school. We were expected to learn all of that at home. Even speaking Navajo was prohibited at school.

Probably, some persons still think traditional education and culture should be learned only at home. In certain cases that would be right, but many parents do not have the knowledge themselves. Consequently, children become more trained in an Anglo way of life and have no (or little) knowledge about their heritage.

About three years ago three of us older Navajo women were selected to teach Indian culture at the Chinle Boarding School through a special program. We were instructors, so we taught the young girls how to work with wool. They learned how to dye the wool with vegetable dyes and how to card and spin it. They learned to make a loom and to weave rugs. We taught them to weave ceremonial baskets; to string beads in various ways to make necklaces, and to do bead-work headbands. The girls also learned to make pillow tops from the small rugs they wove. They were very enthused about their projects, and we enjoyed working with them. They made many beautiful items which they were proud of. I always thought it was a most worthwhile program. The young girls were well behaved and took great interest in their work. Work like that is needed for the young people in the schools. It gives them a great opportunity to learn what their own people have done, and then perhaps they will continue the traditional skills.

Much of our culture was beginning to be forgotten, but now some of it has been restored because our elders did not want it to vanish. That is why our legends, stories and history must be told and published. We are aware that many of our young people do not understand their native tongue. Sadly, this is so because their parents brought them up in the Anglo culture and never spoke Navajo to them. We, as elders, want all of the schools to teach the Navajo language along with the English language. As I said before, some schools have bi-lingual education, and I know that the young people enjoy it because it teaches them to understand and communicate with their elders in Navajo. I have experienced, with my own grandchildren, the fact that not one of them understands me when I speak Navajo. It is pitiful to be like that, especially (as is true in some cases) when the parents do not speak English. Now, however, my grandchildren who attend the public elementary school will begin to learn the Navajo language in class. That is great! I hope they continue the study because I know it is a wonderful opportunity for the Navajo youth. They need to speak their own language just as well as they speak English. The parents should help by speaking Navajo to their children. No one should be ashamed to speak his native language. Another thing we parents should like our children to learn in school, if possible, is Navajo arts and crafts. They can become good basket weavers, pottery makers, rug weavers and silversmiths. All those products are in great demand in the market.

If the above can be done, Navajos will feel at ease because their culture surely will survive and not become extinct. These are my hopes and desires which are making progress and will become realities someday.

I am only a housewife now, and unemployed, but I have work to do at home which keeps me busy all the time. I take care of the sheep; and, sometimes, I get the ambition to card and spin wool, to set up my loom and begin weaving again. I have a lot of wool prepared.

My discussion has been mostly about my own children and how my husband and I raised them. I want to add that we had a strict home life, and my children were made to obey. Now their children

69

are following in their footsteps. I don't know how my grandchildren behave when they are away from their homes, but, so far, we have had no report of misbehavior—which I am happy about. My husband and I are fortunate to be blessed with a large family; and, in our struggle to raise them, we have had no regrets. My husband often has said that he is proud to be their father. We have watched other families where the parents have had big problems with their children. Some of the young people actually take over their parents and use them in whatever ways they can, including trying to get away with unlawful incidents. Their parents are slaves to those offspring who lie idle around the house. According to my knowledge, it is best that the parents begin teaching their children and using discipline in the early years while their minds still are adaptable, can absorb more, learn to obey, think right and be afraid to do the wrong things. Parents really do not want their children to become problems to themselves and others. I can remember that an often-used word by our elders was "danger." If the parents allow a child to do as he pleases, they will be heading for trouble.

I realize that times have changed and that we live in a different world now—not like the one our elders lived in. And as times have changed the people have changed with them. Today, we see young people walking along the highways, hurrying to get to where the action is. Many have become school dropouts, and they do not know what to do with so much leisure time. They gather in bunches and do themselves harm by smoking and indulging in other bad habits. I am aware of some students who leave home in school buses and, when they arrive at school, sneak away to play hooky. The parents think their children are in school. Then, when it is time for the bus to leave for home, they get on board and "innocently" return to their homes.

As parents we must set good examples for our children, so that they will follow in our proper footsteps. A small child will observe everything his father and mother do. If the parents get into a family fight, it hurts them. If the parents are not reliable, that complicates their minds. Then they become rebellious and stubborn, and the situation has its effects on their education. Their minds do not function normally, and soon they decide to leave school.

Some parents drink alchohol in front of their children. When a child witnesses a parent's condition and actions which result from alcoholism, it is bad for the child's morale. Parents must be cautious and not let children see all the bad things adults can do. If one is a parent, it is his or her duty to bring up the child in the right ways. In many cases, a child is neglected or is in the middle of a broken home, which is terrible. A child is innocent, and we should not hurt him or her that way.

Child negligence and desertion occurs, too; and it is a crime. Parents should show more love for their children. Relationships are very sacred, and we should practice a close relationship in our families. Then, when a mother has to reprimand her child, he will return her love by being good. Children have sensitive feelings. Sad, but how true it is that many parents fail to see that! In my family, the most appropriate time that I used to lecture my family was at the dinner table. I gave them short lectures, and I still do when they are home.

71

The father generally is the main one who has the upper hand. A child should be able to look up to his father as the ideal parent. But, if the father drinks and is not reliable, then the child will think "Why not me, too."

In a like manner, a child will pick up any words his parents say; so the parents must be careful about their language around children. Family brawls are bad for a child to witness, making him or her unhappy and irritable. Also, they will not have confidence in their parents. A child's mind is full of great imagination and sensitivity, and it will react to many things.

Parents also must be cautious when they discuss confidential subjects. Children have a keen sense of hearing, and they may hear something the parents don't want them to know. Then, all of a sudden, a child may ask an incredible question in front of family friends. This can be embarrassing. An old person is just the opposite. When he is spoken to, he frequently hears differently because his hearing is not good.

Another thing, scolding and yelling at children all the time is bad practice. Parents are hurting them more that way than by whipping them. One must reason quietly with them. Soft words cannot do any damage. Children need all the affection parents can share with them. Bringing them up right will help them grow into fine adults, and they, too, will follow good examples when they become parents.

Today we hear much about corruption of the young people, and we parents are the ones who must help them. Sure, they are entitled to some good clean fun, but one must not let them get involved in things that are wrong. Some get into deep trouble, and the parents suffer financially and with heartaches.

Why are today's children such big problems? The parents have failed them by not teaching what is right; and they are afraid of their own children. It is sad to see a child in trouble, but whose fault is it? My answer is—the parents'. We parents who have children who never have given us any problems certainly are thankful that we lectured them from the beginning and that they listened to us. Not all children these days are bad; don't misunderstand me. There are children who know what is right and what is wrong, and they behave properly.

I have nearly 20 beautiful grandchildren; so I know what I am talking about. I still lecture to my children and to the grandchildren who are old enough to understand. They listen and never say that I "bug" them. I want my grandchildren to be like their fathers and mothers, I speak to them in English, and then I try to teach them common words in Navajo. I am not boasting that I am a perfect mother and grandmother. My English is not perfect. I preach to my family about the good ways of life because I love them. All parents should bear this in mind and do what I have done. They should show their children that they mean business by being strict once in a while. A timid personality will only lead them apart from you. I think it is heartbreaking when children do not understand their own parents because children need their parents. When children become uncontrolled, the parents weep and say that their children do not want them. I don't think there is such a thing as a child beyond help. Aside from home, there are specially trained counselors who can help them for the asking.

I truly hope that readers will bear in mind all that I have said. They can judge who and what I am—and why I believe that I have made my life a success.

Hoke Denetsosie

I WAS BORN AT THE BASE of the north slope of the Gray Mountain area, not far from where Highway 64 enters from the east into Grand Canyon National Park. My family and relatives had spent several months at their winter camp near Cedar Mountain, close to Red Butte which is located south of the junction of the Colorado River and the Little Colorado. It was in the spring, while enroute back to the summer camp with the sheep, that I was born. The place was a small canyon, one of several tributaries or creek beds that go into the Little Colorado River, less than one-fourth mile from the edge of the creek and about two miles west of the River's gorge.

Recently my mother and I revisited the site. It was a small rocky limestone canyon, with all sides sloping down to the dry creek bed which contained many boulders of all sizes. The place is so rocky that there is very little dirt surface, although one level spot exists with room enough to pitch a small tent. Piles of stones still are there which were used to steady the poles that supported our canvas tent. Next to the spot—a few yards away—is a wagon and truck trail that continues to be used by herdsmen and Navajo families as they move back and forth according to grazing conditions in the general area.

My grandfather, whose name was *Diné Ts'osi,* climbed down with ropes into the Little Colorado River and packed drinking water back up, some of which was used to bathe me. They spent about five days there after my birth; then they continued their journey to the summer camp located on the northeast end of Gray Mountain.

I was born in 1920, and I now (1976) live in the vicinity of Tuba City, on the north side, close to the old public high school. I am of the Towering House People *(Kinyaa'áa nii*—my mother's

73

I was born in a small canyon—a dry creek bed which went into the gorge of the Little Colorado River. It was very rocky, but my parents found a clear dirt spot big enough to pitch a tent.

74 side), and my father's clan is Where the Yucca is Strung Out— *(Hashk'ąą hadzohí).* My father's relatives reside in the region of the Little Colorado River near Leupp, Arizona.

From my infancy to early childhood those were the areas where I was raised. From the day I started to walk my aunts or my mother took me along to herd our large flock of sheep and goats, until I was old enough to take care of them alone. Because the herd was large, it really took two persons to watch over it. There were plenty of coyotes and wildcats.

As I grew to understand things I learned I had many relatives. At that time one of my great-grandmothers was living, as well as a grandmother and grandfather. I had five aunts and one uncle, as well as several grandaunts and granduncles, of whom I saw only a few. My grandmother and great-grandmother told about them. They were living elsewhere on the western part of the Navajo Reservation. Today, only my mother and two aunts and their children are living. The rest have been gone for years. They were very kind and affectionate to me, and I grew to love them very much. Later, when I was in school, I was saddened to learn of their passing away, one by one.

The present Highway 64 was once only a slightly improved dirt road that stretched from the Cameron store. It went due west from the base of Gray Mountain; then it followed the rim of the Little Colorado River gorge and up the higher valleys until it entered the Grand Canyon Park. It passed about one-fourth mile west of our summer sheep camp.

I remember very little of those first years; but, back about 1925 or 1926, I recall that some tourists would pass our camp. Although we lived down in the canyon and our camp was hidden from the road, we always could hear the cars pass because they were very noisy in those days. They did not have mufflers. At first there were only a few. In those remote areas white men or women weren't often seen, but each year more and more travelers passed. Sometimes an aunt and I would graze our sheep near the road, and, then, the Anglos would see us and stop. They would get out their cameras and take our pictures in exchange for some oranges, apples, candy or small amounts of money. I thought we were rich because in those days we could buy many things for a dollar. Those were the first white people I ever saw, except for the trader at Cameron; and, when they talked, we didn't understand.

Eventually, my brothers and sisters were born and soon began to walk and be helpful. Besides assisting our parents and other relatives in sharing the chores and duties of everyday living, we children enjoyed playing in the rugged country around home, like climbing rocks and playing tag among huge boulders. We used to chase cottontail rabbits among the rocks, and they would scurry away to their favorite holes in crevices. We devised ways to use long sticks to poke into the holes and give several twists once a rabbit was located. A stick would grab the loose skin, and we would pull the rabbit out. At home mother would fry the animals for us. The meat was white, tasting something like chicken.

Many times mother would scold us for playing among the rocks because there always was a possibility of coming upon rattlesnakes, which were plentiful. Actually, we saw many varieties of snakes, but, fortunately, we never had a serious problem with them. My mother

Moenkopi, near Tuba City in Arizona, from the east.

76

The dry creek bed, where Hoke was born, of a tributary of Little Colorado River, looking north. The river's gorge is beyond the shadowed area.

was afraid because she was almost bitten by a rattler one time, which was a good reason for her concern when we were playing or herding.

All the beauties of nature would unfold before us in the early summer. In fact, nature probably was our best teacher; and we were curious. We saw many colorful forms of vegetation, and we learned their names from our folks, especially those that were good for food or had other uses. We also learned that there are poisonous plants—some that should not even be touched, certainly not eaten. In the fall many of the plants in our region bore fruit that could be harvested for winter use.

At the base of the Gray Mountain there are no trees, but timber and firewood can be hauled from the mountain top. Usually, though, hogans in our area are made of field stones. Circular walls are formed by laying large flat stones fitted neatly one over the other. Usually the wall is about a foot and a half thick and about six feet high. Logs are cribbed together on top to form the ceiling and support for the roof. There is an opening in the roof's center called a smoke hole. Clay and mud are plastered in the rock cracks and between the logs so that rain and snow cannot penetrate.

In many places along the canyon walls, beneath strata of limestone, there are natural caves large enough so that small rooms can be prepared under the overhanging rocks. These can be enclosed with stone walls plastered with fine adobe clay. One such place was built by my grandfather a few yards northwest from our rock hogans. The room was so tightly made and dry that it was used to store harvested crops hauled from the valley around Tuba City and Moencopi, a Hopi village.

Each fall, after the crops were ripe, the older folk would haul mutton and beef on wagons to the farming communities at Tuba City and Moencopi. They would barter meat for farm produce and any crops that were in season. In this way many Navajo folk formed friendships and acquaintanceships among the Hopi people. During the summer, numerous Hopi dances were (and are) held at the villages; and many Navajo families would make long journeys on horseback and by wagon during those occasions to renew acquaintances, to feast and to trade. When our folk returned with these items some of the fruit was sun-dried, placed in the storeroom and later taken out for winter use.

77

We had three places on top of Gray Mountain where we took our sheep during the summers. The days and nights were cooler by several degrees, and it was a pleasant place to live.

At that time there weren't many young people who had any school learning. The Navajo life style was of a purely traditional nature. Because the country was rugged, harsh and primitive, all members of the family were taught to endure the hard ways.

Young boys and girls were exposed to the elements. They learned the need for physical fitness, and they ran races at dawn and at noon when it was hot. This built stamina. Children were taught to help the family by sharing the chores and duties of everyday living. The boys learned to care for sheep, horses and other domestic animals. The girls learned to help their mothers in preparing wool and in using all knowledge and techniques necessary to the making of a rug, a task at which their mothers already had established themselves as expert weavers. They were taught the Navajo style of homemaking, including learning how to prepare many traditional foods which were grown in the fields, as well as those gleaned from natural sources. They were taught to sew and make traditional clothes from many colorful calicos and other materials that were bought at the trading post.

Everyone was expected to know and learn much basic background knowledge of Navajo culture, the social system, religious concepts and rituals. Children were taught these principles through legends, mythology and songs. Because my grandfather was a medicine man he taught the children many things. Our grandparents even told us about the hardships and miseries they experienced during the period of the "Long Walk" to Fort Sumner and back between 1864 and 1868. Through our social system we learned about clan relationships, and we developed deep respect for our parents and older people because of their native wisdom.

My childhood happiness with my parents and relatives while living the traditional way in natural surroundings was to be shattered about this time, however; and I didn't know of events happening in other parts of Navajoland, much less in the outside world.

I was going to be forced to go to school.

The only knowledge I had of places outside of our locality came from frequent trips on horseback or by wagon to the trading post at Cameron, about eight or 10 miles to the east on the rim of the Little Colorado River gorge. The trader was the first white man I ever knew

An abandoned rock hogan shelter, circa 1924-1928—
one of the former sheep camps located at the base of
Gray Mountain in Arizona on the east side— looking
toward the southwest.

who understood and talked Navajo. I learned later that his Anglo
name was Hubert Richardson and that his Navajo name was the word
for Blue Eyes.

When I was a boy many areas of the western Navajo country
were getting more people, and communities were emerging. Among
these communities two became prominent and were known as the
Tuba City and Leupp agencies. Boarding schools had been established some years earlier, and each fall plans were made to fill them
with students. In order to get full capacity the school authorities
hired young Navajos who had been students and deputized them as
school agents and policemen who went out in mounted groups
among the Navajo families. They forced them, with threats of jail
sentences, to give up their children to fill the schools. In some cases
they even kidnapped the boys and girls. (Since that time many accounts of these indignities to families have been told.)

During one late summer, through the Navajo "grapevine," my parents got information that all children of school age were ordered to go to school and that they would be notified by the mounted police when the time came. My father and mother must have pondered on this and wondered how they could break the news to their children. Because I was a possible candidate to be sent to school, one day my father saddled his horse and told my mother, "My son and I are going for a ride to the trading post." On the way to the post I wondered what was on his mind and why the sudden special treatment. When we arrived at the Cameron store he bought many good things for me. This was his way of telling me that something was on his mind so that I would not be scared. On the way back to the Gray Mountain road he said, "Son, I want you to go to school. Pretty soon some policemen will be coming to ask for children."

I asked him "Where?"

"Over in Leupp," he said. "I hope that you will understand this situation."

But I didn't really understand, for I didn't know what he meant.

Summer passed, fall came, and my parents, my grandparents and other relatives moved to another sheep camp on top of Gray Mountain. Now, every day, my little brothers and sisters were out with the herd because they did not want to be seen.

So one day in the fall of 1926 I was at home with my mother and father when the mounted policemen came to our camp. One of the spokesmen for the group (I later learned his name was Fred Kay, now a noted medicine man) was a young fellow who was working out of the Leupp Boarding School. He said, "We are recruiting children for school. How many are you sending?"

My father and mother replied that they were sending me; and he explained, "We will be spending the night at an all-night sing (Navajo ceremonial) a few miles down the valley at a neighbor's camp. We already have sent some children there to join the others."

My father replied, "We will saddle the horse and be there before sundown."

My grandmother put up a protest against my going to school because I was too small, but it was to no avail. The policemen ignored her. When the time came to leave, my mother put her arms around me and wept silently; then she took a long good look at me and said, "Son, you will be good and brave, won't you?"

I didn't say anything. I just nodded my head.

By evening we rode on horseback to this neighbor's home. Many people were gathered at the medicine hogan because there was an all-night "Beauty Way" sing going on. The people had come on horses and in wagons because hardly any Navajos owned cars or trucks then. At the sing everyone chanted many blessing songs all night, until dawn. Some of the kids managed to stay awake. My father would pass to me a pouch of corn pollen and explain what to do; then I would pass it on to the next person. During the progress of a sing, every so often a pouch of pollen is handed to a person, starting from the doorway clockwise. Each one takes a pinch of pollen and places it on the top of his tongue; another bit is placed on the forehead and the last pinch is offered to Mother Earth, Sky and Sun. All this time the person says silent prayers, asking blessings for well-being. He then passes the pouch to the person on his left, and the same ritual is repeated. After the sing was completed at dawn, we managed to sleep a little until sunrise.

Early in the morning, after we had eaten, the police assembled us near our transportation which consisted of two old black Model "T" Fords. They started to warm up the cars, and the machines just shook all over. Altogether there were 14 boys and girls, all taller than I was. Some of the parents gathered around talking to their kids. Some were weeping. There was a wave of sadness all around. All of us wore our hair long, tied into bundles behind our necks. Just before we climbed into the cars some of the girls' parents got shears, and cut off the hair bundles and kept them. As we moved out everyone wept again, and we all waved good-bys; then we were on our way.

Four policemen went with us, one a driver and the other a chaperon in each car. The highest possible speed was about 15 miles per hour, which we thought at the time was quite fast. My father and other men rode horses alongside, and many times they would disappear in the distance when they were taking short cuts. We traveled eastward past what is now Gray Mountain store and Black Falls. Then we crossed the Little Colorado River, passed the Grand Falls and Sunrise trading post; and, by late afternoon, we arrived at the Leupp Boarding School. We had traveled 55 miles on rugged, dusty, unimproved horse and wagon trails.

81

The boarding school was situated on a barren red clay flat area near the Little Colorado River bed. When we arrived I saw a cluster of large brick buildings, mixed with a number of white frame houses, with here and there a big cottonwood tree. The outer edge of the campus was surrounded by huge dikes. At the south end there were a couple of trading posts several yards apart. The campus also had a high steel tower with a big water tank on top. I used to wonder how they got it up there without dropping it. At times it would leak and would shower the area below with water. Leupp gave me the impression of being a big place. And it was just that, because I never had seen anything like it.

As we were led into a strange big building, the girls suddenly vanished. The bigger boys also were led elsewhere, and that left we smaller ones to an Anglo lady matron who was in charge. They cut our long hair off completely, right down to our scalps because some of us might have had lice. After we took showers, we were given new clothes and shoes. I remember clearly that the small boys wore blue denim coveralls with red trim around the waist and sleeve cuffs. These were brand new, and we thought they were great, but they were the last new clothes we got. Later we wore clothes that had been laundered a lot. School employees washed them so much that they became threadbare and full of patches.

My father came to visit before long and found a boy whom he introduced to me. His name was Rex Monroe, and my father said that he was my cousin—a son of a clan relative. His father's name in English was Little Gambler. My father asked Rex to take care of me because I was small and, in a way, helpless. He did look after me some, but, because he was in other classes, I wasn't with him much except during playtime. Three of my father's younger sisters also were going to school there. They were teenagers; and, when I got lonesome and started to cry, they would come and comfort me. They used to take turns going around with me.

When they enrolled us for classes I didn't have an English name, only a Navajo name, but most of the others didn't have names, either. In the office there were the principal, a teacher and an interpreter.

"What will we name him?" one asked, and another answered, "Let's call him 'Hoke,' after Hoke Smith, a U. S. senator from Georgia." "Denetsosie" was borrowed from my grandfather. My

The crowded Model T Fords went over the rough roads at about 15 miles per hour, which seemed fast to us. My father and other men rode horses beside us.

father was absent, and they didn't know his name. I know now that my name really should have been McCabe.

The first year I didn't attend many classes because of lonesomeness. Being small and young, I couldn't adjust to things, and I cried much of the time.

Conditions at the school were terrible. It was isolated, the nearest town being Winslow, about 30 miles away. Food and other supplies were not too plentiful. We were underfed; so we were constantly hungry. Clothing was not good, and, in winter months, there were epidemics of sickness. Sometimes students died, and the school would close for the rest of the term.

It was run in a military fashion, and rules were very strict. A typical day went like this: Early in the morning at 6 o'clock we rose at the sound of bugles. We washed and dressed; then we lined up in military formation and drilled in the yard. For breakfast, companies formed, and we marched to the dining room, where

83

we all stood at attention with long tables before us. We recited grace aloud, and, after being seated, we proceeded with our meal. If, during the meal, we got too noisy, an attendant, who was the disciplinarian, usually blew a basketball whistle, and all became quiet. After the meal was finished we went into formation again,

At many of the ceremonial "sings" men and boys participated in the traditional sports as horseracing, chicken pulling, rabbit hunting on horseback, footracing and wrest

84

and one of the boys, who had been selected, rose and took a position where he could be heard, holding a thick sheet of metal about 10 inches square with a rope handle, together with a metal rod. He would "bang" away at this metal, while we kept in step and marched single file out of the dining room, and then back to the dormitories until we were properly dismissed.

Some teachers and other workers weren't very friendly. When students made mistakes they often were slapped or whipped by the disciplinarian who usually carried a piece of rope in his hip pocket.

At the end of the term in May parents and other visitors would come to the school. School authorities would set a special day and invite them. A day of feasting, with outdoor activities such as footraces, Navajo style wrestling, horse races, pole climbing, chicken pulling and other events were enjoyed. Horse racing was the favorite of all the events, and there was a lot of betting. That was the beginning of summer vacation. Sometimes there was rabbit hunting.

Many people from miles around came on horses and in wagons. The people couldn't afford automobiles then.

My father and my grandparents would come on horseback to **85** fetch me. With one of them I would ride double, and we would travel more than 50 miles to reach home again.

That year was my introduction to so-called "civilization."

A very unhappy incident happened to me one summer which I will relate. It was the beginning of my second vacation at Leupp. All of the students were ready to leave for home, and the usual feasting and races were going on. My father and grandparents had come for me again. I was very glad to see them, and they were happy to see me. My grandparents wished us to leave for home as soon as the activities were over, but my father had a different plan. He

A Model T Ford—convertible—similar to those mentioned in several places in this book.

wanted to take me to his relatives' place to spend the summer with him. It was some distance north of Leupp. At home at Gray Mountain my parents must have had problems, and they were not living together any more. There was a conflict, and I was confused as to whom to go with that summer. My grandparents insisted that I should go with them, and a small group of people gathered around to help settle the argument. A local noted Navajo leader was asked to intervene between them for a decision. Finally, it was decided that I should go with my father. We traveled on horseback north about 40 miles to my father's relatives who were living near the old Dinnebeto store. (The store has been abandoned since that time.) This was the first time that I met my other grandfather and grandmother *(shináli)* and got to know my aunts and uncles on my father's side. They were very kind to me.

My grandfather's name was Red Camp *(Ch'ah Łichíí)*. Just when I was getting acquainted with them my father decided to move on to some other relatives; and, by the middle of summer, we had visited three homes. We would stay at one place a while and then move on to the next. Most of the time I herded sheep at each place. My father was with me only briefly because he attended a lot of ceremonies (sings) that were held around the area. Usually card games went on during and after the sings, and my father was very fond of card playing. After an absence for some time, he came to see me again one day. He rode in, using his rope as a halter and riding bareback. He had lost his bridle, saddle, saddle blankets and other gear while gambling. I don't remember whether he also lost his horse later.

The people whom I herded sheep for were very nice to me, except the last place. They were mean and strict. They would get me out of my bedroll (usually a sheepskin and a blanket) at dawn and sometimes make me take the herd out without breakfast. My only means of transportation, besides walking, were a burro and an old albino mare. The horse was so lazy and listless that it took a lot of effort on the rider's part to get it going. With me living like that during a hot summer at a constant pace I soon was very dirty, and my hair was unkempt. Even my clothes were sweat-hardened and ragged.

One day, on a late summer afternoon, the man of the household, called "Big Belly Policeman," decided that we would go to a squaw dance (a three-day ceremonial) which was being held not too far away. Having only a couple of horses available as a team for the wagon which was heavy, it was decided that the wagon would be taken apart to lighten it. So, the wagon box was taken off. Then they took the hind wheels off; only the front end was to be used. All the members of the family changed into their best clothes for the occasion, while I remained in rags. The horses were hitched to the old wagon. There were five of us—Mr. and Mrs. Big Belly, their small daughter, Mrs. Big Belly's brother who was a young man, and me.

After the bedding, food and cooking utensils were securely tied to the wagon, four of us climbed on and perched in the space between the two front wheels. With two grown people and two children it was crowded, but we all held on; and we raced off on the homemade chariot, while the young man rode alongside on his horse. There were no brakes; so the wagon was controlled by reining the horses to go slow when necessary. The sun went down. Soon it was dark and a full moon rose above the horizon. It was late at night when we arrived. We camped in the midst of several families who

87

Four of us rattled off in a homemade chariot, with not much space. Mrs. Big Belly's brother rode along on his horse.

Early in the morning of the third day of the squaw dance many horsemen rode at full gallop to the medicine hogan, whooping war cries and firing pistols—a re-enactment of a surprise attack which is part of the ceremony.

had their campfires going, and so we spent the night—the second of the dance.

88

On the first day of the ceremony they had taken the sacred "rattle stick" *(aghaal)* to an old man by the name of "Many Children," who lived near the Cameron Trading Post about 40 miles to the west. Many families had joined him to help with the dance. My folks, being distant relatives to him, had come from Gray Mountain.

It was in the early morning of the third day, just as the sun was coming up (we had spent the night at the main camp), that the Cameron crowd approached over the distant horizon. The horsemen came in, riding at full gallop, to the main medicine hogan. That was a re-enactment of a surprise attack which is part of the squaw dance ritual. They dashed in with whooping war cries and shooting pistols into the sky, circled the hogan and raced back to the approaching crowd. After that was repeated four times it was over. Several yards from the medicine hogan a temporary shelter made of cottonwood trees and branches was built for and by the visiting group.

Early that afternoon the drummer and singers came out in the open, singing circle or round dance songs and beckoning the girls and their partners to come out. Soon lively dancing was in progress, and many people gathered around and watched. My aunts (mother's younger sisters) who were participating in the dance had just taken a "break" and were coming out of the crowd for a stroll when they spotted me. One of them recognized me as I watched the dance while sitting in the back of a neighbor's truck. Two of the girls came over and greeted me in a very nice and friendly manner. One of them stayed and watched over me while the other disappeared in the crowd. Soon, she and another woman came again. One of them ran up, put her arms around me and started weeping. I did not recognize that she was my mother until she told me. They helped me off the truck and led me back to their camp, where I was surprised to find that my maternal grandparents and other relatives also had come to this sing. My folks asked one of the men to do an errand, and he rode to the nearest trading post where he bought some new clothes for me. We went to a creek where I had a bath and a change of clothing.

89

It was my first bath and change for the whole summer. Later that day I was showered with gifts of candy and other goodies which I hadn't had all year. The following day, at the end of the sing, I left with my folks and the others. I did not say goodby to my father because they took me away without his knowledge.

At the Gray Mountain home I spent the rest of the summer getting reacquainted with my brothers and sisters and other relatives.

After two hard years at Leupp my folks decided that I should go to the Tuba City Boarding School because it was nearer our home. That was in the fall of 1928.

The first week of September, 1928, came. During the summer the parents of school-age children had been informed by the Tuba City Agency Superintendent, Mr. C. L. Walker, and other school officials that a day of feasting, outdoor activities and entertainment was to be held, and for parents and guests to bring their children for school enrollment.

Preparation for enrollment at that time was a slow process because travel was by wagon and horseback. Distances were long, and the roads mostly were unimproved wagon trails. Some families started for Tuba City ahead of time and camped near the Agency. There were no lodgings nor regular campgrounds. Then the day came, and the main street of Tuba City was crowded with travelers on horses and in wagons.

I went with Mother, enrolled with other students, and we all were assigned to dormitories and classrooms. Because our folks understood no English, everything was done with the assistance of interpreters. At noon an outdoor cookout was held under huge cottonwood trees. The children and their parents enjoyed stew, big chunks of beef and other food. After lunch we moved to the playground where outdoor activities, many kinds of sports, were held.

In the late afternoon our parents left, and school life began. I found it not much different from Leupp. Everything was rigid and strict. All students, big and small, had to obey the rules. Some older students were picked by the disciplinarian to assist in seeing that the regulations were enforced. That was especially hard on the new young children who were not used to being away from home. Some of them did not adjust readily to the setup, and soon there were runaways, which kept the Agency policemen busy hunting them down and returning them to school. The school's grades were from the beginner through the sixth grade. Small kids had regular classes in reading, writing and counting. After 4 p.m. we were dismissed and allowed to play until 5 o'clock. Then, a bugle called for cleanup, formation and supper time.

The larger boys and girls took classes in the mornings; and in the afternoons the boys helped at the farm and dairy and did other chores, while the girls worked in the laundry, kitchen and dorms. At that time the school farm and dairy provided crops and milk for the students in the dining room.

A typical school day began at 6 o'clock in the morning. The students were awakened by a bugle call—"reveille" (time to get up). They washed, dressed and fixed their beds. Another call made them rush to the outside courtyard and stand in formation until a signal from the dining room—the ringing of a large bell—called them to breakfast. This was repeated morning, noon and evening. As at Leupp, the students marched in formation, entered the dining room and stood at their places. "Grace" was said, and then they were seated. After each meal they were marched out of the building and dismissed.

Before classes began at 9:30 a.m. the students were required to clean the dorms, then get themselves ready for school. Usually there was an inspection before classes. Each Saturday morning the dorms got a special scrubbing and cleaning for the following week. On Saturday afternoons the boys were required to get haircuts and shine

Main building of the Tuba City, Ariz., elementary school—not in existence when Hoke was a boy.

The new Two Gray Hills High School in Tuba City, Ariz., looking south.

Western Navajo Agency (BIA) boarding school campus in the far distance at Tuba City, where Hoke Denetsosie attended. The view is from the east.

their shoes for Sunday inspection and church services. Other time on Saturday and Sunday was free.

For games, besides basketball and football, the larger boys played "shinny" (a ground hockey). Any number of players were chosen by the teams opposing each other. A soft ball was buried in the middle of a field. Two opposing centers would swing clubs and pound the ball out until it became visible. It then was hit to one of the players, and from that time it became a running game. The team that moved the ball over the opposition's goal line made a score.

In the winter, when there was snow, the larger boys would go out, with chaperons, a few miles away from the campus where they would form a circle about a mile across and round up cottontails and jack rabbits. Each boy carried a wooden club. There also were gunmen in the circle to help by shooting rabbits. Sometimes as many as 50 animals would be killed; only a few would escape. After these hunts we would have rabbit for Sunday dinner.

For Sunday church services there was much preparation. After breakfast all the boys and girls would clean up, dress for inspection, assemble outdoors for a hymn-singing session, followed by Sunday school and church. The boys wore woolen olive-gray-green uniforms styled after World War I, with caps and thick-soled shoes. The company officers wore "wrap-arounds" on their legs from below the knees down to the ankles. Later, they wore leather puttees around their calves. When the first puttees were issued some of the boys got a size or so too big; and, when they put the things on, you could see an inch of space around their skinny legs. There was nothing to do but stuff them with white rags to hold them up. It was comical the way a particular officer would stand out front shouting commands—with swollen-looking legs—while school officials would pass inspection nonchalantly, checking for neatness.

The girls wore uniforms, the upper parts known as middies, consisting of white cotton blouses with full-length sleeves and very wide sailor-type collars. Under the collar, around the neck, large triangle-shaped bright red scarves were worn, tied in front. The skirts were a blue-black scottish type, fully pleated and knee length, worn with black stockings and shoes.

In the center of the campus there was a big lawn area, with two spreading cottonwood trees, surrounded by dormitories. Between the trunks of these large trees, in their shade, was a flat wooden platform large enough to hold a piano and a small group of people. On Sunday mornings, after inspection, the companies of boys and girls would form circles on this area of lawn; then, after the hymn books were passed around, the group would sing, led by a slim elderly woman who at one time must have been a concert singer. She would stand on the platform for all to see, while we attempted to sing the hymns in low tones, while her voice would carry above us in a high-pitched soprano. She doubtless got a good workout. She must have liked to sing because she usually wore a smile after each song. This happened every Sunday without fail, unless it was raining or snowing.

After the singing session the students were marched directly to church—Presbyterian, the only church in the community at the time. After we were seated, a doxology (hymn of praise to God) was played by the pianist. The Reverend Mr. Herndon, the preacher, would open the services with a prayer, followed with more singing of hymns. Then, for the next two hours, he would preach to us on righteousness and the evils of sin. Some of us who did not understand the full meaning of the sermons would get bored and fall asleep. With an overheated sanctuary and tight woolen uniforms it was hard to stay awake. But the company officers always were on the alert for this, and the name of each person who fell asleep was written down, to be reported and the culprit called for extra duties as punishment on the following Saturday and Sunday. After the sermon a collection pan with a long handle was passed in front of all those present. Coins in the form of pennies and small change would be offered to show our gratitude for the sermon.

93

Sunday dinners were special—about the only decent meals we had. Roast beef or pork, mashed potatoes, gravy, milk, water and bread were served. For dessert we had apple pie, frosted cake, gingerbread or an apple.

The Babbit Trading Post in Tuba City, Ariz.

In this connection I want to say that some of the student officers were very mean to their squads. Most of the time our desserts were not eaten by us. Instead, apples or pieces of pie or cake were sneaked out in our coat pockets to be given to our captains. That happened so much that our coat pockets would be so stiff and messy that they hardly would bend and we would have a hard time keeping our hands warm on cold days. Those who disobeyed the wishes of the captains usually got a kick in the behind or some other form of punishment, but those things never were reported for fear of reprisals.

The school officials—such as the principal, some teachers, the disciplinarian, the girls' matron, etc.—all practiced various forms of corporal punishment, combined with extra duties for the students, if they thought those things would solve problems. Running away from school, stealing food, talking Navajo and other misbehaviors called for a whipping down in a basement especially provided for that purpose.

These boarding school routines went on from September until the end of May when school was out. Our parents would visit us maybe once a year. On holidays and weekends we stayed at the school grounds, and we would suffer from boredom and loneliness.

A two-room stone cottage was used as a clinic and an operating room. There was one doctor and a nurse, with assistants. (Later, a new hospital, a big dining and kitchen building, a new two-story dorm and another classroom structure were built.)

It was during my second year in Tuba City that I found I was nearsighted, and I had to sit close up front to see what was on the blackboard. I was also one of several children who caught an eye disease known as trachoma. It was prevalent everywhere on the Reservation. An eye specialist was called one day to give us treatment, but, at the time, there were no known drugs that would cure it. The doctors usually scraped the diseased eyelids, which was very painful. In some of the severe cases, like mine, an operation was needed, with further treatment until the condition was cleared. My vision was impaired, and finally I had to wear glasses. In later years this was a handicap to me. It prevented me from entering competitive sports, although I was good at running and other activities.

In the summer of 1929 it was decided by my relatives that we would move from Gray Mountain to a new home at Preston Mesa (Red Mesa) north of Tuba City. My father had died the year before.

My mother, a brother and a sister were living with my maternal grandparents.

It was on a hot July day that the long journey was to begin. The older members of the family had gone ahead some days before. My grandfather told my uncle, one of my aunts, a younger brother and me that we were to drive the large herd of sheep, goats and burros across the hot desert country. The journey was made from the base of Gray Mountain, crossing the Little Colorado River at the Cameron bridge and continuing through the Painted Desert badlands between

95

Preston Mesa, viewed from the southwest.

Cameron and Tuba City. After a week's time we arrived at the foot-hills south of Preston Mesa, a distance of about 60 miles.

At the base of this high red and white sandstone mesa country, covered with juniper and piñon trees, lived a great grandmother and other relatives whom I had not known before. Now they were glad for us to move back for a reunion and to live as close neighbors again. It was there during my formative years on summer vacations from school that I helped with everyday chores, like herding sheep, caring for horses, hauling wood and water, etc. All of us youngsters were exposed to the traditional Navajo life ways, the Navajo social system and religious rituals and concepts. There were many types of ceremonial "sings." We attended and participated in a lot of them. In addition, the menfolk and boys engaged in the traditional forms of entertainment such as horseracing, chicken pulling, hunting rabbits on horseback, footracing and wrestling, which I have mentioned before.

Sixth grade was the highest level of school one could reach at Tuba City. Each year there were many dropouts of students for one reason or another, but not once did I miss school; and I finally reached sixth grade. I had finished those years in an average fashion. In the sixth year I assumed that I had passed for the next grade because I didn't get a certificate.

Then, in the fall of 1932, I transferred to Phoenix Indian Vocational School, a non-reservation institution located in Phoenix, Arizona. This school is one of the several big non-reservation schools in the Western States. More than 35 tribes of Indians from throughout the United States were represented in it, with each tribe speaking a different language. The school was run in a rather strict and old-fashioned conventional way. Academic fields and vocational trades were taught. The grades were from the seventh to twelfth, with the school having facilities for a wide range of studies and programs. Vocational trades included carpentry, painting, masonry work, auto mechanics, leather work, printing, blacksmithing and others. On the school farm there was gardening, as well as caring for hogs, chickens, turkeys and dairy cows.

Activities, besides athletics were drama, various choirs, lettermen's club, school band, orchestral groups and a national guard company.

Also, there were special programs, dances and movies. The movies were called "talkies" because just about that time talking pictures were new and were reaching their popularity.

The girls were taught homemaking, home economics, housekeeping, etc. Only a few students who could afford it went on to higher learning. There were no scholarship funds for college education then.

For religious services on Sundays we had a choice of going to one of the three churches: Protestant, Catholic or Mormon.

When I first went to Phoenix I was dazzled by so many activities and new sights; and trees and vegetation were different from those on the Navajo Reservation. The city of Phoenix was so big that it covered a lot of the "Valley of the Sun" in every direction.

Dormitory life was nothing new to me; so, in time, I became adjusted to things—except for the weather. It was extremely hot, almost unbearable, from about May to October. As for my studies, they were hard, but, eventually, I passed them each year. We were required to learn a trade; so I took up house painting and farming during my junior and senior years. As an avocation I joined the art classes, in which there were few students. There was only one art teacher. She wasn't really equipped with the necessary supplies; so we just used what was provided, and we drew whatever we wished. Mainly the students' subjects were drawn from memory from our homeland scenes and experiences. No attempt was made to teach us the basics of art or advanced studies; so my approach was mostly by trial and error.

I was graduated from the high school in May of 1938.

Being encouraged, and with a much deeper interest in art after finishing school, I took postgraduate work in it. I visited local Anglo artists as much as I could and watched their approaches and techniques, and I got their opinions. Unfortunately, further studies were cut short by the Second World War; so my early art training was brief. During the two years after high school I worked with a new art teacher who had just come out of the Chicago Art Institute. He taught at the Phoenix Indian School, and I assisted him as an apprentice artist. In the summer of 1939 three artists from the school, including me, went to the World's Fair on Treasure Island in San Francisco, observing many exhibitions. I believe it was the next winter that we went to Chicago with a traveling exhibit on Progressive Indian Education from Lawrence, Kansas, with a group of Haskell Institute students (now Haskell Indian Junior College).

In 1940 Dr. Willard W. Beatty, Director of Education for the Bureau of Indian Affairs, Washington D. C., introduced into the schools bilingual and other innovative approaches for school curriculum materials. He employed linguists, writers and illustrators; and, as a result, English-Navajo readers were published.

Ann Nolan Clark, one of the writers, did a number of stories about the everyday life of a little Navajo girl on the Reservation. It later became known as the "Little Herder" series for young Navajo readers. I was chosen to illustrate the books, which was my introduction into the field of illustration. Not knowing any technical approach, I began to study methods and ways of improving my technique as I went along, until all illustrations for the series were finished. In the spring of 1940 I was transferred to the Navajo Cultural Agency at Window Rock under Dr. George Boyce, who was director of Navajo schools over the entire Reservation. I did some work in classroom materials, using the silk screen method of printing. I also assisted local artists who did some work on mural decoration projects. At that time most of the Indian assistants, as we were called then, were very underpaid, with no sign of advancement, no fringe benefits, etc.; and, after four years at Window Rock, I decided to resign my position. I also wanted to see the country and to widen my horizons and outlook on life.

Consequently, I went back to Scottsdale, Arizona, near Phoenix, and I took a job with an Arts & Crafts group which was engaged in leather and textile printing, using the silk screen medium. Within a few months, though, the winter tourist trade in Scottsdale tapered off, sales dwindled and it was time for a summer break; and I went back home to see my relatives for a brief visit. Jobs were scarce everywhere. I went to Flagstaff, then to Williams and on to Grand Canyon National Park (South Rim), where I got a job at the Bright Angel Lodge.

After staying two years, though, I wanted to see new places; so, in the spring, I journeyed to the Kaibab National Forest near Fredonia, Arizona, where my brother-in-law and a sister were working at a lumber camp. I joined them; and, after two summers at lumber camps, we moved to Kanab, Utah, a little Mormon town where my sister worked in the hospital as a nurse and my brother-in-law stayed with a lumber company. A famous western post card company was owned by a cowboy artist named "Dude" Larson who had seen some of my work. We met, he hired me to do western humor cards, and I contracted with him for two years as a cartoonist.

Then, in 1954, in Kanab, I met a noted western author, Jonreed Lauritzen, whose work I admired very much. As a result, we got together on a Navajo story one day, a novel by Mr. Lauritzen entitled "Ordeal of the Young Hunter," describing the early experiences of a young Navajo boy. It was accepted by Little, Brown and Company of Boston, Massachusetts, and still is being published by them. After repeatedly submitting samples of drawings, my work finally was accepted, and I was chosen to illustrate the book.

About 1955 the Bureau of Reclamation, U. S. Department of the Interior, moved one of its branch offices from Denver to Kanab. A crew was surveying the possibility of building a dam and a bridge across the Colorado River at a point called Glen Canyon, some distance down-river from Navajo Mountain. A new highway and a new town site also were being proposed. Many of the people in the locality were hired; and a mass migration to the new town of Page, Arizona, began with construction of a bridge and the Glen Canyon Dam. Among those going to Page were my sister and her family.

From 1960 to 1964 I worked for the Bureau of Reclamation in special services and public relations during construction of the Dam. Mostly I was with a team of photographers doing still and motion pictures documenting the progress of the huge project. I did some work on an artist's conception of the dam, as well as commercial art **99** combining photographs and display work for public relations. With these combined techniques we were able to present fabulous displays, and for me it was a great and rewarding experience. Because of

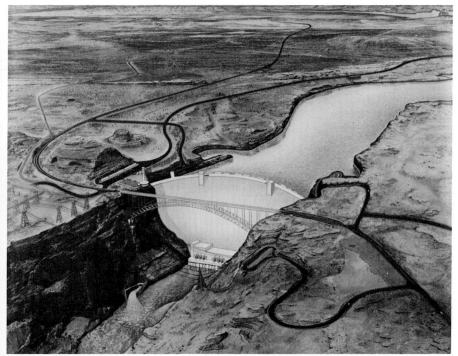

Photo by A. E. Turner,
U. S. Bureau of Reclamation.

*Artist's conception of Glen Canyon dam
and its environs prior to construction.*

A shot from below the huge Glen Canyon Dam at Page, Ariz.—looking east-northeast. The dam forms Lake Powell on the Colorado River.

a new administration in Washington and government spending cutbacks, however, my group was laid off that summer.

Before long, though, a new development occurred. In 1966 a revolutionary new school was established at the base of the northern escarpment of 8,000-foot Black Mountain, near the center of the Navajo Reservation. This experimental Navajo-community-operated school was (and is) known as the Rough Rock Demonstration School.

From the summer of 1967 to 1969 I had the pleasure of working as one of the illustrators there—with a noted Navajo artist, Andrew Tsihnahjinnie.

I liked the fact that some of the important aspects and concepts of the school constituted a unique adventure in community development and local control of education, especially in its involvement of Navajo parents and its leadership by an all-Navajo school board. The school has demonstrated through its philosophy and success that the Navajos can and should be educated to keep their native values and culture while learning the ways of Anglo culture so that they may take their places in the dominant society.

In addition to classroom instruction, the school established a Navajo Curriculum Center, an aspect of which was a materials preparation laboratory that wrote and arranged manuscripts for textbooks and classroom use dealing with significant areas of Navajo culture, history, legends, religion, tribal government, Navajo science and ethnobotony. As one part of our work for a while, Andy and I illustrated a volume of 15 Navajo biographies of prominent historical figures in early Navajo history, as well as current well-known persons. Some books with which we worked consisted of incidents in more recent Navajo history, vividly remembered by the elderly people, or stories which had come down to them from earlier generations of Navajos, originally derived from actual experiences. Much of the material was edited and published by the man who now directs the Navajo Community College Press.

In 1970 I went back to Tuba City to be with my family, and I was employed with the ONEO (Office of Navajo Economic Opportunity), mainly with the Local Community Development Program (LCDP). I worked with my people at the chapter community-"grassroots" levels, and I really learned that the Navajo people had many problems. We conducted group meetings dealing with those problems, and we sought many available resources for assistance. We initiated community projects when funds were available. We gave assistance to needy families and to group programs. As community workers we also served as liaison officers between the Bureau of Indian Affairs Agency and the community people, and we handled leadership training and workshops for our staff. In due time I was promoted to a supervisory (senior supervisor) position and administrative assistant; and I even was recommended to be Agency Director. I declined the recommendation, however.

In October of 1973 I joined the staff of the Navajo and Indian Studies Department at Navajo Community College at Tsaile, Arizona, as one of the artists, primarily illustrating prepared curriculum materials by Navajos, for Navajos and about Navajos, so that they can be utilized by Indian educators as resource materials, as well as by many other persons. A real objective was—and is—to expand in this area of curriculum development at the College, which had been founded in 1969 as the first completely Indian owned and controlled institution of higher learning in the United States. At the College I also have cooperated with another Navajo, Ray Johnson, in doing art work for the many books and other publications of the Navajo Community College Press.

Concluding my account, I wish to mention a few particular thoughts in summary. Having been born into a traditional Navajo way of life, I received my initial formal education, during my childhood, in an Anglo-operated school which had strict and rigid rules. I naturally learned a lot of things, early, from the Anglo society. As I reflect upon those times, my only objections involve the way the schooling was carried out. It was so limited that by the time we left school we were only half prepared to make a living in the dominant world around us. We were to learn later that, in the "outside" world, there was much discrimination and lack of equality, forcing many of us back to our native land. Jobs for Indians were scarce and few. It was by sheer effort and hard work that one was able to make a living.

Since my early life conditions have improved over the years in all areas of our Navajo society. Many changes have taken place, and we have schools with well-trained teachers who do not use harsh methods.

102 The roads have been improved so much that it takes only a few hours to travel where it required days before.

We have more industries and businesses now in Navajoland, and more jobs for both trained and untrained persons.

In addition, there is a tribal educational scholarship fund now for those who aspire to be doctors, nurses, dentists, lawyers, teachers or members of almost any other profession or occupation. Also, our form of tribal government has improved considerably.

Our adaptation to transition from the old life to the new one should help our people in the future. In the final analysis it is our Navajo heritage and the significance of our Navajo beliefs which bind our people—the *Diné*—together through our traditional ceremonialism which helps to make us a great and unique tribe.

For we members of the older generation we have done our part! Today, opportunities for improvement in life constitute a challenge for Navajo youth. Every Navajo child should have the benefit of learning our Navajo ways as well as those of the dominant society. Only by being exposed to both Navajo and Anglo cultures can we be able to distinguish and understand the good things, and the aspects that are not good, about each. One of our traditional Navajo leaders once said, "Navajo schools should strive to prepare their students for life in the modern world, while, at the same time, keeping the best of Navajo tradition and culture."

I think that is wise and fitting.

Hoke Denetsosie, the artist, at a drawing board at Northern Arizona University, Flagstaff, where he was on the summer session staff recently as a consultant in the illustration of children's books to be used by teachers as demonstration material. Standing behind Hoke is Jerry Knowles who was co-director of an Institute on Early Childhood Education. The children were summer demonstration students from the Rocky Ridge BIA boarding school.

103

Hoke, at his drawing board at the Glen Canyon site, working on the artist's conception of the dam.

104

Hoke's wife, Ruth, on the left, and his mother, Lena Butler, standing on the spot where Hoke was born. The view is to the north toward the Little Colorado River gorge.

Hoke and his mother standing near one of the cave storage shelters, with the picture being taken from the east.

David Lansing

MY NAME IS DAVID LANSING, and I live near Red Mesa in the northeastern corner of Arizona. My clan is Within His Cover People (*Bit'ahnii*—my mother's side), and I am born for the Red House People (*Kinłichii' níí*—on my father's side). I have been told that I was born at Aneth, Utah, on March 5, 1901. I will try to relate as much as I can about my life and training.

I grew up near Aneth. I remember a grandfather and a grandmother; also a great grandfather and a great grandmother. We were nomads because we moved here and there with our sheep to such places as Teec Nos Pos, the Dam, Gray Boulder, Black Rock Point, Skinny Water, Salt Water Springs, White Sand, White Mesa and Montezuma Creek. I remember grazing ranges covered with sheep, and mustangs roaming wild in the mountain ranges.

We also cared for cattle that belonged to my close relatives. I remember an aunt and her husband. They raised me as their son. My uncle was a stern man, but he was very kind. He taught me many things. We rose at dawn and ran races. He made me wrestle with him and do other exercises. He taught me how to ride horses and hitch them to the wagon. I also hauled firewood and water for use in our home.

I worked on the farm and around the hogan. My uncle and I did a lot of things together, and I learned much from him. Many times I was tired and did not get enough sleep. I helped him during lambing season. I took care of the sheep, horses and cattle just as he taught me. He kept me out of mischief; so I did not have much time to play like the boys do now. I was busy all the time, learning what to do and what not to do, and I prepared myself for the future.

My uncle made me wrestle with him and do other exercises to make my body strong and tough.

When my aunt and my uncle realized that I was ready to be on my own they told me to go and live as I pleased.

I left home and married a nice woman from Shiprock, New Mexico. We were very happy. Just about that time, however, the **106** stock reduction program came into effect. Many of the Navajo people lost a big majority of their sheep, goats and horses. It was a sad time. After I was married I gradually realized I had more and more responsibilities because I had a family to care for. We had two children, and we lived comfortably; we had sheep, horses and cattle. Later, my wife got sick and died, and one of my children died too; but my older son is still living and has a nice home and a family.

A few years later I remarried. My second wife also was from Shiprock, but we moved to Colorado where I worked in a uranium mine for 10 years. My older brother and sister lived at Red Mesa, and we came to visit them often. They told me not to forget our land because, after they were gone, I would become the owner of it. Soon after I left my job in Colorado and came home my older sister, Zelma, died.

Not long after she passed away my older brother became blind. His name was Kenneth Coalmine. He asked us to come and live closer to him so we could take care of him. We did it, but he, too, died. I am still living on the same homesite with my family. I now have a large family of 11 children, but we get along fine. We have a big house and plenty to eat. All of my children have been or are in school, and some have finished high school. I have one boy going to college in Utah, and he will get his degree this spring (1976). Some of my children have attended the Inter-Mountain High School in Utah. I have two girls at Fort Lewis College in Durango, Colorado, and one in Shiprock High School. The six smaller children are still in Teec Nos Pos grade school. I have lectured to my children as much as I could, and they always have obeyed me and have listened to my lectures. They know what they should do and what they should not do. Our children have great respect for us as their mother and father.

Education is wonderful because a person who is well educated can go a long way. Many opportunities await him. For that reason we want our children to go to school. Times have changed, and education is the only way for young people to keep up with the rapidly progressing world. We want our children to go on to the higher educational institutions. We do not want them to falter along the way. As it is now, there are too many "drop-outs." They become the idle ones who have nothing to do but cause problems in their homes.

Years ago, when I was a boy living at Aneth with my parents, there was a man named *Ba'alili* who lived in the same vicinity. He was a rebel and was very opposed to education. One fall night there was a shoe game going on at our place. I was just a boy, and I wanted to see the game; so my father told me that if I kept the firewood supplied for them I could stay. Now and then I brought the wood in and kept the fire going. When it was near morning I went out to get wood, and I heard someone yelling. I hurried and picked up a few pieces of wood and ran back in. I told the people someone was yelling for help near the east side of the woods. Everyone dropped what he was doing and ran in that direction. Those who stayed behind just stood outside and listened. It was very dark and frightening.

The next day word came that some Navajos had been killed—a man and his wife and their son shot to death. The man who got shot was one of my related elders. He was well known in our area. I suppose it happened because he, too, did not want his children in school.

Not long after the shooting we were living on the farm and harvesting the corn in the fall. We had a cool shelter. One night we heard a lot of shooting not far from where we lived. We were frightened, and no one dared go to where we heard the shots. Later we learned that some U. S. officers had made a surprise attack on *Ba'alili's* home. Some Navajos were killed, and some were taken prisoners; *Ba'alili* was one who was taken into custody. It took place in the fall after *Ba'alili* had discouraged the people about sending their children to school.

A few years later the Reservation was stricken with a bad influenza epidemic, and the sickness took the lives of many Navajo people. Again, this happened in the fall. Most of the people in our area were hit by the flu and laid up in bed for quite a while. There were no hospitals nearby.

108

One old man and wife were not affected by the sickness. The man was a medicine man; so this couple went around from home to home praying for the people. One day they came to our house because all of us were ill. He brought something that looked like a piece of tree bark. He advised all of us to spit in this thing, and we did. He told the same thing to all the real sick people. I do not know what he did with this collected sputum, but about two days after the medicine man paid us his visit, we were all up and around again. The other people he had visited all got well, too. This seemed mysterious, but we were glad to be well again.

A few years later, during the summer months, the horse round-up began on the Reservation. It was part of the stock reduction program. We were told the horses had to have their blood tested and that all the sick ones were to be destroyed. The healthy horses were branded and vaccinated. Navajos who had too many horses had to sell them at a very cheap price, and they were driven away in herds. I don't know where they were taken.

Back in 1924 or 1925 the people in Shiprock and the surrounding areas had been warned about a big flood. The San Juan River was to overflow badly. Consequently, many families moved to the tops of higher hills and on mountains. At that time we were living at Montezuma Creek. The rumor did not bother us; so we stayed where we were and nothing happened.

The people who moved to the mountains left their wagons at the bases and filled them with heavy rocks to weigh them down. All this was silly, but the people can't be blamed for wanting to save themselves and their belongings. A very wise elder who lived in our area told us nothing of the kind was going to take place, and he told us to remain where we were.

Now, most members of my original family have departed. I have only one younger brother and one younger sister still living. They are near each other at the base of the Carrizo Mountain with their families.

About five years ago the neighboring people complained about the land I own. They said I had all the good grazing land, but, because I had the legal documents, there was nothing they could do about it. Besides, I needed the land. We have had very little rain for many years, and the grazing areas are poor. There is hardly any water for our livestock.

I do not know much about our tribal government. Whatever our **109** representatives plan and decide I'll go along with. I know our leaders are working hard for the good of the Navajo people.

As I said, my wife and I do a lot of lecturing to our children. It is good for them to learn at an early stage in their lives. We do our very best to bring them up right. It is a hard job with a large family, and at times things get a little difficult, but we always manage to carry on. We have what we need to live comfortably and contentedly. My wife is a good woman and a very good mother.

Learning to read, write and speak English is important because it is the common language spoken in our country. There isn't much anyone can do without an education today. That is why we encourage our children to stay in school and achieve the requirements which someday will give them good jobs and security for their futures.

Here at home we teach our children the traditional Navajo education. This helps them to enjoy themselves at home as well as in school, and not feel uncomfortable. Their mother teaches the girls to work with wool and to make beautiful rugs like she does. A good income can be earned that way. The boys help me with the livestock and the farm work. They love the outdoor life. They have fun with the lambs and the calves, and they love to ride horses.

The girls know how to keep house and help their mother. I teach my children that the sheep must be cared for and how to do it. The animals provide a good part of our income and our food; so the young ones herd the sheep. In brief, I teach my children what they should do and what they should not do.

Ashie Tsosie

I AM NOT A MAN OF WEALTH. I was born 64 years ago, according to my father. That would be in 1912. I do not remember my mother because she died when I was a small child. I was raised by my father and my sisters. I have brothers and sisters, all older, who are now up in their years. In my family there were 13 children.

I live in the Rough Rock community, Arizona *(Tséch'ízhi)*. I am named by my mother's clan, which is the Salt People *(Áshįįhí)*. My father's clan is the Near the Water People *(Tó'áhaní)*; so I was born FOR that clan. My father was born for the Big Water People *(Tótsohnii)*, and they are my paternal grandfathers.

The Near the Water Clan is closely related to the One Who Walks Around People *(Honághaahnii)*, the Mountain Cove People *(Dziłt̸'ahnii)*, the Tangle People *(Ta'neeszahnii)* and a few others. If they are male I call these clan people "uncles"; if female, I call them "aunts."

My mother's father was of the Start of the Red Streak People *(Deeshchii'nii)*. Their closely related clans are the Red House People *(Kinłichíí'nii)*, Black Streak Wood People *(Tsi naajinii)* and others.

My father's name was Real Tall Man. I was the last one born in the family, the youngest.

My mother originally was from the Tsaile area, near the spot where Navajo Community College now stands, at a place called Pine Tree Spreads Far Out in Sight. That is where some of my relatives now are living, such as my mother's related elders named Salt Clan *(Áshįįhí)* and Dwarf Man, also her brothers and sisters. My father was from the top of Black Mountain, at a place called Red Streak in Water.

After my parents were married, my father took my mother back to his home. They traveled slowly in those days, because horses were their only transportation. From Tsaile they went to Blue Boulder Point and on to Round Rock where they stopped at my mother's relatives' home to rest. Then, they moved on to Valley Store *(T'iis Yáázh Łani)*, between Many Farms and Chinle, to the Salt Water Gap and up Black Mountain to my father's home. It took several days for them to reach their destination.

Many things have changed greatly since then. Now, people travel faster to where they want to go because they have cars and trucks to travel in.

Not long ago I went back to Tsaile and got to know my relatives who lived there. I did not realize that I had so many cousins, aunts, uncles and so on. It made me very happy to meet and know my mother's side of the family.

As I said, I was a young child when my mother died. My father and older sisters worked hard to raise me. They fed me goat's milk, and I had my share of hardships. Today, conditions are different. Babies have plenty to eat and there are all kinds of baby food and milk for them. They get good water to drink and to be kept clean with. During my boyhood days we fetched water from the water holes in the arroyos and the washes. Our parents never heard of sanitation. We drank muddy water; sometimes there were water bugs in it.

Frequently, I think about how my father and sisters struggled to raise the younger members of our family without a mother. I was told that her health began to fail right after I was born and that she died before I was two years old. I am grateful to those who worked hard for me because now I am an elderly man.

About my wife, her clan is the Red House People *(Kinłichii' nii)*, and she is from the Rough Rock area where we are now living. Her closely related elder's name was Little Red House *(Kinłichii'nii Yazhi)* who lived at Rough Rock long ago.

After I grew to realize what was happening around me I often heard my father preach to us about our livelihood. He would say, "My son, it is hard to live without a mother, but we are all trying to work things out the best we can. You are now capable of helping to herd the sheep. I hope you can do your share of the work. Take care of the horses and cattle, too, plus your share of the other chores around the home. Learn all you can now. If you fail to learn

111

anything you will not be a success and you will not have anything to live on." He also would advise us as to how young men who are careless regarding what life is all about become shiftless and are laughed at. He would add, "Your sisters and brothers would be well-to-do but you would be worthless, in rags, without shoes—and hungry."

Those are some of the words of wisdom I listened to in my father's lectures. He was a wise, kind man. It is said that a mother and father are the main loves that a child has. A person may have sisters and brothers, but they do not really love as deeply as the parents. However, they can keep each other happy by laughing at jokes.

My paternal grandfather's name was Tall Big Water. He gave similar advice to my father when father was a boy. My father worked hard to herd sheep and care for the horses and cattle. He inherited his share of the livestock from those beginnings. To this day we still have our livestock.

As a little boy I brought in the firewood, fetched water and did other small chores. As I grew up, I went with my older brothers to herd sheep until I learned how to do it alone. I went into the woods in a wagon to haul firewood; and I went out to fetch the horses and round up the cattle. My father was very understanding and patient. He did not try to rush me; he slowly taught me what I should know. After I reached my teenage years, I did more work. My father forbade me to sleep what he called "late." He made me rise early, at dawn. He would warn me about how pitiful one can be when he is lazy. Sleeping until nearly noon meant poverty. One could not accomplish anything in that way. He explained that sleeping with saliva running from one's mouth is very embarrassing and disgusting and leads to being irritable and hot-tempered.

He said that a person sometimes wants someone to wait on him, to feed him, but my father advised me never to be that kind of person, and he saw to it that I was not to become like one. His lectures were long, but I listened; and I understood when he said, "If you are not lazy you will be welcomed by the Dawn People who will offer you all that is good. It will be up to you, my son."

I knew what it was like to grow up without a mother's love. Sometimes I wished she were with us. When I was an older boy, my work became harder and my brothers were more stern. If I refused to do anything, I was strapped. If I talked back, they would say, "Get a fire poker and put it in his mouth so that he will shut up and go out." So, you see, DISCIPLINE WAS VERY STRICT IN THOSE DAYS. Navajo children dared not have their own way. Grandparents usually told parents to use tight discipline so that children would not take advantage of their parents. In cases where boys or girls were stubborn, or got out of hand, whipping was what they would get to learn to hustle at their parents' orders.

That was what made boys and girls grow up to be obedient and self-reliant.

My oldest brother was very strict and unkind, and I always was afraid of him. Now, as I sometimes think back, it all was for the good of my manhood. I learned what was stored in the future for me, and I was ready.

One day my father was told to enroll two of his children in the boarding school. He refused to do it. His reply was that he needed his children to help him at home to herd the sheep, to tend the horses and cows and to haul firewood. He explained that in the spring, he needed us to do the planting and to care for the farm. The Navajo police came to our home several times to take us to school. In those days, the policemen tried to enforce compulsory education and to enroll school-age children at the Chinle Boarding School, a government institution (Bureau of Indian Affairs). A Navajo policeman, named Little Policeman, went on horseback from

113

Even as a boy I had to go into the forest with a wagon to gather firewood.

114

Whenever Little Policeman came to take me to school my father would greet him as a clan brother, but he always answered "No" when the officer said, "Your children need to be educated."

hogan to hogan telling the parents to enroll their children. My father greeted Little Policeman as a clan brother when he came to our home. Little Policeman said to my father, "Your children need education. What will you do if they are uneducated in the future? Think about this and see if it is for their own benefit that they should be educated. They will help you when they learn to speak English and write."

My father was very stubborn, however, and his answer was "No." He said, "My children have a home, and they all have plenty to do here." Many times the policeman came to our hogan, and my father and the policeman exchanged strong words.

An older brother, whose name was John Nez, and I were of an age to go to school, but we never went because my father wouldn't let us. He had many excuses; so he deprived us of the opportunity to get our education. He just didn't want us to be educated. There were people (his relatives) who lived close to us, and I'm sure they could have helped him with the chores. They wouldn't have allowed him to freeze in the winter, which was one of his excuses. Every fall Little Policeman came to our hogan to get my brother and me. However, my father would tell us to run and hide, or he told us to go after the sheep when he saw Little Policeman coming in the distance on horseback. To this day, I regret that attitude. My father was wrong concerning education. I wish I had gone to school. It is difficult to get a job or to go to a place where no one understands your language.

Finally, Little Policeman gave up coming for us, and we never got a chance to go to school. If my father had let us attend when I was 15 years old I would have learned how to speak English, and I would have had opportunities to get good jobs and to live more comfortably. I often wonder where I would have gone and where I would be now if I had been educated.

115

Now, I am what I am—an uneducated man who does not know a word of English and who never has used a pencil. (I am recording my thoughts on tape in Navajo, and they will be translated into English for printing in a book to be published by the Navajo Community College Press.)

If I had been permitted to go to school and to have been well educated I might have been a teacher or a person sitting in an executive's chair as a director. There are many things that come to my mind now. If I were educated I would teach my children at home, along with their regular class work. I always will blame my father for my being held down in life. Many times when I go to the store or to the Demonstration School the traders or the teachers try to talk to me, but I can only stand dumb because I do not understand them. The best I can do is just smile.

I enjoy the Navajos who speak English and who know how to write—some of the men I knew as boys when I was young. They received their education and were fortunate. They have had good jobs, and some have retired. When I compare myself with these men I feel ignorant and envious. Some are my cousins and other relatives, and I see how they are well dressed. Some are teachers and supervisors. What a change it might have made if my father had let his boys go with Little Policeman to the school! That makes the story of my life.

After my father died I was on my own, and I followed all that he had taught me about the traditional ways. So, approximately 40 years ago, I got a piece of land to settle down on, and I started a farm where I planted alfalfa and corn. I worked hard.

I was a man, and I was determined to make the best that I could of my life. Later, I looked for employment wherever I could find it. I worked as a farmhand for Anglo ranchers. I herded sheep for Anglo sheep growers off the Reservation. I learned self-support from my employers, and they taught me a lot.

When I got married I entered another step in my life. One must get the right mate to have a successful marriage. Together, the two people should share all afflictions and happiness. They should plan and make their decisions together, so that there won't be any bad misunderstandings. That is how I see it. As I have said, I grew up without a mother's love, and I had not known what it was. But I learned what love is after I got married. My first wife died, and I got married again later. The first one was very understanding and good to me. She gave me all the love I never had received before. She took good care of me by keeping our home fire burning for warmth and good cooking. We really shared our happiness and our sorrows. We planned and discussed and decided together about how to make our home delightful. In turn, I did all I could to help her. Keeping the water supply on hand and firewood plentiful, and much other work, is what a man must do at home. And my second wife and I live the same way. She is good to me.

I supported my family the best I could. It is the parents' duty to teach the children what they must learn at home. All three of my boys (by my present wife) are working now. My other son, whose mother died, is living in the neighborhood with his family. All of my children love each other. The last three do not think about their brother as a half brother, but as one belonging among them. My daughter-in-law (his wife) is a sister to my wife; so she is not a stranger to the family.

Another son, Michael, also is married. The youngest one, Tony, is married, too; and all of them love their homes and their jobs. They come to my house often to visit, and my wife and I always have our door open for them. My sons know what traditional life is all about—and also the Anglo culture. They grew up to know about both cultures from the schools they attended, and at home when they were young and during their vacations where they learned from their parents. That was how we raised them. They have had love from both their mother and father, and they have great respect for us.

A wife should be very understanding and good to her husband, giving him the love that he might not have received in his early life, and taking care of him by being a good housekeeper and cook.

Regarding the Navajo people, I suppose they all have taught their children as I have; at least, I hope they have done so. Our children need to know both their Indian Culture and the Anglo Culture. By binding these together securely we can say our children learned and will have the wisdom of the Navajos to share with their children. As we know, today's children must go to school. Education is essential so that they can move out into the world to meet the challenges of self-preservation with determination.

Our children must not forget who they really are. They cannot change themselves. Navajos must know their heritage. They should know their clan relationships and genealogy of their family lines. Many of today's children fail to recognize their family relationship ties. However, I am glad that schools on the Reservation are beginning to teach Indian culture in a variety of courses. That is especially true of the Navajo Community College over at Tsaile on the Reservation in Arizona.

Here at the Rough Rock Demonstration School I was asked to teach the children about their relationships in the family and clan structure. It, and other schools, are teaching in bi-lingual and bi-cultural ways, which should have been done long ago. Most Navajos want their children to learn about their own people in order to restore their cultures. The school here is approximately 10 years old.

Thus, I am not a man with great knowledge. I have told only some of the things that I know about traditional Navajo life, as well as the story of myself. I would advise all who are teaching or interested in this field to work hard. Our children need to know their own language. Many young people today do not speak it, even at home. Also, their parents do not bother to talk to them in our native tongue, or lecture to them as our elders did up until fairly recent years.

118 Making rugs has become strange to many of our young people, but interest is reviving, and things such as rug weaving and basket making are being taught at some places, like Rough Rock and the College. Silversmithing has been a good occupation; and it is being taught, too. Preparing native food, however, is being forgotten, as are other things that our grandmothers and grandfathers loved to do.

I am one of those who encourage the restoration of our Indian culture, and I hope our children will learn both the Anglo and the Indian ways.

Concerning me again—I settled here about 30 years ago, and I have been quite contented. My late brother, named Silversmith's Son *(Átsidí Biyé)* gave me this land I live on years back. My wife is from here. If a man and wife cooperate their marriage can be very happy and successful.

I placed two of my sons, Michael and Tony, in school when they were five years old. From the beginning, I told them they were not going to grow up as I did—uneducated and ignorant. I told them they must learn to read, write and speak English, and to get educations to help them find good jobs and have full lives.

I told them what my father had done to me, how he never had allowed me to attend school. Now, as I record this for publication, they both are high school graduates and have had two years of college work. Both are married and have families. They support themselves; so their mother and I do not have to worry about them. My oldest son (whose mother is dead) also lives near us. We are one happy family, although we live separately. I love them all, and I still feel responsible for them. I have quite a number of grandchildren, now, and our family still is increasing. I feel very happy about it. That is what I have lived for, in spite of all my struggles; and I bless them.

Most Navajos want their children to learn the Anglo culture in school and elsewhere. Then, we also have the traditional knowledge that we want them to learn. The traditional teaching technique is simple. We begin it at a very early stage of a child's life. Today, for one thing, it is very important that our children learn to speak their own language. Then, after they enter school, they have the advantage of knowing how to speak both Navajo and English.

Another important thing our children must understand and appreciate, as I have previously mentioned, is our relationships to those in our families. Long ago our people had great respect for one another. They greeted each other cordially. Expressions such as, My Dear Child *(Shá awéé')*, My Children *(Sha'áłchíní)*, My Cousin, My Aunt, My Uncle and so on were used almost always. Our children of today do not know or use these fine words; so we should teach them so they will know who is related to them and what to call them. I believe that is one of the main reasons for making these recordings in the Navajo language, so that we elders can express our feelings and teachings, and then have them translated into English and printed.

I would advise all the elders who are asked to contribute their thoughts and stories to give all they can. I know we all want the best for our Navajo children. Some older people are consultants in the schools, or will be asked to serve, and I say, "More power to them." The children like to hear such stories, and they want the elders to tell more. I say this because I know—it is part of my work here at Rough Rock.

I thank the Navajo Community College Press for this wonderful opportunity to talk. I always have wanted to help my people in every way I can—to make them understand that we are what we are and that we should not and cannot be changed.

119

Mrs. Bob Martin

THE NAVAJO COMMUNITY COLLEGE PRESS has asked me to tell about my early school days and my traditional education at home, but I want to say, first, that my clan is the Many Hogans People *(Hooghan łání)* and that my sub-clan is the Tangle People *(Ta'-neeszahnii).* I was born at Sanostee, New Mexico, in 1892.

When I was six years old I began to be taught the old established ways of Navajo life. The elders lectured to the young ones about how to live or what was expected of boys and girls at home. For instance, I was told to grind corn, which, in those days was almost our only source of food. There was no near-by trading post to purchase other things to eat. Corn was prepared in various ways, such as in bread and cornmeals.

I helped my parents with the daily chores and learned how to cook traditional foods. The people raised the corn in their sometimes dry fields, hoping for rain. In those times we had more rain than we do now; so the people had good crops to harvest in the fall for winter use. I also went up into the mountains with my parents to gather foods such as wild strawberries and yucca fruits. I helped my mother prepare these native foods, and I ate them and liked them.

We had some old and slow sheep which needed special attention, and, even when very young, I herded them in the pastures.

My parents advised me not to sleep late or be lazy. I was made to rise at dawn to begin my day's work. Sometimes I went out very early to fetch the horses. I sometimes think back and say to myself that they really were the good old days when our elders lectured to us. We were raised with disciplinary action; so we did what we were told to do. One advice the elders gave us was, "Be ready to go on your own; your parents will not live forever for you to depend on them." How true that still is. I have tried my level best to live a good and worthwhile life.

My father took me—a girl—on hunting trips with him into the high mountains. Once we went to the LaSal Range in eastern Utah when I was only six years old. I took care of the horses for him at the camp. Also, I went with my parents to pick piñon nuts as far as Wheatfields where they were abundant. I enjoyed it. The people were friendly and did not say, "This is our land. Go away." Everything was peaceful, and we did not have any trouble.

When I was 10 years old I was enrolled at the Fort Lewis School. I never had been in school; so I did not know a word of English. Fort Lewis was an old Army station at Durango, Colorado, which had been turned into a school for the Indians. There were members of other tribes attending, such as Utes, and Plains Indians, as well as some Chicanos.

121

When I first got there it was frightening, and I almost died of loneliness. It took a year for me to become accustomed. The teachers taught us what we had to learn, and we worked hard to be good students. We did what we were told to do. I enjoyed my school days. At times it was difficult, but I managed to get along well.

During my first summer at Fort Lewis I did not want to go home for vacation. I remained there and worked hard for my employer; and I did what I was told. After all, I was learning things which I never had known before. I enjoyed going to school and being in Durango.

At home, before I started to school, I had to learn to do the traditional Navajo things. My father was a medicine man, and some of my closely related elders were medicine men, too. I learned many good points from them about our own religion. Ever since then, when I attend a ceremony, I sometimes notice a mistake which I know my father would not have allowed to happen. I just think about how he conducted his "sings" long ago, and I know when something is wrong.

Even though I went to school, I never forgot my own religion nor neglected to pray with my offering of corn pollen. Now, in my elderly years, I'm beginning to be forgetful; but I still know the chants and where and when they are sung, just as my father taught me. In my childhood learning days we were told what to do and what we were not to do, or what was taboo. In school, however, all that was different. We learned the Anglo culture. Our advisers, both

Anglo and Navajo, taught us not to be smart alecks or impudent. We never were to mock, laugh or make jokes about an older person. Our elders, around our home on the Reservation, would gather in a council to lecture to the people, especially to the young ones. In their daily lives the children behaved and minded their own business. Their parents kept them busy so they would stay out of mischief. And all was quiet and peaceful among us. When we, the people called Navajos, had sheep in our sheepfolds and horses in the corrals parents made their children tend the livestock. "Herd the sheep, fetch the horses; take the horses or sheep to the waterhole." Those were commands, and we obeyed without any back talk. After the stock reduction period in the 1930s and 1940s all this changed, however. Only a few units of sheep were allowed to a family.

After I left Fort Lewis (I don't recall what year it was), I came to Shiprock, New Mexico, and stayed there a year before I got married. I noticed that the schools were beginning to change; and today they are not like the one at Fort Lewis long ago.

Now that the young people do not herd sheep or care for horses, they have nothing to do at home. There is no farm work because the land is neglected, partly because of dry weather. The situation has changed our people. They have become lazy and cause many problems at home. Some, who are fortunate enough, get themselves educated and obtain good jobs.

Now young people ask us how the elders of long ago (and when I was growing up) lectured to their children and taught them. They come to me and ask the question many times. (Today, I am relating this story to my granddaughter in the Navajo language, and she is recording it.) About the schools changing, I would say the children are more independent and free. What they learn now must be different or they wouldn't be troublesome as they are now. Probably the teachers do not teach them well enough, or the boys and girls are being more than just students. We want our children to settle down and calm themselves.

That is why I willingly say what I want to. I am hoping that some young people will understand what I am talking about and come to their senses. Of course, there are some fine children who behave and are good students; but I mostly am talking to those who need to listen more to what life really is, instead of ignoring their parents' teachings.

We have counselors who come to elderly people and ask how the old-time lectures were given to the young people, how they made the youngsters listen and never become problem children, as some are now. I feel sorry for many parents, and I try to help them in any way I can. I know what they are fighting against.

I now will talk about native foods. My first topic is corn. First, you grind the kernels after they have been dried, and you think of what you are going to make. Then you put a pot of water on the fire or stove. If you are to cook corn dumplings, you make sure the water boils.

While the water is heating you fetch cedar greens and burn them on a screen so that the ashes fall through on to a plate or a tin sheet without the stems.

You have the ground corn (flour) ready in a large bowl. When the cedar greens are burned out, you put the ashes in a small container and add hot water. This liquid then is drained onto the flour just enough to make it a light blue color.

Often you add some boiling water to the cornmeal and cedar ash mixture, and, with your fingers make a blue corn dough. If you are a good Navajo cook, you won't be bothered by the boiling hot water as you mix the dough with your fingers. The elderly women judge a good cook by this, and they praise her for it. Making small balls, you put them into the boiling water, letting them boil for some time, using the stirring sticks to stir very lightly now and then until they are all cooked.

Using the same basic method, you can make blue corn patties on a hot grill stone or griddle. Usually, the stone grill is a fairly thin, flat, wide stone. The Navajo cook offers a little prayer, marking an X in the center, saying, "Let not this rock break in half. I will make good bread on it." Then, putting two regular rocks under each side, you build a fire under the flat one. When it becomes hot you grease it very little and begin making patties and putting them on the grill, being sure they are well done before removing them.

Making sweet corncake is not hard, either. You prepare corn husks first. Then grind enough corn. Have a pit dug in the earth approximately 36 inches across and 12 inches deep, or a little more. A fire is built in the pit and kept from morning until late afternoon.

In the meantime, you mix corn flour with water. Some wheat sprouts are ground real fine to add to the thin corn mixture to make it sweet. Some women nowadays use sugar and raisins to flavor it.

Blue corn patties are made on a thin hot grill stone.
After marking an X in the center, the woman says a
little prayer asking that the rock will not break.

When the cornmeal is mixed well, the pit is lined with corn husks quickly so that no dirt is exposed at all, even to the top. Next, the thin cornmeal is poured into the hot, lined pit. More wide corn husks are used to cover the meal, and a thin layer of damp dirt is placed carefully over the husks. Then hot ashes and hot wood coals go on top. A small fire is kept burning on top all night to cook the upper part.

124

In the morning, the cake is ready to cut out. This requires much work, but the Navajos love to eat it and to share it among relatives.

Another food is regular corn bread, similar to sweet corn bread, but you make the dough a little firmer—not a thin mush.

Some wide corn husks are laid out—open. The dough is put into the corn husks, and the husks are folded firmly, covering the dough like a tamale tied around the middle. Then a small dugout is made in the fireplace and the folded-over husks are placed in a row in it and covered with a thin, damp layer of dirt and hot ashes. The food is baked a few hours, removed from the pit and is ready to eat.

Yucca fruits are different. September is the time to gather them, when they are nice and ripe. I often helped with the gathering. We took goatskins and sacks. We picked the fruits in a pail, dumped them into the goatskin bags and carried them on our backs to a wagon. At home we removed the seeds and then put the fruits into a large container with water and let the mixture boil. (If one prefers dried yucca fruits they are deseeded and laid out to dry in the sun.)

After the fruits have cooked, they are removed from the boiling water and cooled. Then the material is mashed and rolled on a board in six-or eight-inch strips, at least three inches thick. A long corncob is inserted in the middle of a roll, and the whole thing is dried. This preserve can last a long time—more than 12 months, and it will not spoil. It is very delicious.

125

In the winter you can make blue corn dumplings. Put a cupful or a chunk of dry yucca roll in a pan and let it simmer. It will dissolve itself if it is stirred with a stick. Dunk the corn bread and eat it that way, or eat the bread with a spoon as dumplings. It is very good. I make these preserves myself; so I know.

I also prepared my own stone grill to make piki bread. To do it, first select a good-sized flat rock that is hard and not easily broken. Using a piece of granite, smooth the surface of the grill to a nice shine. Grease the grill with sheep fat or sheep brains. (Brains are much better.) Prepare the corn as you do in making blue corn dumplings. Then quickly spread the thin corn batter on the hot stone grill with the palm of the hand, with just one stroke—very thin. If you go over it again, the dough will come off and lump. Yes, your hand may burn, but it is good if it becomes accustomed to the heat because when you work with corn mush and corn bread almost always your hands must be in boiling water for mixing. My hands are kind of cracked and hard, but that is how it is. That is why a child's hands are massaged with a smooth rock, to make them tough.

It is good advice to have plenty of ground corn on hand so that when it is needed you have it. It is very appropriate for a Navajo housewife to have in her home grinding stones, a native grass brush and broom, as well as stirring sticks. They are the main items our people long ago kept in their possession wherever they migrated.

I have all of these right now in my kitchen. The grass brush is used to brush the flour off the grinding stones when I finish grinding corn.

Boxthorn berries are another native food. They are picked into a pail and boiled in water. After they are cooked and cooled, they are ground with the grinding stone and put into a bowl with some sugar. They are delicious.

About piñon nuts, you first roast them in a skillet. Then, with the grinding stones, go over them lightly enough to crack the shells which, of course, must be removed. Into another skillet put some dried corn and roast it until it browns a little. Mix the shelled piñons and roasted corn together; salt the mixture, and it is good for a snack. Making piñon butter is easy, too. Just grind the roasted piñons after they are shelled and make a paste. It is good to spread on bread. Piñon butter can be added to mutton stew, if the meat isn't fat, to give it flavor.

126

Wild mustard seeds grow at Sanostee. I have some in a sack in the house. Do not boil them. They must be ground and are rather bitter, but they are rich and greasy. Many people like them.

Grass seeds also are very good. The seeds are ground, and the flour makes fine tortillas, usually small ones. Long ago, before commercial foods were introduced to the Navajos, a large part of their diet consisted of grass seeds, wild berries and plant roots. Today, of course, we have all kinds of food in the stores.

I learned all of these things from my mother who was very strict. She always had a fire poker on hand to use on me if I disobeyed her orders or was naughty. The elders used to tell us if we were stupid or absent-minded we would be bums and useless in the future.

About sheepherding, at times one or more sheep would go astray from the herd, or a coyote would scare them and cause some to separate from the others. When we youngsters had such experiences we usually were scolded. My mother would say, "I told you to take good care of the flock!" When some sheep moved to another flock, usually we took our whole flock over nearby and got our strays back. That happens whenever herds get too close together.

There are herb medicines for sheep, as well as for people. When they are stricken with coughing and sneezing the people have a cure for it. A good shepherd can sense and see when there is sickness in his flock, and the sheep are given medicine or sprinkled with certain things.

When I became of age I still was at home and had a puberty ceremony. I had not yet gone to school. Until that time my parents lectured me about many subjects.

The first thing done when a Navajo girl comes of age is that her hair is tied in back with a buckskin thong into a loose ponytail. The thong is about an inch wide. The hair in front is combed down. This hair is not cut in bangs and usually is not long, anyway. Leading up to the ceremony, the family women grind corn the first two days. The girl also helps grind it. The girl runs a mile or so to the east early each morning for three days. She is kept busy all the time. Some wheat is buried in damp ground two days before the corncake is to be prepared so that the wheat will sprout. The sprouted wheat is dried and ground. On the day of the ceremony the corn is mixed with water in large containers, and some sprouted and ground wheat is added to the mixture to sweeten it.

Long ago, the people used glucose made by chewing the wheat and spitting into the meal mixture. This is not practiced anymore. **127** I have told before how the sweet corncake is made. A large pit is dug and kept hot with a fire in it; at dusk, the cornmeal mix is poured into the cornhusk-lined hot-pit to bake all night.

On the final day, the medicine man conducts an all-night chant. The chanter sings a few chants or songs over the girl who is coming of age. Then he asks other men to continue. Each sings his songs; and this goes on all night. It is called the "Girl-of-Age" song. She sits and stays awake all night. All the songs are of the Blessing Way—all pertaining to possessions, like rug songs, spindle songs, sheep songs, horse songs, sacred mountain songs and such as these.

The singing continues until dawn. Then the girl quickly takes a purity sponge bath and a shampoo with yucca-root soap. Dressed in pretty traditional clothes and adorned with turquoise, she runs out with dripping wet hair. All the young people follow her. She races to the east and to the west, boys yelling right after her. At the ceremony for me, I ran just a short distance. I was not a fast runner; so some came back before I did. When I finally dragged in I said, "You who outran me will become old before your time, or before me." It is said that one never should outrun the girl coming of age. In any case, the racers all ran into the ceremonial hogan, yelling. The older people who had sung all night remained in the hogan.

At this stage of the ceremony it is time to uncover the baked corncake. The hot ashes are scooped off the top of the cake and cleaned with a grass broom. A woman begins to cut the cake in good-sized diamond-shaped pieces. The medicine man who conducted the ceremony is presented with the heart of the cake; then the others who contributed their songs get pieces to take home. The rest is divided among those who helped with the preparations, as well as relatives.

At Sanostee the kind of a hogan I lived in was the round one. In those days there was no lumber nearby to build houses. The hogans were made from aspen trees which the menfolk went to the mountains to chop and drag out with their horses. Some used young ponderosa pines. In those days, we did not need permits to chop trees; so we got all we needed.

I helped my father drag the logs from the mountains when I was a young girl. He cut the trees down, and the children chopped the bark off. Then we made notches for ropes, tied two or three logs together, and a strong donkey, with ropes tied to its saddle horn, dragged them to where we built our hogan.

128

We were poor and had our hardships. Many times we barely managed to make ends meet. Today, it is so different. The needy get assistance and are cared for.

About water, there was a natural stream that flowed from the mountain near where we lived. We took pails to fetch water. During the dry season we got our water from a shallow dug well.

The menfolk took sweat baths a distance away from the hogan behind a hill. Long ago, the elders considered a sweat bath hut a place of sanctuary. They sang their sacred sweat bath chants, prayed and told their myth stories in it. It also was a good place to discuss problems and to make plans. The sweat hut is a small conical-type hogan, with enough space for four to six men, crowded. It is a sudatorium, with the doorway covered by several blankets. Red-hot rocks are put into the sweat hut and water is poured on them to build up steam.

My parents sometimes bought cotton material from the trading post at Blue Boulder Point. My mother wove rugs and sold them there to buy what we needed. The rugs were roughly woven—not fine rugs like today's. The yarn was spun thick.

To make clothes my mother would buy two or three sacks of flour. When the sacks were empty, she dyed them and made blouses, skirts and other items of clothing for the children. This is not a lie. I am telling the truth. In some ways, my story isn't too pleasant. There were no silver buttons on my blouses, and I had no jewelry when I was a girl. The best thing that happened to me was going to school. The education I got helped me very much.

In my family there were three girls and two boys. Now all of the others are gone. Sometimes I think about my family and get desolated and then weep.

Back to today: I live in a house with all the facilities. I get my compensation monthly, but I have to pay for my land and the utilities. I was proud of my father and mother. They taught me to be what I am. They never permitted me to run freely to ceremonies "because you must keep away if you have no business there. . .Don't go to squaw dances alone. . .Never gossip or cause trouble among other people—you could cause a fight that may end in tragedy somehow." These were my parents' words of wisdom and I have abided by them to this day.

My paternal grandfather's name was Yellow Mustache. He and his wife went to Fort Sumner (Bosque Redondo) when the Navajos were exiled. My father was born there; he was two years old when his people returned to their homeland.

129

The reason a girl should not go to a squaw dance is that once you go, you will want to attend again and again. Soon your mind will keep on making you want to go where the "action is." Now, however, I go to squaw dances and other gathering places just to renew acquaintances and to meet old and new friends. Not often, though. Recently, there was a squaw dance not too far from here, but I did not go. I have some relatives living not far away, though; and when they had a squaw dance, I went just to help them.

My story, from here, will pertain to my education. I was 10 years old when I entered school. It was in the fall when all the crops were ripe and ready to harvest. I did not know a word of English, but my father wanted me to be educated. He said, "Daughter, you will go to school at Fort Lewis." So, in two days, we were ready to leave. My father brought in the horses early that day. He saddled one for me, one for himself and another for my mother, and the three of us left. In those days Navajos traveled mostly by horseback on the horse trails, and we went by Table Mesa. We traveled north until we came to the home of one of my sisters, where we spent the night. The following day we continued our journey. We traveled slowly and came to a place that was thick-wooded, with many piñon trees and cedars; the sage brush was thick, too.

We saw Ute Indian tepees here and there because we were in the Ute country. My father had a close friend who lived there. His name was "The Late Stump Man's Son." We stopped at his place to rest. My father always took his rifle with him wherever he went. The next morning he got up extra early and left. He was a good hunter. Not long afterward, we heard shots.

All the men ran with their knives. Some of the Utes went, too. They all wanted to help butcher. My father had killed two deer; and, several hours later, the men came back with their loads of deer meat. In those days there were no hunting regulations, and the people got their game without permits.

We spent another night there. My mother prepared some meat to dry and put it far up on a tree. On the second day, when the sun was high, we continued our journey. We traveled all day and spent another night in the woods along the way. In the morning we left early. Late in the afternoon we finally reached our destination.

130

We went directly to the superintendent's office at the Fort Lewis School in Durango, Colorado. He had an interpreter with him. I was scared and wondered what they would do to me since I did not know a word of English. My father said he had brought me to enroll in the school. The superintendent accepted me with much kindness and told me to go to the girls' dormitory. My mother took me there. The dormitory attendant told me to take a bath first. I discarded my traditional clothes. I was given a brand new pair of shoes, a dress, underclothes and stockings. I washed my hair and combed it neatly. I felt so good all dressed up in my new clothes and was very refreshed. I turned myself around admiring my clothes. It made me happy. It was in 1902.

That night I was given another dress. I learned this was called a nightgown, to be slept in; and I slept in a nice clean bed with white sheets. All this was strange to me, and I thought of my sheepskins that I had slept on at home.

The next morning I suddenly became homesick. I felt so lonely that I began to weep, and someone told me not to cry. It was time to eat. We were told to go to the washroom, which was in the basement of the girls' dormitory. We washed our faces and hands. Then we were told to line up, and we marched to the dining hall. The dining hall was very large, with many tables. We were told to be very quiet; someone was to say grace before we ate. After grace was said we sat down and were served our breakfast. The food was strange and did not taste good to me; so I did not eat. After the many others had finished eating, a bell rang, and we marched out of the dining hall back to the dorm. We were told to clean up for classes. I was lonely, and I kept on crying. When we were ready, we lined up to march to the school building.

My parents just simply had left me there and did not come back to see me this next day. I suppose they left for home right after they enrolled me.

When I came to my classroom I was given a stick called a pencil, a large piece of paper and also a book of A B Cs. The teacher told me to learn how to write—to copy the letters. At first, I scratched lines all over the paper, trying to learn.

I stayed in school the whole year. At Christmas, we all received a large present. It was an assortment of new clothes. They were beautiful, and I was all excited and so thankful. There was a new dress, shoes, stockings and underclothes. This made me very happy, and I was proud of them. Back home my mother had made my clothes from flour sacks. How lucky I am, I thought. I had grown up in a poor home. When I was a little girl I hardly wore any shoes, or any kind of store-bought clothes. Here at school we had plenty to eat, and warm clothes.

As my school days went along, the older students helped me as I learned. The second year, I really knew what "yes" and "no" meant, and I could write some things; but I did not understand my teacher at all. We could only communicate by sign language. However, with the help of the older students, I began to learn, and soon I could say a few words in English; but learning was very slow.

Soon it was vacation time again, and the parents began to come for their children to take them home. My parents did not appear until very late, after most of the students were gone. Finally, my father came for me, but I refused to go home. I actually wanted to stay. A man came to the school to recruit girls and boys for summer employment. We were placed in private homes to work as house-keepers. I learned a lot that summer—how to cook, wash and iron clothes and keep the house clean. My employer was a nice lady who taught me how to work. In the fall I went back to school. We wore black shoes and black stockings. We were measured for our new dresses. The girls in the sewing class made the dresses from bolts of assorted cotton materials.

I was very fortunate to get my education free. There was no one to tell you that you were a government employee, or that your income was so much you had to pay for your child's books and clothes in those days. As I said, we had good clothes to wear and good food to eat.

131

One important incident occurred in my life that I think I should mention. One day, some girls were planning to run away from school. They came to me and asked if I could run fast or walk far. I told them I was able to do both. They invited me to join them. We planned to leave when the rest of the students had gone to the dining hall. When it was time, we hid ourselves; and, when the others marched to the dining hall, we ran into a ditch not far from the girls' dorm. (When I think back, I know that I was foolish to do such a stupid thing.) After all was clear, we made our "getaway." We had not gone far, though, when I got tired. The other girls told me to go back because I was too slow and was a problem to them. They warned me about the wolves in the woods and that we would have to run fast to escape them. They told me I'd never make it, that the wolves would eat me; so I turned back toward the school. I believed the girls. I was afraid; and, climbing a tree to find where the school was, I saw that it was not far away.

Suddenly I heard voices, and I saw three big boys approaching not far from where I was. They were following our footprints. One said, "They went this way and there are three sets of footprints." They came closer to me. "There are only two now," said one boy. I clung close to the tree, scared to death and kept very quiet. In the distance I could see the students marching from the dining hall. The boys kept looking around, then one looked up and saw me. "Come down quickly," he commanded. I climbed down, but when I was almost down, he grabbed my dress and pulled me down to the ground roughly, and he scolded me. I was trembling and shaken up. These big boys took care of the farm and the horses at the school.

The boys told me to hurry back to school; so I ran as fast as I could to the dorm. The matron scolded me and chased me upstairs to bed without any supper. I was very hungry, but I knew I deserved the punishment.

The next day, the school superintendent and his wife came to me. They both questioned me, "Who planned the runaway? Where are the other girls?"

I told them what had been done and how they had gone on and had left me behind. They warned me that if I did it again the school would punish me harder—that I would be hanged on a tree. I believed them; so I did not run away again. The other girls never came back. I do not know what happened to them.

Fort Lewis was a wonderful school, and I learned a lot there. I worked during summers for families in town, and I earned money

After the effort to escape failed, the boys saw me in the tree, pulled me to the ground roughly and scolded me. I really was trembling.

and learned good things. Besides our regular academic work, we had vocational classes where we learned to cook, sew and keep house.

The schools of today are very, very different. The parents now **133** furnish their children's clothes, and some schools teach Indian cultures. One of the best places for that is Navajo Community College at Tsaile, where the students are taught their traditional culture and about their religion.

As I have told you, my formal education began in my adult years. During the early stages of my life I was taught the traditional Navajo ways.

My father began putting me on a horse when I was five years old; and by my sixth birthday I was a pretty good rider. In those days the parents expected their children to do anything that was asked of them. They did not tolerate laziness and excuses. I was kept busy all the time, doing chores around the hogan until the end of the day. I even went hunting with my father to the La Sal Range in Utah. I took care of the hunters' horses. Life was hard, but interesting, during those childhood days; and I had valuable experiences.

Later, when I finally entered school, I had to work hard to learn; and, because I was already mature, learning was not easy. Today's school children are very different from those in former days.

I do not really understand why; it is just a fact. I believe that children who have confidence in their parents and listen to their teachings at home are the ones who will be more successful in life. I easily can judge an individual by what he or she does and says. The boys and girls who had parents who taught them the good ways of life and lived up to those ways are the ones who obtained an education. They have good jobs. Some have become teachers and are teaching their own people in different communities all over the Reservation, like at the College at Tsaile. We are very proud of these young people and others who are helping the Navajos to live better.

We want more of our children to succeed. We want them to be well educated. Some schools have changed. We are told that a person who works for the Indian Service should get his children into public schools or elsewhere. But I think all our children are entitled to an equal education without discrimination. Long ago, no one said such things to our people. According to my judgment, the schools then were far better than they are now. Today's facilities are much better, of course; but a more important point is that, years back, we were made to learn with disciplinary rules which were good for us. We knew we had to learn—or else!

I always am happy to tell about my life and to answer questions. I know that it is for the good of our young people; so I try to cooperate in every possible way. If I know that my experiences can be used to help others, then I am satisfied—and happy.

Buck Austin

MY MOTHER'S CLAN is the Bitterwater People *(Tódích'íí'nii)*; so that also is my clan. My father's clan is the Reed People *(Lók'-aa' diné'é)* so I was "born for" that clan in 1909. My father was born for the Coyote Pass People *(Mą'ii deeshgiizhinii)* or Jemez. They were my paternal grandparents. My mother was born for the Charcoal Streaked division of the Water's Edge People *(Naaneesht'ézhí Tábąąhá)*. They were my maternal grandparents. My later father was a great counselor and teacher in Navajo traditions.

Education in the Navajo traditional ways began (and sometimes still is carried on) from the fireplace. For example, one should not accumulate trash around it. It still is said that there always should be a fire poker in the household. The poker long ago became known as the eyes of the fire. In the old days the woman had her own and the man of the family had one, too. That was the custom when man was first created, as the legends tell.

Long ago there were many varieties of plants and plant seeds that were used for food by the *Diné* (the Navajos or the People); and there was abundant wildlife on the mountain ranges. Elk, deer and antelope roamed in the forests; and there were many rabbits, rats and prairie dogs in the valleys. The valleys were covered with all kinds of vegetation. There was no famine in those days, and hunger was unknown. The people planted and produced their crops. They had plenty of rain to make the crops and the vegetation grow. Many fields were full of tall fresh corn. That is the way it was, as told by our elders.

Many years passed, and warfare began to take place among the tribes and with the Spaniards. Wars with the Hopis, Utes and Piautes began an era in the history of the Navajos who, in a way, became fugitives—always fleeing to save themselves from being captured or killed. They hardly had time to gather food or to work on their farms. Many went without food for days. Small children were victims of starvation and the enemy. Then, from about 1864 to 1868, many of the Navajos were exiled to Fort Sumner over on the other side of New Mexico. Some Navajos, however, who lived on Navajo Mountain, in the general area that is now Page, Arizona, as well as in the Kaibito area and in many canyons, stayed behind and managed to raise some crops and herd their sheep. Those people were not hungry.

The elders lectured to the young people all hours of the night. It really was education. The youngsters were advised to rise with the dawn and race to the east, no matter what the season. "Sleeping with your face in the dirt is not good for you," they told the young people. "The enemy will overpower you in a duel if you are a weakling. You will be his prisoner or his victim, lying on the ground with a crow-feather arrow in you." (I think that was the lowest type of arrow.) "If you are a strong well-developed man, you may be a brave warrior who gives his life—a hero lying in the midst of all the eagle-tail-feathered arrows. If you are a coward, an old spear will finish you with just one stroke."

The old ones used to add, "A young man has to prove himself worthy by being a brave warrior; he must learn to be alert at all times, to be swift and a skillful marksman. If he encounters a barricade of arrows and spears, none will penetrate him. He will be unharmed and spared. He will have learned to maneuver himself swiftly and to protect himself. A man's early training as a runner, and taking ice-water baths, will make him a real man. If he has raced on Mother Earth, and, for some reason, she wants to claim him back, he will conquer the challenge and prolong his life to old age because he is a strong man. While racing at dawn, if one unfortunately has a mishap and Talking God wants to claim his life, a real good man would not allow it to happen. One shows his desire to live by proving his abilities. When an enemy attacks with his gun pointing at a good man, the gun might fail to discharge and he will be spared."

Those were some of the words of wisdom the children were taught in the never-ending old-time lectures.

If a Navajo ignored the lectures and preferred to sleep, he never would amount to anything. If one did not race at dawn, he would

In the evenings and at night an elder or medicine man would tell stories of the legendary life of the Navajos, especially about Monster Slayer and his twin brother, Child of Water. Trash was not allowed to be around the hogan, and a fire poker always was nearby.

just wish for all the good things. When he would see a man with new clothes and fine moccasins he would wish he had them because he was barefooted and without anything of value in his possession. Such a man would be in rags, ashamed of himself and very miserable.

137

On the other hand, if a person would race at dawn, his life probably would be fulfilled with all the blessings of riches. The Holy People would greet him and appreciate him. They would present the person with whatever was good. Talking God would meet a Navajo with soft goods and Calling God would meet him with hard goods. Behind them the moon would come as a beautiful horse, followed by the sun with a variety of horses for him. So one should run among all these Holy People, the Dawn People. One should not let this wonderful opportunity pass him. If the Holy People chose someone, that person would be blessed with beautiful fat horses and sheep, also cows.

From all these gifts one could prosper in the older times and be a real man. If one was a failure and did not care to listen, and did all the wrong things, temptation would lead him to filth, rags and hunger. Then he would be barefooted with cracked and blistered feet;

and his barefoot trails would be visible, with blood on the rocks. The people would laugh at him; his in-laws would laugh at him. Others would ride their fat horses while he was on foot. This might have led him to a cliff where his trail ended. Then his in-laws would say "He ended his worthless life here," and just laugh.

Parents would not want this to happen to a son. If he were blessed with good fat horses, he would ride them. Now, thinking about this word, I am sure the elders were prophesying the vehicle trails of the modern age. The foot trails and the horse trails all have disappeared. Now it is only the never-ending roads and highways.

Traditional education also included caring for the family stock. Our elders say that, at the break of day, a person commenced herding the sheep to where there was good pasture. In turn, the sheep would provide him with new shoes and new clothing, or whatever was needed in the household. He took the horses to where there was plenty of fresh grass and water; and, in turn, the horses provided transportation. To be a part of his own livestock a Navajo breathed his animals' breath and inhaled the odor of their dung. Through smell, a horse or sheep would recognize its owner anywhere and would not be afraid. They would accept him as one of themselves. During lamb marketing time, the sheep would not loathe the owner for selling the lambs; or, when he sold a calf, the cow still would be a part of him. The money a Navajo received for the sales would buy what he wanted. That was a payment or reward from one's livestock for being good to them.

138

A young man began from scratch in his farming education by clearing the land; then came the cultivation and the planting. When the corn began to grow, he hoed out the weeds. Corn was the main source of food for the people long ago. It was counted on to feed the children. Everything that was done on a farm was educational for the young people.

When a young Navajo man had learned to work on his farm and how to take good care of his livestock, then he would be well prepared to have a family. If he were not interested in learning, he would just be a "wandering bum" and would expect to get meals from other people. Later he would get together with a run-around girl, and get her into trouble by making her pregnant. Then, he might abandon her because he could not support her; or, if not, he probably would take his family to some relatives or friends where there was food. This would become a habit, and the people who knew him would say, "Here comes that bum with his hungry family. Put the food away. Go out and get the sheep out of the fold." They would say these things because they were tired of feeding his family and providing whatever he begged to have, like lending him a riding horse.

Such things were all teachings of the parents to their children. They did not want bad habits to develop in their children's lives. Education in the traditional Navajo ways was based mainly on preparing to earn a livelihood in the future. By staying on the right path, and not following the bad path which leads into many temptations, one would not have to suffer the consequences. People would know the reputation of a man and woman; and they would not trust them nor want them around should they follow the wrong paths.

Education in religion was taught by the elders, too. They said, "One must have an arrowhead in his possession at all times. It represents his protection prayer. Also, he should have a bag of corn pollen. It becomes his daily offering for all the blessings of good things. If one desires to learn a special ceremony of the Blessing Way, he would be of service to many of his people and would strengthen their morale and keep them in harmony with one another."

This might apply to a man, a woman, a girl, a boy—or even little children. The people appreciated such a person and had great respect for the services rendered to them. They recognized competence and depended upon him or her for years to come. The people welcomed such persons into their homes. When they saw one approaching they would say, "Here comes your grandfather (or grandmother); bring him (or her) in and spread out the best sheepskin. Also, prepare a good meal for him (or her), and take care of the horse."

During my youth I had horses and sheep and cattle, and I cared for them. Now I live a different life. In a way, it is the life of a doctor—going around healing the sick with the medicine herbs. The big responsibility of a medicine man lies in his hands.

If a man has poor knowledge of a ceremony and is careless with the sacred protection prayers, the people will say, "He used to be a well-to-do man with horses and sheep, but he became lazy and useless." It is just a matter of what one really wants to be—a success or a failure. The arrowhead and corn pollen pouch can lead a person on a good corn pollen path, and his success will make the people recognize and accept him. When he attends the sings at different locations, they will welcome him. They will feed him well and give him lodging, including his horse and family (if they are with him). The hospitality will continue until the ceremony is over. If one had no transportation, they gladly will furnish it. The people have great respect for their medicine men who are competent and render their services the right way.

In the education of girls, they, like boys, were told to rise at dawn and race, and to take cold water baths. If a girl did these early exercises her hair would grow long and beautiful; it would shine and wave in the breeze like the rippling waters. Her complexion would glow like the sunlight. She also was advised to begin her tasks at the break of day, taking her grinding stones outside of the hogan to grind corn, a task which would make wrists and arms strong and harden the palms of the hands. It would strengthen the backbone, too. The older women taught the girl how to grind the corn. It was

140

Girls and boys had to run to the east every morning for exercise and to avoid becoming lazy, and older women taught the girls to grind corn so that they could prepare their own for their puberty ceremonies.

a "must" so that when she came of age she could grind her own corn for her puberty ceremony cake. If she were lazy and did not want to learn, when she came of age she would be sitting crying over the grinding stones because she did not know how to use them. When a girl matured and got married the in-laws would criticize and laugh at her because she did not know anything. These were words of wisdom—to encourage a young girl to learn and to do her daily routine chores of homelife in the traditional Navajo way. She was taught how to build a fire and use the fire poker, as well as how to cook to satisfy her husband of the future.

The elders judged a woman by ability when they selected her to be an in-law. They expected her to be well trained and prepared for the future and generally educated in housekeeping and caring for her husband, as well as her children. The man had the responsibility of the farm and caring for the livestock. The heavier duties were in his hands.

141

The young girl also was taught to make all the assorted Indian corn breads. When she was told to make tortillas, and she kept burning her hands and gave up too soon and cried, she never would be called a woman and be accepted as a wife. A girl was taught to work with wool, too—carding, spinning and weaving. She would make saddle blankets for her husband and beautiful rugs to be proud of.

Some essential items in the household were the grinding stones, a grass broom, stirring sticks, and, best of all, the fire poker. She had to possess all of these and know how to use them. If she did not know how, her husband would leave her because he would get tired of doing things for his wife. A mother-in-law surely would ask a wife to weave a rug for her, or to grind some corn or to make tortillas or piki bread. What would the young wife do if she did not know how to prepare these foods: sweet tamales, milk griddle cakes, fresh ground corn bread, sweet cake? The girl child also was introduced to all the tools of the weaver—the batten stick, the spindle and the carder. She was taught how to do all of a woman's work. That was the life of a girl growing into womanhood not too many years ago.

Today, it is all changed. Young girls do not want to do anything they are told. Very few learn to weave or to cook traditional foods.

And parents do not lecture much to their children anymore. The girls now look like boys—wearing pants. Some have ponytails, like a girl just coming of age. I gave a speech to some young people recently, and my subject was hair styles the women wear today. I mentioned to them that wearing their hair hanging down was very wrong and that they were not proving anything by wearing it that way.

Long ago, when the clansmen were returning to the Navajo Nation, they were attacked by the Arrow People. The Navajos requested the wind to erase their footprints so the enemy could not follow them. That was done by means of their sacred rituals. At that time the women were advised to let their hair hang loose during the ceremony, but, after it was over, they were to tie it up again. The years passed, and a famine struck the Navajos. Through their sacred ceremony they requested some rain. The women were advised again to let their hair hang loose until the ceremony was over. Then they tied it up. Whenever there was a woman involved in a ceremony, she let her hair down until she was advised to tie it back up, but it was not to be loose at any other time.

Today, women and girls go around with their hair hanging down most of the time, and they are violating the traditional rule. Only when there is a ceremony should the women have their hair down. When I told those things the girls in the audience only shook their heads. It was at the Rough Rock school. But these were the teachings the girls received long ago.

Now, many of those fine teachings are forgotten, and the women follow hardly any of them.

Formerly, a young girl was taught how to handle the lambs and kids during lambing time and how to save as many lambs as she could. Also, she was taught how to take care of her husband who did much of the hard work to keep his family. She was taught to cooperate with her husband and to work by his side. That resulted in a successful marriage.

Charlie Brown

MY FELLOW PEOPLE AND FRIENDS, I am 74 years old and live in Nazlini, Arizona. My clan is Yucca Fruit Strung Out in a Line *(Hashk'ąą hadzohí)*, born for the Towering House Clan *(Kinyąą' ia nii)*; Near the Water People *(Tó'áhaní)* is my maternal grandfather's clan and Red Running Into Water *(Táchíí'nii)* is my paternal grandfather's clan.

Much happened in the past to the Navajos. We were told in the 1930s that we had many more horses and sheep than were allowed, which brought on the livestock reduction program by the government. They took herds of our horses away for about $5 each. After a short time the same thing happened to the sheep and goats, but we received only $1, or even less, for them. This I can recall, but I cannot seem to remember the exact years in which it all happened. The same thing came about on all areas of the Reservation, I think.

After the horses were reduced, a lot of Navajos were on foot, and the need for horses became a problem. That I saw!

During that experience we were told that only one individual in a family could have horses, and then very few. As the years went by, however, some men had about five. Officials said that, later, certain laws about allocations of livestock would be provided, but for a long time they kept saying, "The laws have not been passed yet."

Horses, sheep and goats were taken from us. It once was said in our traditions that all Navajos were to have livestock; but, today, it seems that many of our children are empty-handed. Before reduction, the young men had plenty of horses for their enjoyment and their means of travel, but the white men took most of them away or shot them. Today, it seems that horses are a chore and a trouble for us. As they increase in number we are told of certain boundary lines belonging to us (where we can use the land), and their grazing takes away forage that could be eaten better by sheep or cattle. Also, many of them are not good horses.

It all added up to hardship and distress for many years for the Navajos, right down to the present generation. Even some of our own habits and products seem to have vanished. Many times I think about this as I work among the people and as I travel to different places.

Furthermore, I was told as a boy how our Navajo people were herded to Fort Sumner (Bosque Redondo or *Hwééldi*) far over in the eastern part of New Mexico. Later, a small part of our land was returned to the people so that they could start life over again after they moved back from Fort Sumner. From that time on the Navajos increased to a great number.

144

Beginning as a child, I experienced running at the break of dawn and, in winter, throwing snow upon ourselves or rolling in it. We were taught: "Go run in the early dawn. Who is going to support you when you grow older if you can't do that? You'll just be as though you were stabbed with a crow's feather, and all curled up—helpless." Today, I believe this to be a good thing—getting up and around in the early mornings. I have known older Navajo men who were wise and who used to say, "Running will make you strong and will help you learn knowledge." Today, this still is being preached by some older men and women because they know it to be true from the experiences they have had.

It is said that the main diet at the beginning of Navajo history was berries and grass seed. I realize, though, that, while some of the Navajos were eating those things, not all of them ate the same types of food. When it was the time of piñon nut ripening, they ate those too. From yuccas came the yucca fruit. Also, wild onions and various other kinds of plants were in their diets. Not too long ago I saw these foods still used as a regular meal by some people. Yucca fruit remains part of the diet of some Navajos; also wild berries that grow in the mountains. The Navajos gathered the berries and prepared them in a special way so they could be stored and would last for quite a while. They then were cooked or treated in ways to be useful in households.

We who were poor seemed to be dependent on the soil; our lives depended much on cornfields. It was a blessing when at times we had good crops. That is what I counted on for myself and to take care of my children.

In the far past, the Navajos lived in dirt hogans. Even when I was a boy we grew up in shelters made of pitched poles with dirt for the exterior, and at times some of the dirt would fall on us. We can be thankful for the nice homes that many of us have today. In addition, a certain amount of land can be allotted to us for planting our crops.

At the time our people were being rounded up to be herded to Fort Sumner, they had cornfields which were ruined on purpose by Kit Carson's soldiers running their horses through them. Our elderly men and women tell stories pertaining to it. In Canyon de Chelly and elsewhere the peach orchards and other trees were destroyed, too. The Ute Indians had been our enemies long before that, and there was much fighting with them. I have been told stories of such fighting.

145

Besides the Utes, the Navajos had enemies like the Apaches and the Spaniards. The Navajos were blamed for being thieves, but mostly they acted for self-protection or in retaliation. Others said the Navajos were "just plain coyotes," but conflicts finally were settled after the return from the Long Walk (Fort Sumner). At one time it looked like the Navajos would be killed off by their enemies. Today we still have many problems, but the Tribe has an income, and we are being helped by the government in Washington, and there is no actual fighting with our neighbors.

Our elders told us that we have four sacred mountains surrounding us. One of them is Blanca Peak (white) on the east, which is our strength. Another is Mount Taylor (blue or turquoise) on the south, which is our strength, too, and which our medicine men tell about in the ceremony of the Blessing Way. They bless it with corn pollen. The others are the San Francisco Peaks (yellow) on the west and the La Plata Mountains (black) on the north. Huerfano Mountain and Gobernador Knob also were made for us and are highly regarded.

Years ago, men would gather together and tell stories of the past and teach one another certain ceremonial songs. Many songs and stories have been handed down to this day. We had many different types of ceremonies, and we still keep most of them; but, as time goes by, we are losing our elderly people who told the stories of the past and the very beginning of the Navajos. Elderly medicine men also know the true ways of ceremonies and prayers.

Some medicine men were singing in a certain ceremony last summer when lightning struck down two people. One medicine man

When we were very young we were made to run toward the east at dawn, even through the snow on the coldest days of winter; or we threw snow on ourselves. The idea was to make Navajo children strong and hardy.

146

We poor people seemed to depend on the soil, and especially for the corn that could be grown, for our living. It was a blessing when, at times, we had rain and good crops.

tried his best to revive them, but the two showed no life. So, another medicine man was brought around—one who could perform a special ceremony. He started his prayers and songs, and the two who had been lifeless (at least unconscious) arose again. I believe in this—in what the medicine men sing and pray. I believe in the Navajo ceremonials. My main activity is in the sweat house ceremony, where only the males are allowed to go to take sweat baths.

Today there are many religious denominations on the Reservation. In the early days there were only two main ones. For years, now, the Mormons and others have been among them. I wonder why the Anglos have so many forms of religion. The Mormons have many teachings, as do the Catholics, Presbyterians and the others. I seem to be confused at times, and I still choose the Navajo ceremonies because I believe in the medicine men who have corn pollen of which to partake. I want the Navajo singing and prayers. I want the corn pollen and the Navajo medicines. That, I think, is the right way.

147

When I lived in Chinle I was told to become a policeman, which I did for four years. They also told me to be a chapter officer for the community. I did that. I was on the Community Action Committee, too. I also was a member of the school board, and I spoke to the students. To this day, that is still part of my work. I also was a member of the Land Board Committee. I always have been busy.

I never had an education. Back in the days when schools were not as common as now, I used to cry to go, but I always was turned down with "No, you herd sheep here." That was the reason I put all of my children through school. At times, I think of how things are complicated by the lack of an education.

Nowadays our young generation doesn't seem to listen or care about the education that is being provided for them. That is why mothers and fathers should talk to their boys and girls about right and wrong. As for myself, I talked to my children of what I knew was good for them. I said, "Do your best in everything, for I have tried to tell you what is right. Go and gain knowledge for your own future because I won't be telling you what to do the rest of your lives. It is up to each one; how much ability you have allows you to make things worthwhile, not only for yourself but for others. Take care of yourselves, from your head to your toes."

My children still come around and help me and take care of me; I also am kept informed as to where they are living and working.

It is up to parents to teach children the right way, especially about education, and to let them know that only the best is wanted for their schooling. Young people should know that education makes jobs available.

Nowadays most Navajos live the modern way. But, if we were still living by the old ways of the past, with each individual having his own livestock (and still making use of the values we had), I think the situation would be much better.

148

Part of the La Plata range in southwest Colorado. According to Navajo legend, the color associated with the La Platas is black.

Deescheeny Nez Tracy

MY CLAN IS A LARGE ONE whose members live here and there from west of Tuba City, Arizona, across hundreds of miles to the eastern part of the Reservation in New Mexico. It is the Start of the Red Streak People *(Deeshchii'nii)*.

When the four original clans began to migrate they separated into new clans. The first grandmother from whom I am descended was of the Black Streak Wood People *(Tsi'naajinii)*. Those people lived at the foot of Blanca Peak *(Sis Naajini)* at a place called Dark Rain Rays Descend.

In a legend two girl children were taken from a family, one of them to a place called Slumber Rock; and she became the beginning of the clan of Sleep Rock People *(Tsénahabiłnii)*. The other maiden came to a place called Red Cliff Gorge. She became the first Start of the Red Streak People. Thus, people just stopped at locations where they chose to make their settlements, and clans were named according to the description of the location. The three clans were group related. Many Navajos who belong to these clans do not know the relationships, especially the young people. They have little knowledge of clan ties. In fact, some do not know what a clan really is.

Later, a young girl came to Red Bottom Rock, and she became the first of the Red Bottom People *(Tł'áashchi'í)*. This added another related clan, making four. Their adopted clan is the Red House People *(Kinłichii'' nii)*, who really came from the Pueblo Indians. They migrated into the Red Streak People who adopted them. The Many Goats People *(Tł'ízí łání)* also make a related clan. All are scattered to various points of the Reservation now. All of them are one group that are related from the Black Streak Wood People clan. These clans should have respect for one another. They should not intermarry, but, today, such group relationships are not rightfully observed and followed. It may be because the Navajo Nation now is very much over-populated. However, we who are in our elderly age still respect our relationships. The tribal census count now shows that there are 150,000 or more Navajos.

I was born FOR the Bitter Water Clan *(Tódích'íí'nii)*, on my father's side. It is one of the original clans, known as Children of Changing Woman.

My mother's name was Start of Red Streak Woman, and she died of old age. She was born for Near the Water People *(Tó'áhaní)*. It also is an original clan which Changing Woman created long ago.

150

My visitor (interviewer) says he is of the Towering House clan *(Kinyąą'áa nii)* . It is slightly related to me; so I greeted the man as my paternal grandson. Before we met today we did not know one another. By introduction we recognized our clans and realized we are related. [The interviewer was Hoke Denetsosie, who wrote a chapter in this book and was one of its artists—EDITOR'S NOTE.]

We elders want the young people to learn to respect their clans, as we did years ago. We think it is important, and we do not want it to be forgotten. Today, projects and programs are working on the problem in order to help the young people find themselves. At Navajo Community College I have spoken to the students on clan relationships several times. I did not go into great detail. It always was in a class where the students were Navajos, other Indians and Anglos. That made it complicated, and I know that some did not understand what I was saying or my real meanings. I spoke in Navajo. I could tell that those were not really interested.

I have made many public speeches, but I still have a difficult time organizing a talk to make it interesting and understandable. Speaking before an audience of different tribes and Anglos is hard because of saying a few words at a time and then waiting until they are translated. A person may forget what he has just said and repeat himself, which bores his listeners. Probably recording this way is better because then only Navajos can listen to the tape, and they will understand what it is all about. Anglos and others will read my account after it is translated and printed.

I was born at Ganado, Arizona, where the local chapter house stands now. There were landmarks from the remains of our shade shack posts until the chapter house was built there recently. I have seen those posts, and I know I was born there in 1900 in the middle of July, during the full moon.

151

Ganado, Ariz., from the south toward the north.

I am not a medicine man, and I have little knowledge of the rituals. My family was poor and my mother had to support us. She wove rugs and sold them in order to buy what we needed. Now, in some schools girls are learning the art of weaving. They work with wool, and the trade is one of the sources of income that our people depend upon. During shearing time the women select the best wool to work with. It is processed by carding, spinning it to the right size for the loom, dyeing and then weaving. The spun wool is made various colors. Vegetable dyes are used a lot by many women because buyers prefer such rugs. They gather the plants, roots and barks that are needed for dyeing. When we see various types of real Navajo rugs in stores or at the Arts and Crafts Guild we admire them. They are made beautifully. Some designs are so attractive that it is hard to believe they were done by hand. Truly, they are a result of traditional education, the young ladies learning the art at home.

Another art is silversmithing. The first workers made copper and brass conchos and buttons. After silver was introduced they began to make numerous other things. Today there are many silversmiths, making squash blossom necklaces, rings, bracelets and other beautiful jewelry with turquoise and other valued stones. Some are made with gold. Young people are learning to be silversmiths because it is a good money-making art. The white man is credited with bringing the tools and other equipment used in modern silversmithing. Tools of long ago are no longer in use today. We are aware of the white man's knowledge, inventions and discoveries, and that is what makes our world progress. Science is a wonderful thing.

It has been more than a hundred years since our Navajo forefathers were released from their confinement at Fort Sumner. They made a compromise with the white men; and one promise, before getting freedom, was to allow the children to attend school. So, today, most of the schools on the Reservation are full to capacity.

I grew as a boy during times of hardship. There was very little food or clothing. The few trading posts that existed were not e-quipped with much merchandise or food like today. Young people now are fortunate to have their parents buy for them what they need. My family had only a few head of sheep when I was a child.

I was told that my mother and grandmother were alone when I was born at the break of dawn. My mother had a hard time delivering me, and she later said that I almost killed her. I also was told that I took my first step when I was 12 months old, which is about the right time for a child to begin walking.

I shall tell you briefly a story pertaining to Navajo history-mythology. The legend is carried on by our elders and medicine men.

Long ago, Changing Woman (also known as White Shell Woman) bore two boys—twins—on the summit of Gobernador Knob *(Ch'-óol'íí)*. It took place during the monster era. The man-eating creatures were a great menace to the People. (Ruins of ancient people are all over the Reservation and other places close by.) The Holy People gathered in a council discussing what should be done to get rid of the monsters. That was why Changing Woman was born—so that she would bring forth two great warriors who could destroy the monsters. She reared her sons in a little hogan in an underground dugout, concealed by a huge flat rock, in order to keep them safe. That is why we have dugout cellars to preserve our perishable belongings and harvested crops. Changing Woman was pregnant nine months before the twins were born. Thus, when the surface people came into existence it was said the women should be pregnant nine months before babies would be born. She kept her baby boys underground in the hogan; and, on the twelfth day, when their mother came to feed them, they were walking. Today it is 12 months before a child begins to walk, but the figure "12" still is true.

The twins grew up strong and healthy. They were the children of the Sun. Stories say that he was the father. Later, the twins took a long journey to their father's home on the western ocean. They went on the journey for a special purpose—to get weapons to save the people. They did destroy the evil monsters, and the people began to grow in numbers and to live at peace again.

I have said that I am not a medicine man, but I feel that I am a competent consultant. We have a saying that as long as one has hands to work with, a mind to think with, eyes to see with, ears to hear with and legs to stand on, he has his life to live—as long as the Great Spirit allows. And, if one is a capable person, he can think back to the past and forward to the future. That is how life goes on.

153

Talking about rug-making again, it really is hard work. A woman can spend many days, or weeks—even months—weaving a rug. It is a very tiresome job; but, when it finally is completed, she and her family rejoice because they will have money to buy some of the things they want.

Grinding corn also used to be a hard job for the women, and it still is when they do it. The corn flour is used to prepare many types of corn bread, gruels, mush or puddings. The women long ago knew how to prepare such native foods. Candy and other delicacies were unheard of. Very seldom did sugar, coffee and commercial flour appear on trading post shelves.

Native foods are very nutritious and give plenty of energy for long periods of time. Eating lots of such food keeps a person's teeth clean and makes them last longer. Children in times past had few cavities and seldom had to have teeth pulled.

The people planted corn, squash and beans. Fruit trees, melons and other vegetables were introduced by Anglos or by other Indian tribes.

When I was six years old I began to understand my surroundings. I remember that we ate a lot of corn, prepared in various ways. I was eight years old when I was told I had to prepare myself for manhood. I had to rise very early in the mornings. I was not allowed to sleep past sunrise. In the winter, when it snowed, I was forced to take snow baths. Also, all year long I ran a long distance very early each morning if I did not have to fetch the horses. My mother was very strict, and she lectured to me far into the nights about good living. In the winter, when the snow was knee deep, my mother would build a good fire in the hogan. Then, at dawn, she chased me outside into the deep snow without my clothes. If I hesitated, she threw me into the snow and then warmed me by the fire. She did it because she loved me and wanted me to become a "man." It was done so that my body could endure the cold weather and make me strong and healthy. There was no such thing as catching a cold. The wise man would say, "If you come face to face with an obstacle you can overcome it easily. You develop quick and strong legs, strong lungs, strong resistance and a strong voice. By doing that you are prepared for cold or hot weather, hunger or thirst, even sickness." That is why my mother taught me how to be ready for these emergencies. Yelling as loud as a person can while running either in cold or hot weather makes the voice strong, also the lungs and legs.

154

Twisting the body while running develops strong muscles and limbers them up. Exercising by wrestling with a tree stump will make your arms strong and develop muscles generally. Then, when one is healthy and strong he or she is almost immune to sickness and will reach an old age. If one is lazy and sleeps late, he or she will be weak and shiftless; sickness and poverty will be at the door.

That person may spend a lot of money on healing ceremonies to keep going because he or she never developed the body; and the mind will be weak. There will be problems all the time. All of this teaching was part of my traditional education, and I remember it well. For example, after my mother had thrown me into the snow a few times I realized I had to do it; so I jumped right in.

I remember breaking ice eight inches thick in the pond which was almost a mile from home. At dawn I raced to the pond. Then, when I had broken a hole large enough for me, I took a plunge into the icy water—naked. I ran home with my body covered with frost and my hair hanging down in icicles. I had to take either a snow bath or an ice water plunge.

My mother once said, "When you take a plunge into the water there are many good things beneath the ice, and you must jump in to get them. When you do, you will be covered with those things, and you will bring them home as gifts you have earned. Wealth and health are shut in under the ice; so it is up to the individual to get them. The ones who have ambition and energy are those who are capable of getting the good things. The ones who are lazy and won't help themselves never will have a chance to sit on a good fat horse or own fat sheep."

These are words of wisdom to the young people from the old-time elders. Racing at early dawn also holds good fortune for a person. One who rises early and races will be gifted and blessed, even if he or she comes from a poor family. Success eventually will come to the individual who earns it. A person with a good sound mind is dependable. A man who is a failure has many problems, especially after he gets married and begins having children. He will possess little with which he can keep his family. His children will be hungry, and he may have to depend on his relatives to feed them. The welfare of his children is the number one priority a man must prepare himself for, if he is to be ready to support a family.

In hot weather one should run up a high hill without stopping. He cannot find wealth at the foot of the hill or halfway up. Success is waiting for him at the top. All traditional education refers to good horses and fat sheep, and they are at the top of the hill. It takes a lot of sweat and thirst, but it is very rewarding. I did all that my mother taught me. At first I thought there were no horses waiting on the hilltop or riches under the ice, but I understood what she meant after I began to have my own livestock. I treasure what I have worked so hard for all my life. My mother was right; and she raised me herself. My father was not with us.

155

In the year 1918, soon after the first World War, the great influenza epidemic hit our country. Many Navajos died from the horrible sickness because we did not have hospitals or medicines. It was the same year that the Ganado Lake dam went under construction, and I first began working. John (Don) Lorenzo Hubbell and his two sons had their trading post at Ganado. It now is a National historical site. Ganado Lake is a Navajo recreation area. The Hubbells were great friends to the Navajo people. They helped many of them. Old Don Lorenzo was half Spanish through his mother, and the Navajos called him Old Mexican *(Naakaii Sani)*. He had opened the trading post back about 1878. He had married a Spanish woman, and they had four children—two boys and two girls. One boy was Ramon; the other Lorenzo, Jr. The girls were Barbara and Adele. The family owned a number of trading posts. The old man died about 1930.

Ramon made the suggestion for the lake project, and he took a delegation to Washington to get approval. His interest and promotion paid off. The Bureau of Reclamation approved the idea. The Hubbells provided the mule teams that were used to pull the dirt scoops. Ramon hired me to work with the teams and as a caretaker

*A portion of the old Hubbell Trading Post
at Ganado, Ariz., looking toward the west.*

156 for the mules. He was like a father to me. He taught me how to manage the animals. He was Spanish-American and I a Navajo, but he treated me like his own son, and I loved him for it.

I worked on the dam construction all summer and part of that fall. In October the flu epidemic hit the construction crew; so work was shut down. We had been paid $1.25 a day. It was my first earned money; and I had no complaints, although we worked very hard—sometimes for 10 hours a day.

I supported my mother because she had worked hard to bring me up. I thought I should repay my debts to her. I was glad that she had made me a strong and healthy man with the early exercises she had forced on me. She also had taught me how to farm, to work hard at it and not let the weeds get out of control in the cornfields.

A farm is very special and cannot be neglected because it provides food. Five things that are very valuable and require a lot of attention are the corn, horses, cattle, sheep and goats. For many generations they were our sources of survival.

At an early age Navajo children used to be taught to care for those things. The girls also had their lessons, working with wool and learning to cook traditional foods. They, too, exercised by racing and by grinding corn to develop strong arms and backs. Nowadays, many young people fail to listen to their parents. As I have mentioned, I did listen, and you see me at the age of 76—still strong and healthy. My life has been filled with good things. My horses and cattle are fat and beautiful, and my sheep are well taken care of. Not one horse has a sore back or is over-ridden. Navajos still judge by the appearance of farm and livestock.

Back in the 1930s everything changed suddenly when livestock reduction was forced upon the Navajos. They blamed John Collier, the Indian Commissioner, when they lost their stock. Many thousands of sheep, goats and horses were taken away or were destroyed before their eyes.

We are grateful to our leaders of more than 100 years ago who signed the Treaty of 1868 that promised education for our children. Education is wonderful. Among other things, Navajos learned to improve their living conditions and now can maintain nice clean houses. Many have modern facilities, like electricity and gas to cook **157** and to heat their homes, as well as running hot and cold water and bathrooms. These all make life easier. Many of us don't have to haul or chop firewood now, or haul drinking water. I moved into my new house a little over two years ago, and all I do is press a button or turn a knob, and I get all the conveniences of a nice comfortable home. At first, it seemed strange and uncomfortable to me, but I got accustomed to it. It took a while before I realized that it was not a dream. I am uneducated, but my children all have their educations, and they taught me all that I needed to know about the home.

To sit on a good horse and to have fat sheep and cattle a man must not be lazy, and he must help himself.

When I was a child my mother said she needed me at home; and she refused to let me attend school. So, I had no knowledge in the English language until my children taught me a few words.

When I speak to people at meetings or talk to students, I traditionally greet my audience with "My friends," "My grandchildren," "My children" or whatever relates to brotherhood. Being friendly and respectful to everyone can prolong a person's life, while jealousy and hate are evil and lead only to loneliness, ill health and tragedy. We must learn to avoid unpleasantness as much as possible. As parents we want to have happy homes so that our children can enjoy life and live comfortably.

Regarding religion, I regret to say that many Navajo people now are careless about their beliefs; and some ceremonies are forgotten or have become extinct because nobody has relearned the chants. Now, we want to keep all that are left.

158

Today, many of our people have chosen the Anglo religions and have turned against their own. Many churches are on the Reservation now, and the missionaries have converted numerous Navajos to Christian beliefs. The churches are well organized, and each has its own president or head man, which make for strong organization. We do not have such an organization like this in our religion to keep us together. That is one reason it gradually is fading away. We see some of our most sacred ceremonies used as social gatherings. Some people have little respect for our sacred religion, but others still have faith and depend on our healing ceremonies when they are in need.

Large tents are set up for revival camp meetings, and many of our people fill them. This helps to make them turn away from the Navajo religion; even some of our medicine men cast their healing paraphernalia aside to join the Christians, and most young people have little interest in the long and tedious task of learning ceremonies. They do not ask questions or inquire about the legends pertaining to the ceremonies.

As I said before, we must learn our clan relationships. Our young people do not know who they are because no one has told them. When you ask, "What clan are you?" they often reply, "I don't know." Some who do know are reluctant to tell because they are afraid that boyfriends or girlfriends may be related to them. That is one reason persons should ask before they begin going together or getting married. Until not long ago, our people lived up to the rule of clan relatives not marrying, even though there possibly was no real blood relationship. The elders strongly lectured to the young people about their relatives. They forbade their children to intermarry. Navajos should honor and respect all who are related. It will help in living a long life, with prosperity. That is a part of traditional education.

Anglo education is important, too, of course. Our children go to school to learn that culture and the English language. They return home during the summers, and some of the girls practice what they learned in being good housekeepers and good cooks. The boys try to find employment to keep themselves busy. They teach their parents at home about improvements in living conditions, and that is what I mean by education being important. My main regret is that I never had a chance to be educated.

The white man is very generous. He shares his knowledge by teaching our children what they need to know. A big problem is that our children are taught the Anglo culture, and, then, when they return home, some are uncomfortable. They do not want to live in primitive dwelling places. They are unhappy; and some leave their homes or do not want to go there after school is out. They are accustomed to soft beds, clean clothes, plenty of water, electricity, etc.

As I have said, I am not educated, except in the traditional way, but I respect education, especially in the Navajo way; and I have some knowledge of our history and mythology. I have faith in our culture. Learning to be a good medicine man, whom the people can rely on, takes at least four or five years (perhaps 10 or 12) of studying and listening. It is something like going to a university; and the time put into the training is tiresome. The lessons mostly are given at night, with the instructor constantly at hand. Prolonged sitting without sleep is strenuous. To become a Christian takes only a short time—a few lessons and prayers, and you are converted. To be a priest or preacher requires a lot of study. Prayers in our ceremonies are very long; and some are said four times, eight times, even 12 times. Twenty-four is the limit; so you see what I mean by "long." Some say they can be repeated up to 40 times.

The prayers were granted to the Navajos by the Holy People long ago. I don't know if any medicine men still carry their prayers to that extent. I heard that one from the Black Mountain area still does. Long, long ago there were songs about sheep being created. They were called the sheep songs. Also, horses had their songs. Those

159

songs told that they were all made from vegetation in places that were to provide their food and their medicine. Sadly, this mostly is forgotten now. Only a few still are known and used. Many of the sacred songs that were known to produce rain clouds are either forgotten or the people have become careless with them. They have little respect for them now. That is why much of our land is barren. There is no moisture for the vegetation to grow. Long ago the medicine men performed rain rituals requesting rain, and they had knowledge in the Rain Way. They used special offerings of pollen and placement of the variegated sacred stones. They had much faith in the ritual, and it actually brought dark clouds and rain. That great gift was granted to the people by the Holy Divinities. In churches, the ministers or priests pray for goodness for the people. I often have asked them why they do not pray for rain, and I get the reply, "We try to." Why is it we have little rain?

160

There is another religion which some people adopted not long ago. It is the peyote ritual. I don't know whether they pray for rain. I have no part in this cult and not much with other churches. My belief remains with the Navajo religion. I do not make comparisons to other churches, saying which is the best. I just stick to my own native beliefs. I believe in freedom of religion, though. Everyone can be what he wants. As for me, I have successfully lived my 76 years in good health. So far, I haven't had a single ceremony performed in my behalf, thanks to my mother for bringing me up as she did.

Long ago the people had rituals for "good health and long life." There were songs and prayers, also herb medicines. Much of that knowledge, too, is forgotten and lost. It was so important that I don't know why the people didn't keep it. And that is why we must preserve all that we have left today. Gathering all of the information that is vital and keeping it on records or tapes, or printing it in books, can be our Bible, like the white man has. We must continue using our healing ceremonies. Medicine men must be trained to make it possible. We need their services for our sick people. Many have requested that I tell the ceremonial legends, but I am telling the truth when I say that I have no great knowledge of them.

After the people were taken in exile to Fort Sumner (Bosque Redondo or *Hwééldi)* the most noted medicine men were asked to perform special ceremonies so the people could gain their freedom and return to their homeland safely. That was done according to what the Holy People had instructed at the beginning of our history.

There may be some medicine men left who have knowledge of the ceremonies which brought our people back to begin new lives for themselves. As we all know, the Navajos have increased tremendously from the handful who survived the hardships and sufferings, or who had escaped being rounded up on the Reservation, from maybe 12,000 to about 150,000.

All was going well, and the people had increased their livestock very rapidly, when along came John Collier and stomped his big foot on our sheep, goats and horses—and crushed them before our eyes. We believe that is when the rain went with the sheep. If it hadn't happened we would have rain and green ranges with sheep grazing all over. Now we have only small units to our permits, and the sandstorms erase a herd's hoof prints in seconds. Where there once stood large sheepfolds, now there are little ones, or nothing. **161** Dust blows in those places. That is how it is at Ganado. We try to fill our permits, but many folds are left empty. The people are partly

Nowadays sandstorms erase our small herds' hoof prints in seconds, and dust piles up where there once were large sheepfolds—or there are only small ones.

at fault by some of them ceasing to care for sheep. They have forgotten the songs and prayers which produce more livestock. Many are hungry for mutton, but they buy their meat supplies from the grocery stores when they can afford to do so. Those who are fortunate still have mutton on their tables. In our area there once grew abundant vegetation for grazing, but it is gone and only harmful weeds grow heavily, which kill our sheep when they eat too many of them. There are the locoweeds *(Ch'il'aghání)* and owl's foot. They have yellow flowers and look pretty, but they don't smell good. They can be poisonous to livestock. They are enemies, like the evil monsters of long ago. These plants can survive without much moisture because they are evil plants and grow abundantly on the ranges. Good grazing areas are hard to find, and the people lose many sheep because of bad plants. I know because I herded sheep until just recently. I began to get tired; so my children forbade me to herd. I was a good farmer, too. I worked on three farms, and they produced abundant crops. Now there is hardly any rain, and I'm tired. I do not do heavy work anymore. My farms are idle. Sand dunes are all one sees there now. Years back, when we had more rain, the people depended on their farms. Today, many are lazy, and few plant corn or squash. Some lucky people have irrigated farms and use them.

162

Without so much farming, unemployment is high on the Reservation. Many of the young people cannot find jobs, and the No. 1 problem is drinking. Many who are unemployed turn to drink because they have nothing else to do. Some who are working spend much of their earnings for liquor, and they end up in jail. Some lose their jobs. On paydays we see them swarm into surrounding towns like Gallup, Holbrook, Winslow, Flagstaff and Farmington to get drunk, and some don't return.

A majority of our people do not know how to save their money. As soon as they are paid they spend every cent and find themselves penniless the next day. When one of them wants to buy a car he goes to a second-hand car lot, probably off the Reservation. He purchases an automobile which he thinks looks neat, but he fails to check the real condition of the car. He is proud and happy about it, and he drives away, anxious to show off; but, before he gets back home, the car stalls on a hill, and he walks the rest of the way. There are many crooked car dealers who cheat the Indians because they know that many are ignorant and not aware of what makes a good buy. They only want the money. A car is wonderful to have, and it gets a person where he wants to go faster, but he must realize the expense, and he must KNOW the dealer.

I understand a little about the white men. From their beginning they were gifted with wisdom—knowledge, inventions and great discoveries. They have scientific minds and have done wonders in this world in the fields of medicine, science, manufacturing, commerce and all others, including machinery devices. They even got to the moon. Who knows where else they will go!

It was predicted long ago that the Holy People would be angered if in any way we tried to bother the moon or the sun. At the beginning the moon and the sun were lifted upward by the Wind People and placed in their respective locations, where they are now. Maybe the Wind People are angry, because we have more windstorms and hurricanes on the earth. Is it the wrath of the Wind People because the white men tromped on the moon? The world is changing. It seems like conditions are worse today. Even here on the Reservation our tribal government has it controversies. More problems develop, and our children are right in the midst of it all. Things may get better, however, if we all have faith in the Great Spirit and ask him to guide us back into the road of the pollen. If we turn against our religion and mock our ceremonies, using the ceremonial sites for social affairs, then someday we will suffer the consequences. More and more people will weaken and go crazy. The use of drugs and bad smoking and drinking habits will produce even more addicts and alcoholics, most of whom will end in disaster. As I see it, people have no willpower. They weaken at the sight of a bottle of wine. They gulp it all down in a few swallows, to the last drop. Most do not know how to drink socially. Those who have money to spend run to the nearest liquor establishment, not thinking first of family needs. Later, when they find themselves in jail, they remember their families and ask help to get out. Their money is gone, and they are hungry. I have seen many who have gone to workshops or to rehabilitation centers fall back upon drinking again.

As I record this story of my life and thoughts about Navajo history and traditional culture I think of how people these days have telephones, telegrams, television and radio systems to communicate to the far ends of the world. And I believe that in some way radios, tape recorders, etc. have corrupted many minds. Our young people spend their money on those things to occupy more of their time at

163

home. They do not listen to their parents or other elders, and they do not care to work. From the silly music they compose their own songs which they sing and giggle about at the squaw dances and other ceremonial affairs. They have lost respect for, and faith in, our sacred ceremonies. The squaw dance is a healing ceremony, NOT a Navajo social dance, as some call it, where people drink and make up stupid songs to amuse themselves with. It is ridiculous and shameful, but it is how many of our sacred healing ceremonies go today. The young people see all of those bad things on television, and learn and copy all they see—drinking parties, sex, prostitutes, addicts and narcotics rings, murder and all kinds of violence. They are enemies to the human body. I do not drink or smoke or do evil, and that is why I am very critical. I never wasted my money on such things. I take care of myself, and that is the reason I have lived so long without a single "sing" (healing ceremony) done for me. A person who comes in contact with a lot of sick people with contagious ailments will pick up the germs and become sick later. The same idea applies to coming in contact with the evils of television and today's life.

164

I seldom go anywhere now. I stay close to my home, unless it is necessary to go out. I am using myself and my good health as an example because I hope some people may realize how precious a human life is. The Great Spirit gave us a limited time to live, and we should not take our lives for granted or spoil them. Until fairly recent years our cornfields were our life-givers. Corn was the main source of food. In fact, the farm was where most of our food came from—food that made us strong and healthy. But today we have all kinds of useless foods; some are just imitations; many are harmful sweets and candies, pastries, sodas, and so on. That is where people get different kinds of ailments—toothaches, stomach aches, colds, blood disease, high blood preasure, heart attacks and more. In the homes the refrigerators are full of pop and Kool-Aid. Our children sit in front of the TV and consume gallons of pop into all hours of the nights. When morning comes they want to sleep until noon. That is life to them. We seldom hear about a person running at dawn yelling at the top of his voice, or the screams that come from taking an ice-cold plunge or rolling in the snow. We hear only the screaming of the radios and stereo players. Who is to blame? The white man made the inventions.

Another problem I want to mention is that the young do not speak their native tongue as they used to do. I have a bunch of grandchildren, both boys and girls, who do not know how to speak Navajo. It is hard for me to communicate with them because I do not understand them, and they do not understand me. All they yell is "Grandpa," and I say "What." They laugh and shake their heads when I speak to them. Parents should speak to their children in Navajo while they still are very young. We must not let our native tongue or our culture become extinct, and practice in speaking Navajo will help keep them.

People should be aware of what is happening today. Money earned is worth less than the cost of living, and that cost keeps right on rising. What about the future? The Navajos may have to go back to their native foods to survive. That would mean working our farms again and gathering native foods, like seeds, berries and roots. It is difficult to raise crops now, with the lack of moisture. Also, **165** the price of wool is low, and the trading posts do not buy mutton from us anymore. All the meat the consumers buy comes from the packing companies. We do not know how old the meat is because it is kept frozen. Meat and other things we buy may be three or four months old, maybe much older, and that may be the cause of the children having upset stomachs. The outpatient clinics are packed full all the time in the hospitals and elsewhere. There is more sickness and misery among the people today. Many women are plump and short, and the men are pot-bellied and short, too.

Years ago, the men were slim, tall, brawny and healthy. There were hardly any fat men or women because they kept themselves busy all the time. Modern conveniences give more leisure time today, and the people have become lazy.

Now, for my final part of this recording, I want to tell about my main job—my work experience. Just how I learned to be good at my trade may sound unbelievable because, in a way, I don't understand how I did it. I have told you I am an uneducated man. Nevertheless, although I have no knowledge of the English language and cannot write, I learned a fine trade.

In 1922, at the Ganado Mission, a white man (he was an Italian) was supervising the construction of the stone buildings for the school there. He had a crew of the same nationality who were professional stone masons. There was one particular man, an elderly one, that I worked with. The foreman of the crew hired me to lift the heavy stones for that man and to keep him well supplied with concrete, mud or cement. We were working on the powerhouse. A Presbyterian white minister was the first superintendent of the mission school. His name was Mr. Mitchell, but the Navajos called him Slim Missionary. He worked very hard to establish that mission school for the Navajos. He could speak Navajo fluently. He was a good man, and he helped me to get employment with the construction crew. Each mason had a Navajo helper. I watched the elderly man chisel the stones into rectangular or square shaped blocks. I did not know at first how it was done. He used a small sledge hammer and a chisel to cut the stones. When the man was busy working at something else I would pick up his tools and to do what he did. I practiced every chance I got. When I first watched him it looked real easy to do, and I wanted to learn. I was just a young man then, but my eagerness persuaded me to learn fast. The man was happy that I took an interest in the trade.

166

I watched the professional stone mason chisel the stones into the shapes that he wanted; then I practiced and learned to do it well.

Not long afterward he let me do a little work until I got the hang of it. We worked together real well. In about a month's time we completed the walls of the building, and the carpenter crew took over. That was the beginning of my first job as a stone mason; and I went on to help construct other stone buildings in that area. Every year one more building was added to the mission school. I was well on the way to becoming a real good stone mason. We constructed the buildings that had to be done, and, after that, I naturally was laid off.

A few years later the government provided a special project for the people, and I worked with it. I don't remember what year it was, but I believe it was during the livestock reduction period. The people were told to build houses for themselves; so a crew of men moved from one location to another, building homes on a voluntary basis. No one got paid for the work. The men only helped one another. Food was furnished by the family whose house we were working on.

I have told you about the Hubbells—old Don Lorenzo and his sons, Ramon and Lorenzo, Jr.—who had the first trading post at Ganado. Later, they hired a crew of stone masons to construct a building adjacent to the trading post. I was one of those masons. Our foreman was a Navajo man named James. He had gone to school and had vocational training in stone masonry. The other hired men knew little about it, and we had a hard time getting the work done. My experience of a few years before helped me, though. I was the only one who could cut the stones and block them because I remembered how it was done. We completed the building in about three months. The roof was made from narrow ponderosa pine logs, and the building still stands in the same way we built it.

Several years later construction was started on the Window Rock headquarters (the Navajo capital) of the Bureau of Indian Affairs. When the government took away most of our livestock it had promised employment for the people so they could earn money to support themselves. I worked at Window Rock on the construction of those buildings. After that, I was well recognized for my ability as a stone mason. For example, a man who owned sheep gave me 60 head to build him a stone house a few miles west of Ganado. Another man also hired me to build a house in the same area, but he gave me only 50 head of sheep for the work. Those stone houses still stand, but they now are abandoned and wind-beaten.

It was in midwinter when I heard that more construction was in progress at Window Rock. There were not many automobiles then. We traveled mostly by horses and wagons. The place where I lived was called Bitter Water. It is where I live now.

After I had completed the stone houses near Ganado I decided to find employment at Window Rock again; so I packed my horse with all the necessary tools, bedding and some food supplies. When I arrived there, construction was progressing slowly. The stones were being hauled in from the rock quarry to where the men were working on the foundations. I looked at what they were doing, and it did not

167

look good to me. I supposed that most of them were inexperienced and were just learning. I went to the employment office and was hired. When I reported for work the foreman gave me some instructions on how it was done. I knew all of that; so I got my tools out and began cutting the stones into perfect shapes, and I laid them evenly. After the foreman saw my work he assigned me to the more difficult job of blocking in the corners of the walls. Our construction superintendent was a white man. The stone mason foreman was James Salt, a Navajo. He kept himself busy running from one section to the other where the masons were working. Some were cutting the stones and blocking them, while others laid them. I did my own cutting of the stones—the way I wanted—and laid the cornerstones for the walls. Most of the men were earning a four-dollar-a-day rate. My wage, though, was eight dollars a day because I was well experienced and my qualifications were good.

168

That was how I was employed, even though I had no education. I had learned by experience. It is just a matter of setting your mind on what you really want to do and getting involved in it. I worked at Window Rock the rest of the winter, until April. By that time some of the men had become good stone masons because I had taught them how it was done. The administration building was completed, and construction closed down temporarily. I left Window Rock and went home because I had a lot of work to do in planting; besides, it was lambing time and sheep shearing time.

The next fall, construction began again at Window Rock. That time it was the power plant. After we had finished building the walls, the men who were working on the huge chimney were afraid to go any higher then 25 feet; so three of us offered to finish the job. The chimney was 130 feet tall after its completion. We did it in about a month. Just recently that chimney was torn down and the whole plant was remodeled because it does not burn coal anymore. The furnaces are gone, replaced with huge generators for a heating system.

After the powerhouse was completed we constructed the Navajo Council chambers. That is where the laws and regulations are made and where the Navajo government is planned for the people. I again did the difficult work of laying the cornerstones for the walls. I shaped the stones that were rounded into curves, and I blocked the long stones for the windows. Curving the stones is hard work. We also had done it when we built the big chimney for the powerhouse.

Next, we constructed other buildings—the employees' buildings, the houses in the residential section on the hillside, apartments, etc. When all the houses were completed I began working at Fort Defiance on the new hospital. We had a government inspector from Washington who checked our work at the end of each day. He approved mine and always complimented me. He said I did an excellent job and accomplished more than the other men. I got far ahead of all the professional stone masons; and, for that reason, they did not like me and rarely spoke to me. (Some of those men lost their jobs because of mistakes they made and for other reasons), but I did my best and stayed on the job. There always will be jealousy. That was the way it was against me, but I paid no attention to it. When we had finished all the walls no one wanted the job of stacking the tall chimney; and another Navajo mason and I constructed it, and it still stands. The man I worked with was a good mason, too. I knew him only as Yellow Horse's nephew.

169

I left my job before the chimney was completed; we only had about three feet to go. It was spring, and I had to do much planting and other work at home. The white man who supervised the construction rated me as one of the best stone masons he had known.

Later, I helped build the new powerhouse at Fort Defiance. It was different there because I had to work with a hard crew. The men were Anglos—tough and ill-tempered. I managed to work with them, but I tried to keep out of their way. After the building was completed, they built the chimney themselves. I left in the late fall. Later, I helped construct more houses at Fort Defiance and other places where I was recommended.

In recent years concrete blocks have been used instead of native stone for building houses. They are cheaper to work with and lighter to handle than stones. When they were new I did not know how to lay them until I watched and saw how it was done. Then I began working them as the other masons did.

When the government school at Thoreau, New Mexico, was under construction I got word to work there. They needed some good brick and concrete block layers. The BIA area office sent a letter asking me to report for work. Some men had been laid off because of lack of experience. Only a few were on the job when I got there, and the work they were doing was slow. When I reached Gallup, a man named Carl Todacheene, of Shiprock, took me to Thoreau where I was to begin work. He introduced me to the construction supervisor, a black man.

Window Rock, Ariz., capital of the Navajo Nation, with the actual rock formation in upper center and the Council Chambers in the foreground.

"This man is a skillful block layer," said Carl. The man looked me over and laughed. "Him?" he replied. "Naw! not him." He told us he had to lay off many men who said they could work, and he had his doubts about me, too. He wanted to test me first. He handed me a trowel and gave me five minutes to fill in a section that had been left open. First, I got the concrete blocks and stood them up where I needed them. Then, I slapped some cement on the trowel and quickly spread it on the tops of the blocks that were already set. Next, I placed the blocks real evenly, first putting cement on each one as I layed it in. After that I scraped off all the excess cement, cleaned and smoothed each one.

The supervisor watched as I finished, in less than five minutes, the job he had told me to do. He laughed again and said, "You're hired." I reported for work the following day at 8 o'clock. Again, though, I had to leave in the spring. My family, as usual, needed me at home for the spring planting, the lambing and the shearing.

We thought we got a good wage rate back then, when masons generally earned about $3.25 an hour. Today, however, a stone mason's pay is several times that amount.

I had a good career to look forward to when I was classified as a professional stone mason and bricklayer. I received offers and worked at various places in the country. They included Phoenix, Arizona; Barstow, California; Stewart, Nevada, and Carson, Nevada. I became a member of the union; so, wherever I was needed, I would go. I turned down some jobs because I had farms to work on and livestock to tend.

In all the places I worked not once did I sign my name. I used only my thumbprints when I had to sign applications or a paycheck. After my long years of successful work experience many do not believe that I cannot write or speak English. But, even with that handicap, I learned an excellent trade, and I worked hard to be a good stone mason. I am proud of myself. All the supervisors I have worked for have given me good ratings. I also am a qualified bricklayer. I added that trade by experience and determination. **171**

I have supervised construction projects on the Reservation. Some men who had school training in stone masonry and bricklaying worked under me, even though I am a non-educated man. One of the construction jobs I supervised was the tribal jail building at Lupton, Arizona, a few years ago. Mr. Henry Whipple, who was our construc-

A portion of Fort Defiance, Ariz., looking toward the west.

tion superintendent at Window Rock, knew my skills as a cinder-block layer and placed me in that position. I had constructed cinder-block (or concrete block) houses here and there on the Reservation. I also had supervised the construction of the jail building at Navajo Springs near Navajo Mountain and at Chinle, Arizona. I also helped construct the large Civic Center at Window Rock. I laid the rock tiles in the washrooms of the Civic Center.

Then, while I was working with the construction crew on the new police and judicial building at Window Rock, I received a notice of retirement. I had earned it, and my social security benefit is my income now. I do not depend on any livestock. My children take care of what is left of the livestock after the reduction program.

172 I have described my work experiences and how I became an expert stone mason. I am using myself as an example of how one can become a good, skillful worker in any trade he likes; and I hope that many young people will think carefully about my story so that some-day they, too, will be successful and become good workers.

I am glad that I have taught some men to be fine stone masons. I feel that I have done my share, especially now that my thoughts and the story of my life have been recorded for publishing in a book by the Navajo Community College Press. Finally, I am happy that this material—along with accounts by a number of other elderly Navajos—will be used in the College's curriculum and will be read by Indians and non-Indians all over the country. Perhaps it will contribute to a better understanding of my people.

Paul Blatchford

MY FATHER WAS AN ANGLO, and my mother was a Navajo, a member of the Mud clan *(Hashtł'ishnii)*, born for the Red Running Into Water clan *(Táchii'nii)*. Therefore, I am of the Mud clan. I am 57 years old and live in the Tuba City community.

As a girl, my mother lived around Toadlena, New Mexico; and, at about the age of 10, she was brought in by the Indian police to help fill a wagon caravan going to Tohatchi, New Mexico. Then, from Tohatchi, the children were taken to Gallup, New Mexico; and from there they embarked on the Santa Fe train to the Sherman Indian School at Riverside, California. My father was born in Superior, Wisconsin.

I am a descendant of the great Chief Manuelito who helped mightily in getting the Navajos freed from captivity at Fort Sumner *(Hwééldi)* and returned to their homeland after the terrible Long Walk. He was my great-grandfather. My grandfather's name was Paul Homer Manuelito. I used to travel by horse to his home.

After I had gone through school, sometimes I would think back to the summer of 1922. Traveling on horseback with my cousins and grandfather, we started early one morning from Cottonwood Pass, which is 10 miles or so east of Crystal, New Mexico. Around 10 o'clock in the morning we came to a half-roofed log cabin, and I was curious as to who lived in it. My grandfather ordered us to stop and let the horses rest. He began to unravel his story by saying: "This is where the government set up its first workshop after the Fort Sumner troubles when I was a young man. Your great-grandfather was a smart man whose real habitat was the Blue Mountain range in Utah. He forded the San Juan River many times, and this is one of the places where he made a speech. This building was called the first 'blacksmith shop.' He told his people to learn as much as they could. Also, he said that when the treaty of 1868 was signed between the Navajos and the United States, he (Chief Manuelito) had asked that the government put schools on our Reservation and let the people learn as long as the San Juan River shall run; so, now, I want you boys, if you ever have a chance to go to school, never to turn your backs on it."

My education started back in 1921 at the age of five. The parents of my two cousins, ages 9 and 10, and my parents got together and agreed to send us to the Christian School at Rehoboth, New Mexico. I was living at the old sawmill 13 miles north of Fort Defiance at the time.

As I recalled afterward, we boys never knew that we were being tricked, and it was really our curiosity that got us into the Model-T car the day we left for school. When my oldest cousin cried out, "The white man is taking us to school," it dawned on me that he was right! I could just picture my grandfather when he had said, "If you ever have a chance to go to school, never turn your back on it."

My two cousins had stayed at my home for a week and a half, and, one day, a Model-T appeared. We didn't know that the white man, Mr. Bascher, was going to pick us up; so our parents told us to just take a ride in the car and see if we liked it. We got in and off we went. I was the interpreter.

We stopped at the Fort Defiance Trading Post, the driver bought us some candy and we went on again, bouncing up and down while sitting in the back seat. The roads were rough—nothing but wagon trails. There was no road maintainance. It never had been heard of in those days.

It was about two o'clock in the afternoon, as we passed Window Rock, when my two cousins started crying. They said we were being hauled away to school somewhere, and they told me to have the white man driver stop and let them out of the car. I said, "No," and they cried all the way to Rehoboth. But when they saw those other children playing around on the school grounds they stopped crying.

On our first morning the dormitory matron turned on the lights and told everybody to wash; so we got up, fixed our beds the best we could and washed. Then the bell rang, and everybody started running except us. We didn't know what to do until the matron came and scolded us saying, "Hurry! You have to line up outside."

The school was a military setup, and the matron placed us toward the end of the group—in Company C. We wore the Holland military uniform altered to our size. We marched to the dining room; we marched back to the dormitory, and we marched to our classrooms. We marched to church Sunday mornings. At our dormitory I noticed an addition to the building. It had a small, cellar-type window which I looked through, and I saw two boys. They were runaway boys, chained to a big iron ball. They told me that a punishment for runaways from school was to be put in jail.

Everything went fine until the last part of January, 1922. It was a nice Sunday, and we three decided to run away in the afternoon. That night we slept in the open; and, all night, the mountain lions yelled. We didn't have coats, but we had heavy long-johns, and the three of us took turns sleeping in the middle for warmth. The next day, before noon, we saw a Model-T going toward Fort Defiance, and we thought we could hitchhike. The car belonged to a state policeman—a trap. They found the numbers marked on our long-johns at the neck, and we were returned to the school.

Corporal punishment was identical at every school, whether it was a government or a church mission school. They showed us different lengths and widths of straps. When students ran away they were told to pull their pants down, lean over a bench and receive 25 straps. Next time they ran away they received more. Also, if one was late for line-ups in going to dinner or to class, one was placed in what they called the belt line. There were two lines facing each other, four feet apart, and the person started from one end, running from right to left—and all those who could swing with their right arms, swung their belts at the person. Then he turned back and the other line gave him a strapping. Also, if anyone wet the bed, he or she had to carry the mattress around in the square between the girls' dormitory and the boys' dormitory—and had to continue to carry that mattress around all day long.

Those were some of our punishments while in school.

The police force would find runaways and take them back to school. When someone was "absent without leave" the school notified the police, and they would search for him or her.

The general curriculum in the schools was history, arithmetic, English and penmanship, which were taught the first half of each day; while the other half was used to clean up dormitories and perform other jobs if the person was one of the younger students. The

175

Through a window I could see into the cellar where two boys were chained to a big iron ball. They had run away from school, and that was the punishment.

One day a Model T came and took my two cousins and me away to school

school offered vocational training in the early days for the older students, and it was taught the last half of the school day.

The memories of how children were treated—and punished for every little thing they did—made me want my children to live at home. I felt that they could attend school nearby, but not a boarding school or a mission school away from home.

Parents in those days, however, had nothing to say about the schools, although they did gripe and complain regarding how the kids were punished. The police forced those kids to go to school, and I know many parents whose teardrops fell—but they couldn't do anything about it. If the parents resisted the policemen, they (the parents) were put in jail; so there really was nothing they could do.

In 1946 we finally got the special five-year program, and I think it was the start of better education on the Reservation. Many children were older and were sent to the five-year program. Afterward, they came back to the Reservation and got married, and from there on they thought more about education, especially for their own children. To this day, we have had better schools than in years gone by because many of the Indian children are able to live at home and attend day schools. But, the problem still isn't solved because we don't have enough schools on the Reservation to keep all of our children here. Maybe 30 percent leave the Reservation to be educated.

I am the counsellor for the Public School Board in Tuba City. We have three Indians on the board and two Anglos. There is more concern these days about the schools, and many Navajos are participating at board meetings. We really have better schools than in the early days, and more subjects are being offered. As progress continues we will have new subjects available which never have been offered to Indian students. The studies are much different today than they were in the early days, and the parents now are involved in choosing the subjects to be taught in public schools. They have a chance to take part in the education of their children, and that is one of the main reasons for our better schools.

Years ago the government principals did their own planning, and they probably received their orders on how they should run the schools and the subjects to be taught directly from Washington. That is as far as they could go because they had no assistance or direction from the Indian people toward educating the children. But now we have school boards that willingly hear the desires of the

177

people on subjects to be taught in the schools. The people question why a subject is offered in a school off the Reservation but not in Reservation schools. For instance, in Tuba City we didn't teach auto mechanics in our high school. We had carpentry, and the Indians on the board felt that auto mechanics should be taught to our students as well. The reason it couldn't be taught was that there was not enough money to cover it.

But we kept trying. We expressed our desire in the proposed budget and then hoped that we could obtain enough money so that by the fall of the next year auto mechanics and other trades could be offered. We felt that many young people going through high school needed that kind of education so that when they graduated they would have trades.

178 In the early days the highest grade children reached was the eighth. However, they did learn how to be plumbers and carpenters in vocational training classes. After 1946, however, vocational training was discontinued, but it now is being placed in the schools again. The importance of vocational training was that high school students either could find jobs and start working upon graduation or possibly they could go on to college if they had saved enough money earned from their vocation.

Many reports are received from the people saying that they prefer the public schools so they can keep their children at home. But there are still the problems of missing the school bus, or children staying away from classes to attend dances at the Community Center, etc. It is a matter of discipline. The majority of parents like to keep their children at home, with the need of more guidance for the first year; however, the next year, the parents prefer the boarding schools to public schools. They feel it is better at the boarding schools than having children run away off the Reservation because of problems at home.

The government policy for vocational training began at the 8th-grade level with a safe subject. I mean that the students were not required to operate machines but did things that were safer for the beginning learner in the vocational training program. In gardening, for example, a person learned the methods of irrigation and cultivation; also, the plants that will grow at different elevations, and, finally the methods for harvesting. Also we had animal husbandry— how to raise rabbits, the names and the different types, and how to raise chickens, the various names and the different types, and how to raise pigs and the different types and the names of each type, etc. This education even included how to raise pigeons, and the knowledge of how they live. Dairying also was offered. Almost all government schools had it. In this course of study, the student learned how to milk a cow, how to treat milch cows, how to separate the cream from the milk and how to feed a milk-producing cow.

At the 9th-grade level the student was ready for technical vocational training, and the individual had a choice of three trades. A three-month period was allowed to learn the first trade; the next three-month period the second trade was learned, and then the remaining three months were used for the third choice made by the student.

The next fall, when the students entered the 10th grade, they had an opportunity to change to another trade, or they could remain in one of the three trades taken the previous year if it was to be the final choice for a vocation. I took about everything that was offered. I studied gardening, animal care, milch cows, cabinet making, stone masonry, brick laying, plumbing and carpentry.

179

After high school I went to Phoenix Indian School because I understood that only P.I.S. and one other school offered vocational training after finishing high school. It was the closer of the two, and both offered vocational training for all Indians in the United States. The trade areas that I never studied in high school but I learned at Phoenix were electricity, radio, telephone and diesel mechanics.

In the early 1920s, while school attendance was increasing, transportation was very slow, and the hauling of food to the schools was difficult. In order to have fresh fruit and vegetables available, all mission schools and B.I.A. schools were forced to seek out or develop a farming area in the nearby vicinity to raise potatoes, pinto beans, corn, tomatoes, carrots and turnips; some schools even planted fruit trees. There was also some exchanging of various products among schools. Whatever one had in surplus it would exchange with another school; and cellars in those days were very common. There were plenty of wild rabbits; and, for special occasions, the older boys would get up and hunt for them right after breakfast, bringing them in before dinner time. It happened for such important meals as Thanksgiving and Christmas dinners. In later years, after the farming was well under way and turkeys were being raised, there was a surplus of those birds, and their meat was used instead of jackrabbit for special events.

The Tuba City BIA school was first opened in the Blue Canyon area after the Executive Order of 1882. It was down in Blue Canyon that the officials started a little farm, but, with more and more children coming to school, they had to buy out the Mormons who lived at what is presently Tuba City. That boarding school still is in existence. The Mormons developed the farming area around Tuba City, becoming the major food suppliers for the Kayenta and Leupp Boarding Schools. They also had a big dairy farm; and meat also was supplied from Tuba City. Today, the slaughter house still stands in the Cerby Valley, but it might never be used again.

In the early curriculum for Navajo children, kindergarten was provided for the beginners. It included playing with blocks and learning to sing "Mary Had a Little Lamb" and "Ten Little Indian Boys"; playing games, with everyone holding hands, forming a circle and moving around in that circle singing "Ring Around the Rosie." They also sang "Farmer in the Dell"—and it was always stressed: "Speak English! Speak English!" Next came the first grade. It was the year to learn to distinguish the letters of the alphabet and to learn to write in capital letters. That was drilled every day until Christmas. After Christmas the vowels were learned. Vowels were printed on cards, and the teacher would stack them on her desk, picking them up one at a time with the whole class saying the vowels in unison. Learning to write the vowels, together with the rest of the alphabet in capital letters, making words, followed; and that was drilled until school was out. Always the big stress was: "Speak English! Speak English! Don't speak Navajo! Don't speak Navajo!"

Then, students of the second grade learned to read simple words. They were drilled until Christmas, always with the same: "Speak English! Speak English!"

After Christmas the teacher could communicate with the second graders and she would explain, "Now you have learned how to read, and when you get into the next grade you are supposed to be able to read a book." Books provided at first were about "Little Black Sambo" and "Little Red Riding Hood"; and, then, the following year the pupils entered third grade. That was the year classes became divided into periods. For example, 45 minutes of spelling was the first period, and the second period was for penmanship. The work in penmanship lasted for about half an hour, and then we went to morning recess. After the recess, about an hour and a half to lunch time was utilized in learning basic arithmetic.

In the afternoon, after 1 o'clock, we started with one and a half hours of English—a long subject, then a 15-minute recess. After recess, we spent the time reading until 4 o'clock when we went back to our dormitory.

Fourth grade was the same as third grade, but more strict; and it really was difficult to pass after one reached the fifth grade. I knew some students who just stayed in that grade. As for me, I did not return to the same school. I registered to transfer to the Albuquerque Indian School. I told them that I was ready for sixth grade, and they took my word. That is the way I passed myself, and I never had any trouble from there on. In the sixth grade we learned spelling, English, history and arithmetic.

The seventh and eighth grades were the same as the sixth grade; and the ninth grade changed the curriculum to different subjects such as biology, geometry, algebra, English, science and history. The subjects from that grade on didn't change much throughout high school.

181

That was the way our curriculum was during our school days. For a lot of the later years we went to school half a day, learned a trade in the other half, and, the next morning, went back to the classroom.

That was how education was carried on among the Navajos when I was young; and, in spite of many hardships, harsh discipline and problems that I have discussed, students generally did learn much—and I am glad that I was able to get what was considered a full education at the time.

John Dick

I HAVE LIVED AT ROUGH ROCK all my life. My clan is Red Running Into Water People *(Táchíí'nii)*. My maternal related clans are the Tobacco People, *(Nát'oh Dine'é)*, Charcoal Streaked People, *(Naaeesht'ézhí)*, and Deer People (a division of Red Streak Running into Water), *(Bįį Dine'é Táchíí'nii)*.

My mother was born for the Water Flows Together People *(Tó' aheedlíinii)*, which is the clan of my maternal grandfather. My father's clan was the Start of the Red Streak People *(Deeshchii'nii)*. His related clans are the Many Goats People *(Tł'izi Łani)*, Black Streak Wood People *(Tsi'naajinii)* and the Red House People *(Kinłichíí'nii)*; and he was born for the Salt People, *(Áshįįhí)*.

All the clans I have mentioned are my related clans from both my father and mother. According to the records, I am 68 years old (1976). No one ever told me about my early childhood days.

When I was 17 or 18 years old I realized what life really was about. I understood clearly what my father, uncle and mother meant when they taught me all about living in the traditional Navajo way. I learned what not to do and what not to say, and I still know these things very well. My parents were wise; they knew what they were teaching. To this day I look back and say to myself, "It is completely true what my parents taught me." During my younger days I never talked back or made smart remarks to my mother and father. I always listened to their long lectures and advice.

I am not an ill-tempered man, and I have learned to control myself. I never have had any trouble with anyone in any place. I mind my own business, and I believe in self-respect and respect for others. My parents and grandparents always said "let alone be"—

in other words, "Don't stir up trouble." I always have kept this in mind and lived accordingly.

I was not given a wife until I was 30 years old because my parents considered me too young. They always advised me to leave the girls alone. I felt that I was not ready to take on heavy responsibilities; so I listened to them.

After I got married I left my home, knowing, then, that I was ready to begin life on my own. I built a home for my wife, and we began having children. That taught me much about the big responsibilities that were mine. It began right after the first child came and has continued ever since.

Each child is different, no two are alike. Although they all are the children of a man and his wife, their characteristics and personalities differ. But, when listening to lectures they are alike; all that parents have learned should be repeated to their children.

183

It has not been too long since education first came to our Reservation. At first, about 100 years ago and for some time, many of the people were opposed to education. Only a few allowed their children to enroll in school. Probably none of those students received high school diplomas, and higher education likely was not ever known. As for me, I am uneducated, even though strong attempts were made to enforce compulsory education when I was a boy. A law man would come to our home to take me to school, but each time my father would say, "No, he is the only one I have whose job is to herd the goats," and he begged the man to leave us alone. The Navajo policeman was Curley Hair, of the Water Flows Together clan, *(Tó'aheedlíinii)*; he was from Chinle, Arizona. My father was related to his clan.

Mother always butchered a fat young goat when the policeman came. I suppose she did this as a friendly gesture so he would leave us alone. I always wished I could go to school, but my father begged the authorities not to take me. He would ask, "Whom will I depend on to help me? My sons are all I have." My older brother and I were the only ones who were of school age at the time.

I worked very hard at home, and no one felt sorry for me, even when I was tired and hungry. All the work had to be done.

My father was strict. He whipped me when I got stubborn or out of hand. My parents forbade me to sleep late, and, at the break of dawn, I was out doing exercises—running or taking cold baths. When told to do something I never hesitated or said a word back.

I just hurried, slipped on my shoes and ran out to do it. I never defended myself with an excuse. Discipline was hard, and I was afraid to disobey. Whatever was told to me had to be done.

Now, when I think back to the lectures our wise elders gave us and compare them to the present time, things have not changed much. Maybe, in a way, they have because we parents of today want our children to take advantage of the opportunities that approach them so they can learn more. We cannot deny them these opportunities by saying we need the children at home now. For my part, I still have to live with my problems. I struggle along because things were done (or not done) that way.

I have learned the traditional Navajo education—caring for sheep and horses, and a lot of other things. They are part of my life, and they provide for part of my daily needs. There is a lot to learn just about horses—rising at daybreak to fetch them, feeding them and taking them to the water hole. When I was young many wild mustangs roamed the ranges; so our horse corrals were full to capacity. Now only a few stand close to our hogans. When I would go out after the horses my father forbade me to ride them. He would say, "Do not ride back on one. Bring them home on foot; run with the horses, so you can develop strong legs and be a fast runner."

I do have a confession to make: Once in a while I cheated. When I was where no one could see me, I would rope a tame horse and ride off to get the other ones. When I got closer to home I would loose the horse that I used and innocently bring them all back on foot the rest of the way. What a life! When I couldn't catch a horse I would do it all on foot—the hard way. I think everyone has a notion to try and get away with something like that at times.

After I began working, as a child, my parents did not make life easy for me. My grandparents' words were harsh, too. That was how I was brought up. At times I was so weary I just felt like sitting and crying, but, after thinking, I knew I never could be a man if I acted like that; so I had to endure hard labor. Today I doubt that anyone lectures to children as my parents did to me. Instead, the young people are running over their parents. They are the ones who give the orders to their parents and their elders. The young people of today are rude; mockery is their specialty. Not all are like that, though; some do have great respect. I am fortunate that I had men of wisdom to teach me self-respect and make me what I am. Years back, no one dared to speak out concerning his or her elders. We were not allowed to go to any public gathering if we had no business there.

184

When I went for the horses soon after dawn my father forbade me to ride them, saying, "Bring them home on foot—run with the horses so that you will develop strong legs and be a fast runner."

As I remember, times were hard in my early days, with the people struggling to survive; there was hunger and need for warm clothing. Everything was very scarce. There were no supermarkets or department stores like we have today, and outside employment was unheard of. The people were ignorant and generally stayed close to their homes. They did not know how to support themselves, except by farming and raising animals; earning money was strange to them. It was the women who were the "bread winners." The whole family depended on the women. They had wool to work with. They carded and spun the wool and then wove rugs, which they took to trade for food and what little clothing they could buy. I say this because I was one who depended on my wife and mother. Many times my shoes were so worn from herding sheep that my toes were exposed. I was never ashamed of the fact that we were not a well-to-do-family.

Some of the elders who knew me can verify my story because they watched me grow up. After I was married I really struggled to make ends meet as best I could. Today we are aware of the changes that have taken place.

185

When I was a boy the women were the main bread-winners. After the sheep were sheared, the ladies carded, spun and wove the wool into rugs which they took to the trading post to barter for food and the little clothing that they could get.

We have grocery stores filled with food; clothing markets full of clothes, and other shops equipped with whatever we wish to pur-chase—if we have the money. Now, fortunately, I have a job, and I can support my family without trouble. In past years I took good care of my horses; so, now, I have the nice ones that I want, and I feel that I am rewarded.

I have worked very hard for what I now have—horses and sheep, and I am well satisfied. I have meat on our table, wool for women-folk to weave with and horses to ride.

I was never lazy, and I herded sheep all my life until just recent-ly when I was offered a job at the Rough Rock Demonstration School. The people chose me according to what I have just told you. They are the references I used to get my job. Now I leave the sheep-herding to someone else. I feel I have had my share of that work load. As I have said, I am well satisfied with the accomplishments I have made. Without the wisdom from my elders and my parents, all of this could not have been possible, and I am very grateful to them. If I lived a shiftless life, doing the wrong things, like drinking alcohol and gambling, I never would have been a strong man. My life has been good, and the credit goes to my parents. If parents are fine counselors they expect their offspring to utilize what they have learned by teaching their children likewise. The experiences that a person has will be his guide to teach from. He never will forget who made him what he is.

Traditional Navajo education is very important in having a good sound mind and body. You are told to rise at dawn, run races early, trot with the horses and yell loudly as you run to develop strong lungs and a strong voice. You inhale the sharp, fresh air, and you greet the dawn with an open mind to begin the day's work. If you can endure frigid weather you will have a strong resistance.

All of these things depend mainly upon you. If you lack self-determination, you are a failure. That is how I grew up. The people in my area all know who I am because I do not keep myself hidden in my hogan. I am where people can see me. I do not live behind a mountain in a remote region. My home here is at a spot called Spreading Aspens in the Rough Rock Area, where my forefathers lived for more than a century. From here my grandfathers and grand-mothers left for Fort Sumner (Bosque Redondo or *Hwééldi*) more than 100 years ago when the Navajos were rounded up and driven like cattle hundreds of miles to the east side of New Mexico. Their

187

burial grounds and old hogan ruins are still visible here. I feel this is where I belong, and I will stay to the end. Our community has grown a lot compared to a few years ago.

Many people, by marriages, have come to live here; some come looking for employment at the original demonstration school and the new high school. At many large gatherings I speak to my people when asked to do so. I speak in Navajo. I know very little English. (I am recording this story in Navajo.) I explain to them the importance of traditional and academic education. I tell the people I am stuck here for good unless a charming lady lures me away. I say if that happens I may leave. It is just to make them laugh because everybody knows me and my family. It always is a wise gesture to keep your listeners in a good humor.

188

Some of our own local people have gone elsewhere to find employment or for marriage purposes. I think it is a struggle, though, to move to strange places.

As I said before, it really has not been long since the first schools were built on our Reservation so that our children could be educated. We are grateful to our great leaders who made it possible.

The white men are intruders. They came into our peaceful land to build their trading posts all over the Reservation. We were forced for many years to trade with them for food and clothing, but some of the traders were (and are) crooked. They knew (and still know) that many Navajos do not understand the value of money or what they want to buy; they often have been cheated by the traders who gave the Navajos only half the value of a rug or a piece of jewelry and then sold them for much more. That way the traders made more of a profit, especially when they made the Navajos take payment in food and merchandise which is priced very high. Thus, the Navajo consumers for a long time have paid very dearly for the food they got at the trading posts. They finally are realizing, though, what the traders are doing to them and why those traders are becoming richer. They want to get our money, but we now have a tribal legal aid department. It did some investigating all over the Reservation on the questionable deals the traders have been giving the Navajos. Lately we have had trader regulations that are enforced.

Here at Rough Rock a Navajo Demonstration School was built about 1966. It is a place where traditional education is taught. The Navajos themselves run the school, but it has changed somewhat. The people in our "community" (hundreds of square miles) said,

"We have depended on Washington too long; let's have a school to help the government. So the new buildings, built by the Bureau of Indian Affairs, were turned over to the *Diné* (the People). In spite of all our efforts to make it run smoothly, the government is interfering and criticizing the administration and faculty, making us all miserable. We thought we were helping the government, but it seems like we only are adding another problem. The Navajos who work here are using what they have learned at the government schools they attended. However, we are not going to give up. The problems we have we will, by all means, solve the best way we know how.

Education, both Anglo and traditional, must go side by side. Our children need to learn both. Their history and their culture cannot die out. Our children need to look back and see how our people lived. Then they can compare, to see how much we have progressed.

189

A Navajo does not look into the future. He lets the future take its own course; but a white man studies the future and makes preparations for whatever will come. We have young people who have reached a point in their education where they can be teachers on the Reservation, or hold other positions, but too many are dropouts from school. It is like putting something through a sieve—some fall through, others stay behind.

There is a time limit on our lives from the moment we come into the world. It is granted only by the Great Spirit. At birth, each boy and girl receives a different sacred wind to give life. Life can last from one minute to old age. If the Great Spirit wishes, a person will live to a ripe old age. Traditionally, this is a blessed gift to be thankful for—if you have lived a fruitful life.

No two people are alike. We have different colored skins, and different languages. It is that way all over the world. We think differently, do things differently, and live differently. Even in one family, each child is different from the others in characteristics and personalities. They may be shy, stubborn, tough, roudy, ill-tempered or stuttering; or they may be just the opposite. Some change as they grow, but others stay the same.

If a person looks up to the good way of life he has a fair chance at success. He probably will be rewarded with good health and prosperity. It is up to the individual to make this come true. The most valuable expression in the Navajo language is the one for self-determination. Don't ever forget that! Everyone should know the importance of *taa ho' 'ajiti'iigo t'eiya* (self-determination). Our elders taught us that. If you are a failure you are not a man. If you are a man words should not hurt you. If you are a coward, or have no spine, and do not want to hear what is said, then forget it. You're sunk.

With all the necessary exercises you will develop into a strong man. That does not mean you have to develop your muscles to grapple with someone. You must be made strong to be on your own and do the work a man must do. You have to tackle your farm work and the other hard work that must be done. That is why you must develop your health and muscles. In your early days you should be made to take snow baths and ice water plunges to endure cold weather. During hot weather you should run and jump to train yourself to endure the heat. Cold and heat are some obstacles you must overcome. Also, you are advised to take emetics to discharge all the acid fluids accumulated inside you, and this will clean out your system. It also will purify you so you can have a clear sound mind. When you are full of unclean fluids you become miserable and irritated. That is why you must race at dawn and have an emetic herb in your possession at all times. The most important thing is to have a sweat house where you really can sweat out all the unclean pores and feel refreshed again.

190

That is all part of the Navajo education which one must learn. No one urges you to sleep late, if you want to become a real man. Lessons like knowing how to live on very little food, water and rest help you confront unexpected situations, and you have a better chance to survive.

As I said before, I am an uneducated man; I never stepped into a classroom as a boy, but I grew up learning my traditional training at home. Now you see me as a man. I often wonder how I got a job without an education; but what I am doing now is for a good cause. It is never too late to learn; so I try to learn something new every day.

As I go along with my work as a counselor and a consultant, I also give lectures to the children and tell them stories. My speeches pertain to what my elders taught me. I have no right to take things from the lectures of others. I only give my talks from the lessons I have learned from my parents and other older people. From the time I began working for the school I have helped many who have needed my assistance. My work takes me to many important meetings in various schools. I have traveled to large cities on planes to attend

In my work as a counselor and consultant I often lecture the children about good behavior and Navajo culture, and I tell them stories.

In my present position with the Rough Rock Demonstration School I have traveled by plane several times to big cities to attend conferences pertaining to education.

conferences pertaining to education. This helps us to get grants to keep our school going.

For much of my life I have seen planes go by in the sky, but I never dreamed I'd be traveling in one someday—going to faraway places in just a short time.

Through my interpreter I present the problems we have at Rough Rock and tell many officials and others what we are trying to do for our people—both the old and the young. They all are interested, and they listen.

All of that is good experience for me, and I get to see new and strange places, and I learn how to get around in them. The outside world is very different compared to our small communities here on the Reservation. It is interesting to be out in the white man's world. It's hard to believe that all these incredible things are happening to me.

192

I am the president of the school board here at Rough Rock. It is my duty to do all I can for our school. Many problems have to be discussed, and decisions must be made. People may judge me as a timid soul, but I am not. When I begin talking there is no end to what I have to say. I do not keep anything back that I feel must be said. I have been the president for three years now. I try to do my job to satisfy my people. That is why they choose me. My aim always has been to keep up the standards of a good school to educate my people—to have a school to be proud of. Here we have traditional Navajo doctors (commonly known as medicine men) in training. We have instructors to teach these things so the trainees will know how to carry on the traditions. We do not want our healing ceremonies to phase out.

Long ago, Navajo religion was spread out to all points of our land. Medicine men were plentiful, so one did not have to go far to get one. Today they are scarce. A person has to travel many miles to get the kind of medicine man he or she needs.

Our people live to a great extent on the blessings and holiness of all these sacred ceremonies. At the beginning the Holy People granted them to us. Our elders taught us to respect them and to keep them sacred and holy. This, too, is part of my work. I am a Navajo healer or medicine man. I have been a medicine man for seven years. I know the people have confidence in me because I never have heard complaints or criticisms. Many come to thank me for helping them. That makes me feel happy because I have great faith in my religion, and I conduct my ceremonies with reverence.

I have been a Navajo healer or medicine man for more than seven years, and I have helped many sick persons.

About education, all of my children have had their learning, and I am proud of it. It is what I desired for them. I did not want them to be uneducated like me. I always wanted them to return to their people and show their appreciation by helping them. That is exactly what they are doing now, and that is the way it should be. All young people should help their parents. After all, parents worked hard to support them and bring them up. Young educated people should show their appreciation by helping their elders now and then. It's the least they can do to repay their debts.

I have a very big family. I have sons-in-law, daughters-in-law and wonderful grandchildren. They all have good hearts for me, and I love them. My dear wife passed away several months ago, in the spring, which was sudden and heart-breaking. But I have my children to live for and pride in my work. Those things keep me busy and my mind off my heartaches and loneliness. I try to keep my chil-

193

dren close by. My heart is with them because they mean so much to me. I have no intention of ever deserting them. I love them too much to hurt them. I worked hard to get what I want for them—horses, sheep, cattle and good homes. I still provide them with some things that they need. I keep my door wide open for them when they come home to visit. I try to offer them the best. Especially now that their mother is gone, I feel it is my duty to be a good father to them. I am a man who considers all men equal. No one is different; all are my brothers, sisters and children. I speak to them like that. I have respect for all people. We were placed on this earth ages ago—all created equal. The real value of riches is in our bodies. Whatever we are adorned with—turquoise necklaces, pendants, bracelets, rings or beautiful clothes—all these are just ornaments to admire. Our bodies are more valuable than all of those so-called riches. That is why we must not destroy one another or make fun of one another. One should never tell a person he is poor; nor should he ever laugh at a woman, for she is the seed of Mother Earth. She was the first one to be placed on the earth. She reproduced, as a seed does, and she bore children from which more people evolved. If you make fun of a woman, it is said that you really are making fun of your own mother. In fact, never laugh at your sisters, brothers or your father. Those are some of the things I teach my people here at the school.

194

At one time, the land on which I live was empty, except for us. We were the only inhabitants (my wife and I), but soon our family began to increase, and more houses were added in the area. Other people moved in, and the community began to grow. Now, more people are requesting home sites, and there is not much space left. The people are beginning to have problems and disputes among themselves over pieces of land they want to build their homes on.

I was taught not to be a busybody; so I always have stayed out of trouble and minded my own affairs. I have no hard feelings against anyone. I have come to know the needs of my people, and, with that in mind, I prefer to stay within my own territory; I have my children's welfare to look after. I have taught them to be friendly to everyone and not to have any misunderstandings with our neighbors or others. They know what I mean. About more people, our Navajo population has increased to a great number—maybe 150,000—in all areas of the Reservation, and they are spread out to all points.

We hear about the sacred mountain—the San Francisco Peaks *(Dook'o'oosłííd)*—being disrupted by the white people for some housing and developments. We, as Navajos, love our sacred mountains—Blanca Peak *(Sis Naajiní)* is in the east, Mount Taylor *(Tsoodził)* is in the south, the San Francisco Peaks *(Dook'o'oosłííd)* are in the west and the La Plata Range *(Dibé Nitsaa)* stands in the north. Then, we have Huerfano Mountain *(Dził Ná'odiłii)* and the Gobernado Knob *(Ch'óol'í'í)*; and we dwell within the big area bounded by those mountains. We do not want them harmed or destroyed. To us the mountains are sacred, and there are holy beings living in them. That is why we do not want them harmed. To become a part of these sacred mountains we have sacred mountain soil charms in our possession, which we cherish. They are our guidance and our protection. All we ask is that the white people leave our sacred mountains alone.

Mt. Blanca in Colorado, one of the Navajos' sacred mountains. Its color is white.

The white men are intruders. They came from other countries to invade us. They have taken control of our land, and we are crowded into a so-called "Reservation." Now they are trying to destroy our lives, our hearts and our minds. At the beginning, our mountains were given life with a puff of smoke. Assorted mountain tobacco was planted on them for us to use; so we depend on these mountains to fill our smoking pipes and to make corn-husk cigarettes for our sacred smoking rituals.

As a man of medicine, I have begged the intruders to preserve our sacred grounds. Many times, when I give a speech before people of all races I plead with them to leave us alone.

There are many things our white friends are doing that we are grateful for, but we do not want them to meddle with our sacred mountains. There are other mountain ranges on our Reservation that also have mythological stories connected with them, and they also are sacred. We have heard our elders tell about them. They are very holy to us; if harm is done to them, we, too, will be harmed.

There are foolish rumors among our people that are untrue. Last spring someone was spreading a rumor about bad things that are going to happen very soon. It is ridiculous, but some believe it. There are predictions told by our elders long ago, but they are not to happen for a long time yet. There will be signs to let us know when these will come to pass. Things like that should not be heard now; they are frightening and are not good for morale. There are so many good things to talk about; and, with a limited amount of time, we can tell only so much.

Now I will briefly talk about the history of our tribal government. It was not long ago that our tribal delegation was organized. Before that we had what were called chiefs or orators who spoke for the people or to the people in gathering places. That was after the people came back from Fort Sumner and even before they were exiled. They first returned to Fort Wingate, New Mexico, and then to Fort Defiance in Arizona. It was more than a hundred years ago. The Navajos had a headquarters, known as the Central Agency, at Fort Defiance. Delegates, chosen later by the government's superintendent, came to the agency on horseback and wagons in those days to attend their sessions. Some chapter houses were constructed later, and chapter officers worked with their delegates to help the people with their problems. Later, the Navajo capital was located at Window Rock, Arizona. That is where our tribal administration began really to exist. Before that the Navajo people knew nothing about tribal government. They had depended on the federal government all the time since the Long Walk of the 1860s. Agency officials spoke to the leaders by interpretation about their needs and how to run a discussion session.

The first Tribal Chairman was Henry Chee Dodge of Crystal, New Mexico. He was a great leader. During his leadership the people

196

began to understand their problems. They learned how to discuss them and to make decisions. When the first real tribal government was established at Window Rock, a stronger organization was formed. It controlled all tribal affairs, with a chairman and a vice chairman, and with a complete administration. The tribal government was running along smoothly for a while, until fairly recently when our leaders got too involved in politics; so we now have controversies among our tribal leaders. We choose our own tribal councilmen through elections in the chapters. Our Tribal Chairman and Vice Chairman are also chosen in this manner—Reservation-wide.

We have chapter precincts where we vote and where the candidates do their campaigning. They promise, if elected, to do this and that for the people, but such promises seldom are carried out. All this has separated our people into groups and in certain areas created conflicts and confusions. In spite of the differences of opinion, all matters seem eventually to go back to the federal government. Washington has the "say so," as long as we are wards of the government. Most documents go through their channels for final approval before the tribal administration can do anything, especially moneywise. All important resolutions that are approved by the Tribal Council have to go through the proper channels, too.

Of course, the Council has control of tribal affairs, but still we know that Washington is superior. So we still depend on the federal people.

As I mentioned previously, our early Navajo leaders worked from one Central Agency at Fort Defiance. It was the only place where there was "action." The leaders convened there to discuss their problems. Suddenly, everything changed—natural gas was discovered on the Reservation. Henry Chee Dodge made a speech at a Nightway chant near here. I heard him myself. He said, "We now will stand united as a sovereign nation. The natural gas royalties will grow fast. This will deposit revenues into our tribal treasury for our use. Our Reservation will be made larger when we purchase more land. There are other natural resources on the Reservation, such as lumber and coal, from which more money will be deposited. The Tribal Council will control the money."

He strongly opposed the "per capita" the people were asking from the natural gas revenues. "Let us reserve the monies in the treasury so we can have a tribal fund to fall back upon when we need it. Getting your share of the per capita will not last," he told the people. This all became a reality. The tribal funds are used for the Navajo administration at Window Rock.

There are many branches with different departments all over the Reservation now. They are using the tribal funds. Every four years we have our tribal election. In some areas new councilmen are selected, and we elect or re-elect a Tribal Council Chairman. We hear that the tribal funds are getting low. Then again we hear a cheerful side—that we have some increase in the treasury. The people on the Reservation chew on each others' necks over this. I think we should keep depositing into our tribal fund to make it increase more, like Chee Dodge said.

We realize the conditions in our country now. The cost of living has climbed to a high point of inflation. Each one of us needs a lot of money just for food and clothing; especially for our young people. And they want only the clothes that are more expensive. If they can't get what they want, they become troublesome. That is what we are up against. Today the burden is heavy. What about tomorrow's children? Every day more come into the world. We on the Reservation are overpopulated, and the living status is not high enough to take care of us.

198

Some of the schools that our children attended have been shut down because of financial problems. There are just too many children to be accommodated, I suppose. We hear on the radios and in the newspapers about Washington aiding the foreign countries with billions of dollars. All that money could be used for education, building of more schools, more good hospitals, better roads and irrigated farm land for the Indian people. We need more employment. In some areas we still have rugged dirt roads to our schools and communities. With all the money being poured out to other countries, all we get here is a penny now and then, and what good is it? None, as far as I'm concerned. Then, too, a lot of money has been spent on foreign wars that really should not concern our country. Here in the United States the government used to draft able young citizens to serve in the armed forces. They sometimes went to war so we could "have peace." Some of our loved ones never returned from the wars. I should think war veterans deserve something better than they are getting—not much more than just pats on the back. It is very disgusting, and I often wish I could grab the government by the shoulders and drag it in front of the people so that it would understand what we are talking about. We have many complaints that remain unsolved because nothing is done about them. Many of our war veterans came back disabled; some left their minds behind, and more are affected by the horrible experiences of the war. What is being done for these unfortunate victims. Not too much! We only see them suffer. We are truly concerned about those who gave so much for their country. We try to get help for them through various sources, but the government should have complete responsibility for looking after the veterans.

We are aware of the situation our schools are in. Most of them are full to their capacities. Some are very overcrowded, and an increase in school-age children is expected every year. Some of the institutions are having financial problems because of having so many students. Recently there have been setbacks in the school budgets **199** from the state and the federal government. Also, there is a shortage of teachers. At the beginning, when the Navajo children first began to attend the government schools, they received their clothes when they enrolled. The government (Bureau of Indian Affairs) issued clothes and footwear. Later this changed, and the parents were advised to buy the school clothes. Some of the real needy families had a big problem trying to get new clothes for their children, especially if they were large families. Children often do not go to school when it starts because they don't have proper clothes. Another important matter is that some teachers are not teaching the children all they need to learn. Of course, some are fine teachers, but others only want their paychecks, and they do not care whether a child learns to read, write or speak English. In recent years the Navajo people have wanted to teach their own children. That was the big reason why the demonstration school was built here at Rough Rock. We did fine for a while, until the government began to interfere by criticizing our efforts. This only complicated things for the faculty, administration and others who were trying their best to do good work.

The government tries to tell us it is the only thing that can educate Indian children, but we know that we have qualified teachers who are more reliable than most Anglos and have had good training.

We have so much to talk about, and so many problems to discuss, but some Navajos do not want to get involved and to come forth with what is on their minds. We want them all to be parts of their communities by helping with projects that create better environments, but too many of them have become weak-minded because they prefer to hang on to their wine bottles. That is our biggest problem now. Many of our once good elders have turned into alcoholics, which makes it very hard to communicate with them.

Also, a large number of our people have been converted to different church denominations which turn them against their own Navajo religion and culture. Only a few of us remain faithful and have our prayers and chants. Our elders should have continued to tell their stories; then our religion would have been made stronger and we still would have enough medicine men to serve our people where they are needed. They never should have ceased their lectures to the young people. When I was a boy, my parents went out to get the elders to lecture to us. They lectured far into the night as we sat and listened. They talked mostly about livelihood and what we should not do or say.

200

Now the young people hate lectures. Such talks "bug" them, and they do not listen. Our elders used harsh words even when we did not do wrong, and they were effective. Now, the modern young people's lack of discipline has put them above their parents. We older ones are crying for help to get our children to settle down; and we are afraid to ask some wise counselor to speak to them because he would ask, "Why is he or she doing this?" The young boys and girls would not trust us; so it would be a wasted effort. We know we have a tremendous job ahead. We can only stress our efforts to a certain limit—and hope for improvement gradually in the future.

I believe I have said enough. I have told you all about my own life, as well as other matters pertaining to the betterment of our people; and I am glad that my talk will be printed—along with accounts by other elderly Navajos—in a book by the Navajo Community College Press, and that my story and the whole book will be useful to Navajos of all ages around the Reservation—perhaps to Indians in general and to the Anglo people all over the United States.

Jeanette Blake

WHEN I WAS YOUNG, schools were just beginning to be an important part of Navajo life, and I started when I was six years old. I traveled on horseback to Tuba City from Navajo Canyon; and I rode a horse to school until I was 15.

I am now almost 74 years old, a member of the Bitter Water clan *(Tódíchíí'nii)*, born for the Black Streak Wood People *(Tsi' najinii)*. I live at Red Rock, Arizona.

One summer, when I was a student, I was chasing some horses when my own horse started bucking, and I fell off, injuring my leg. Because of the injury I returned to school late in the year. Also, my mother was very ill, which was another reason for staying home. Because of this absence my father was told, "You are keeping your children away from school," but I didn't think my father was being stingy with me. After my leg became well again I returned to school, accompanied not by my father but by a cousin on my father's side. His name was Mr. One Who Pokes With Knife.

Later, we moved from Navajo Canyon to Standing Rock. While we were living there, a Navajo man brought two white men to our place. One of the white men, Mr. Robertson, was a range rider. He handcuffed my father and took him to Kaibito. Not long after they left, my mother and I followed them. My father was angry with the white men for what they had done; he grabbed a stick and tried to hit one of them. He was stopped by a Navajo man named Mr. Ugly Educated. Because of it, however, my father was put in jail. When we arrived at Kaibito he had been locked up already, but he was released after my mother begged them to free him. We spent the night on a hill nearby. The next day we left. Even after we had arrived at our home, I didn't know what the plan was that they had discussed.

I left for school, and I soon turned 15; also I received word that my father had been killed. I'm not sure how it happened, but they said that the trader had loaned guns to the white men. My father was at Mr. Navajo Mountain's place, where a Navajo ceremony was being held. While there, it was predicted that he soon would be shot. Before long, several white men arrived at the place; and he was shot—right among the people in a hogan—three times before he fell. Some people's belongings were made bloody. The white men warned the people, saying, "If one of you tries to go for help, you also will be killed." So nobody tried to leave. The womenfolk had to be helped out. That is how it was told. I did not see the incident; I'm only telling what I remember.

One of my father's brothers, Mr. Smiley, followed the killers to Kaibito, but they already had left the area. He continued on toward Tuba City. I don't know where he finally turned back. Not long afterward, they were caught and taken away, so I heard.

A young person sometimes does not pay real close attention to what is being said. That is why I can't remember about this incident very well.

We were quite prosperous. We had three flocks of sheep in separate corrals. We also had horses and cattle. My parents had four children—three girls and one boy. The family later lived satisfactorily in Tuba City. We did not buy clothes in a store as we do nowadays. Instead, they were made from fabric the government furnished.

When I was a child there were many in school—I think about 200, and we were all well behaved. The school was good, but no speaking in Navajo was allowed. That really was stressed. I don't know why it was, except that they just wanted us to learn English and to be like the white people. We were not allowed to use makeup.

After we grew older, the students went their separate ways. Some of the boys and girls left for another school. They were taken in a wagon, pulled by four white mules. They did not go to Phoenix or to Sherman in Riverside, California, but to Flagstaff, Arizona. From there they left on a train for some other place.

Now, today, children are going to nice schools, but they are not well mannered. When you tell them to do something, they won't do it. At school they are instructed, but once they come home they lie around reading books and other materials. When we try to teach them in helping around home, they don't want do to it.

When I was going to school we didn't have vocational training, learning different trade projects and so on. It was just school.

I was trying to round up some horses when the one I was riding started bucking. I fell off and injured my leg.

The food was shipped in from somewhere. There were no paved roads. For example, there was a dirt road leading from the sheep dipping right on through into the sagebrush. There were only horse and wagon trails. Today, however, there are different roads leading into Tuba City. The road that we use now from Tuba City goes on to A Rock That Was Jagged Once, on to Dog Springs and then to Hair in Water—which leads to Kaibito, Arizona. We traveled this road on horseback, never by car. Horses were used all the time and were the only means of travel to school.

At the beginning of schooling, in kindergarten, we mostly played. Then, in first grade, we started learning the names of animals. We also started learning arithmetic and began reading some. We did a lot of reading. I really can't remember much of it, though. Whenever anybody speaks to me in English, in turn, I can answer them in English. I never reached eighth grade; I only got as far as half

203

of sixth grade. I don't know what I liked best about school. However, it is good to understand the white man's language. When he talks to you, you are able to give a reply right off or answer his question. This is being able to communicate—like in getting letters, that is when you make use of reading them yourself and not needing a translator.

I didn't like the punishment that was used in school. If anyone talked in Navajo, that week the person's name would be written down. On Saturday the punishment came—boys' pants would be brought in, which the girls had to wear; the boys who were caught speaking Navajo were forced to put on girls' clothing. They would go around this way where they would be seen—the girls in boys' pants and the boys in short dresses. As for myself, I never had to put the pants on as punishment for talking in Navajo. If anyone ran away from school and was caught, he or she was locked up and could not go outside for about one week, maybe. At that time, a student was kept and locked in the school, not a jail.

204

The school was all right with my mother and father. There were four of us children who were placed in school, but one passed away while attending.

In early days, before schools were started, the older men and women taught the children. They would say, "One is not supposed to sleep after the sun rises. It's not good to sleep when the sun is up. Run after fortune—who else is going to feed you? Go, run." That is what they would say. If we were asleep, we would be forced to get up. "Go, get in the water," they would tell us. "Get the grinding stones and go outside and grind, even though it's cold." People ground meal that way through the years. I did it as a girl; and I still grind outside. At first, in the winter, the grinding stones felt cold but after a while they became warm. Also, the older folk would say to me, "Go after the horses; boys are not the only ones who go for them." So, I would go after the horses and herd them back toward our hogan. That was how I grew up.

My father was strict with us and would whip us. My father would say, "One of these days I won't be around, and in the days to come I want you to be useful. But, if you are stupid, and get a man and give birth, your children will be reaching out with crooked fingers, begging." To this day, I remember those things. Now our children are going forward in life; and, from all sides, they come and visit us.

Schooling now is conducted well in Shonto. I am pleased with it. "If only we had had schools like that," I say. Shonto is doing very well.

Yes, today I am satisfied with the schools. "If I were only young and able to go to school again," I wish to myself. I never had a real good education, and I never had a chance to "go away to school" to an off-Reservation institution. However, my native Navajo training in the family was good, and I had enough schooling to get along with Anglo society; so I am fairly satisfied.

If a girl was heard talking Navajo her name was written down, and one form of punishment was to make her wear a pair of boy's pants. In those times girls did not wear jeans and pants as they do today. Boys, for the same offense, had to wear a girl's clothing.

William Cadman

MY FRIENDS CALL ME BILL. I am pretty well known here at Fort Defiance, Arizona, but I was born near Tohatchi, New Mexico, at a spot called Willows Extended Red. These places are on the Navajo Reservation.

I was born on August 8, 1916, and my mother is still living. She is of the Edge of Water People *(Tábaahá)*. My father is deceased. His name was Carl, and he was well known. He was of the Red Running Into Water People *(Táchii'nii)*.

I belong to the Edge of Water People (my mother's clan), and I was born FOR the Red Running Into Water People (my father's clan). I was not reared by my parents. My father worked on the West Coast, somewhere in California, all the time we children were growing up, and my mother was with him. There were five children in my family. Today, only two of us are living.

Our parents left us with a grandfather and a grandmother, and we were raised by them. My grandfather was a man of wisdom who lectured to me a lot. My grandmother told me once that, when I was a small child, I almost died. They did not expect me to live; so they had to take me out of the hogan into a bough shelter which was built hastily some distance away. That was the Navajo custom when a person was about to die in his or her home. If death had occurred in the hogan, according to tradition my grandparents would have had to abandon it.

However, on that day we had an unexpected visitor. A man came on horseback. He was a well known medicine man whose name was Crippled Man, from Fort Defiance. Crippled Man was on his way home after he had performed a ceremony. I suppose he stopped for a short visit because he was a good friend of my grandfather. It was just a coincidence; and my grandfather immediately asked him if he could help me.

Because the medicine man had all of his ceremonial equipment with him, there was no problem. He conducted a healing ceremony over me that night. The next day my high fever subsided, and I soon recovered. And here I am today.

When I began to understand my surroundings as a boy, I was in a school at Tohatchi. At that time I lived at Pointed Bend, a short distance southwest of Tohatchi. My grandfather had enrolled me in school in 1922 when I was six years old. He wanted me to have an education. (Only one old building still stands.) I attended until I was in the fourth grade. During that year a disease called trachoma spread among Navajo school children. There was only one hospital on the Reservation—at Fort Defiance; and all the children afflicted with the disease were transported to that hospital. I was one of them. Many of the children and adults were getting their eyes scraped, and their eyes were treated daily.

In 1926 I went to school at Fort Defiance, where I stayed for two years. We had our regular vacation during the summer, and, over those three months, most children herded sheep and helped with the chores at home.

In the fall we returned to school. I completed my fifth and sixth grades at Fort Defiance. However, while I was at home my grandfather taught me many things. He made me get up early each morning to do exercises. I ran out and fetched the family horses, fed them and took them to the water hole. At that time we used horses for farm work and transportation.

Also, in those days the Navajos had more sheep and cattle than they do today. Now the sheep are limited; in fact, so is all stock. I helped my grandfather take care of the horses and the sheep. That was important in a typical family.

I remember we had rabbit hunts on certain Saturdays. When one was planned I rose real early and fetched all my grandfather's horses for the big event. We left the horses in the corral until noon. That way we were sure they had enough time to digest what they had eaten and to let their bellies go down. Then, with enthusiasm, I saddled the horses. Neighboring people gathered and mounted the horses, and away we went on our hunt. It was great fun. I was not afraid of any kind of horse. I tamed wild mustangs that roamed

207

the range, and then I rode them. My grandfather taught me how to work on the farm and how to haul firewood and water to our hogan. We hauled water in two large wooden barrels in the wagon for two or three miles. When it rained we carried the water in pails from the water holes that the rain had filled. I also learned the kinds of firewood that were best to cook with, and we would go into the forest in our wagon to haul that wood back to our home.

In those days no one said the water from a pond was contaminated and unfit to drink. We drank from water holes which were full of tadpoles. We strained the water through a cloth so that we wouldn't swallow tadpoles or other things, but we never boiled the water first. Now no one dares to drink that kind of water. The Tribe's sanitation department has representatives go among the people teaching them about sanitation.

208

As you have guessed, I grew up in a poor family. We had sheep and horses, but my grandfather never possessed much. Many times we suffered from hunger and weariness. My grandmother gave us goat milk when it was available. She prepared various kinds of corn breads, puddings and mush. Once in a great while she butchered a sheep and we had mutton to eat. During the rainy season we loved to go with grandpa to drown out the prairie dogs. It was very exciting. All the boys took long clubs. When grandpa got a prairie dog out of its hole we clubbed it to death. We sometimes collected a dozen or so prairie dogs and used them for food.

My grandmother cleaned, singed and dressed them neatly. She put them in a row in a hot pit prepared for roasting, and they were real good. Today the public health department has forbidden the people to eat prairie dogs. It claims that they carry diseases.

When I was a boy there were hardly any sweets like candies, soda pop and gum in the trading posts, which were the only places where we could purchase what we needed to buy. We had no supermarkets.

Our main dishes on the table were Navajo tortillos, fried potatoes, coffee, corn bread of various kinds and mush from dried corn. In the summer we had fresh corn prepared in various ways. Another typical Navajo dish was mutton stew with fry bread. We ate simple meals; nothing lavish. No hamburgers or hotdogs or cokes!

After each vacation we returned to the boarding school, and I learned a lot at Fort Defiance. I ran away twice because I was lonely.

My grandfather taught me how to saddle a horse—and how to ride it, tame or wild.

I had no idea that some day I would be living here at Fort Defiance permanently, and now I am sure that my actions were just foolishness. My grandfather would bring me back to school, and he always encouraged me to get as much education as I could. Now, I am grateful for it, and I appreciate his efforts.

During later years in school I learned how to be a good farmer. We planted fresh vegetables for the children, and weeded and irrigated the gardens.

I worked in the carpentry shop and learned that trade, too. I also worked in the bakery and learned to make bread and pastries. The system was made possible by letting the older students attend their academic classes for half a day and vocational classes for the second half, with rotation among tasks every month during the school year. Today, students have only an hour in the shops and more academic work in their classrooms. The schools I attended were all government Bureau of Indian Affairs schools. Now, we still have BIA schools, but there are more public schools. And there still are missionary schools. The government school at Fort Defiance has been gone for a long time, and most of the brick buildings have been destroyed.

When I was young we had two main types of churches—the Roman Catholic and the Protestant. Missionaries went among the people with interpreters and taught the gospel and better living. Some of the Navajos were converted, which divided the Navajos into two groups. One would say, "I'm a Catholic"; the other would say, "I'm a Protestant" (although many of them still hung on to their Navajo religion). A few became true Christians and had nothing more to do with the Navajo religious beliefs. Today, however, we have all kinds of church denominations on the Reservation. Originally, the Navajos began to go from one church to the other, not knowing which one to belong to. This confused them. At the boarding school we all had to go to church every Sunday and learn how to pray, read the Bible, memorize our catachism and learn what a church is all about. The members of my family still attend every Sunday. I have faith in my church, and I also have faith in the Navajo religion. I have great respect for all of the healing ceremonies, and I use the services of our medicine men. The Catholic Church does not criticize the Navajo religion. I believe that the Catholic and Navajo religions are similar. The Catholic priest says, "The Navajos pray and respect the sun, the moon and the sky. These are all heavenly. In their prayers the Great Spirit is the real Divinity." That is why I have faith in both religions.

But to take up my schooling again: In the fall of 1928 I was taken to the Albuquerque Indian School. Other boys and girls were transferred with me. I was in the seventh grade then; and I stayed until I was graduated from the 12th grade. It was a government BIA school.

During the years that I had attended the Fort Defiance boarding school it was like a military setup. We wore uniforms on special occasions. We had precision drills in companies, each with its captain. We lined up in companies to have roll call every time we went to classes and to the dining hall, and we marched in step to the captains' calls.

The boys' adviser in the dormitory was a very strict disciplinarian. I suppose the girls had one, too, because we saw them marching. We had drill contests by companies. All of the early military training as a boy came in handy when I was drafted into the armed forced during World War II.

Two views of Tohatchi, N. M., as it looks today.

I had good training in farming at the Albuquerque Indian School. We raised fresh vegetables for the school kitchen, including corn, potatoes, carrots, cabbage, beets, onions, beans and other foods. In the fall we learned how to harvest the late crops and store them in dugout cellars. It was very good training, and now I know **211** just what to do. I use my training, and we have plenty of vegetables in our family.

My grandfather did not approve of eating candy. There was not much at the trading post, anyway. We never had any money to spend. Some young Navajos didn't know what money was until we began to earn it.

In 1936 I graduated from high school. I had hoped to get a higher education, but my father and mother were unable to help me financially. Students today who want higher education can get scholarships from the Tribe and other sources, but we could not do that. They also have more opportunities after graduation than we did. The students in my younger days had to pay their own tuition for higher education; so I never had a chance to go farther.

I returned home right after graduation. My grandfather and grandmother were happy to have me with them again. They were very old by that time. Later that summer my grandfather became ill and died, which was the most unhappy experience I ever had had. My loss was great because he was the one who had brought me up. I mourned for almost four years, but I finally got over it. Then I told my grandmother I was going to look for employment somewhere. I knew I must get out into the world on my own, and I was depending on my high school diploma.

I left home in 1937 and went to Window Rock, Arizona, to apply for a job. At that time the government had begun a new program called Day Schools. The children were brought in buses directly from their homes to school, and they were returned after school.

Two days after I had applied for a job I received a notice of employment from Window Rock. The BIA office had approved my application. I was told to report to Window Rock as soon as possible, and I was right there the following day. I was hired as a bus driver for the Day School at Lower Greasewood near Ganado, Arizona. I picked up the children at their widely separated homes in the mornings, took them to school and, later, back home. My salary was low— fifty dollars a month. But it seemed big to me. Today, those who work for the government earn much more money, and they are paid every two weeks. At that time we waited a whole month for pay checks. However, food and other prices were not high like today.

I worked at Greasewood only a year. Then I was transferred to the Steamboat Day School as a bus driver. Steamboat is not far north of Lower Greasewood. That school is not in operation now, but the buildings still are there. Some Navajos who work at the Toyie Boarding School live in the houses. The old classrooms are used as workshops for various departments of the Office of Navajo Economic Opportunity, and for other purposes.

During the time I was at the Steamboat school there was a lady working as a cook. I always saw her there when we ate, and we got acquainted. Later we were married. My wife, Perry, is the daughter of the late Bear Springs Man, a well-known medicine man. He knew the Night Way Chant. It was a great loss to the Navajos when he died. My wife and I still are making our living together. Perry is of The Red House People *(Kinłichíí'nii)* and was born for the Big Water People *(Tótsohnii)*. We have six children—all grown and married. And we have some grandchildren now.

After we left Steamboat we worked at Kinlichee (Arizona) school for several years. Next, we were transferred to the Crownpoint Agency in New Mexico, at Whitehorse Lake Day School. My wife still was the cook, and I was the bus driver. We worked there for two years.

Then World War II broke out overseas, and all the male citizens had to register if they were 18 or more years old. I went to Santa Fe, New Mexico, to register and have my physical examination. Then I returned to work.

In 1942 we were moved back to Steamboat. Not long after that I received my induction notice, and I was drafted into the armed forces. I had to leave my wife. We had no children yet, but she was expecting one. I went to San Diego, California, to Camp Pendleton, in the Marine Corps. I took my boot training there and became one of the Navajo Code Talkers.

The Navajo language was used as a code system for communication. That is, we talked in Navajo (as well as in code) to send secret messages on the radio to the battle fronts in enemy (Japanese) territory. Navajo is said to be one of the most difficult languages to understand and to decode. We carried radios on our backs and transmitted vital messages in Navajo code. The enemy forces were absolutely stunned, and they never figured out what we were talking about. That really was something which helped a lot in winning the war in the Pacific. It took a long time for the American people to recognize the significance of the Navajo Marine Code Talkers, but now we are famous nation-wide. We have an organization with our headquarters at Window Rock, and we have meetings and carry on various activities.

In 1975 some of the members participated in the Rose Bowl parade in Pasadena, California. Every year, the Navajo Code Talkers have a convention at a chosen place in the United States. We are honored by being invited to special events throughout the country. About twenty-five years passed before Americans really understood what the Navajo Code Talkers had done for their country.

213

When I received an honorable discharge in 1946 I came back to the Reservation where I was employed at Fort Defiance by the government as a construction worker. We built some stone buildings there. Later I applied for a job with the police department and became a Navajo policeman. I worked in that department for 12 years, and I did my duty in enforcing the law. We apprehended all the violaters that we could.

When the Navajo tribal administration took over the police department I resigned because I had been working for the government all those years, and I wanted to earn my retirement benefits from the Bureau of Indian Affairs. Police headquarters were at Fort Defiance then. Now the whole central organization has been moved to Window Rock where new administration and confinement quarters have been constructed.

214

As a policeman I performed to the best of my ability. We hear people complain about the rough handling of prisoners, but I considered myself a peace officer, I never did any of that. I worked hard and got myself up to the highest rank of Chief of Police. It was the high point in my life. It is very difficult to be head of a large department like that. Many responsibilities are before you. I managed to run my administration smoothly, though, and I got along fine with all my personnel.

After my resignation from the police department I began working for the Window Rock Public School. It is located at Fort Defiance but it is called by that name. Window Rock Public School was moved to Fort Defiance a number of years ago because of lack of space for enlargement where it had been located. The new school was constructed at Fort Defiance, and it kept its name. I like my position here, especially the opportunities to work with and help the students. I have been at the school 15 years. I am very close to retirement. I have lived at Fort Defiance ever since I became a Navajo policeman. I am an active chapter member, attending meetings regularly.

In 1966—an election year for the Navajo chapter officers—the local people asked me to be a candidate for chapter president. I had come to know the people and their problems; so I agreed. I wanted to help my people, although I had no experience in that area. I won the election and became head of the local chapter. After I had served my four-year term I was re-elected for another four years. During this last election I had no opponent; so now I am serving my third term. Being a chapter officer is a very hard task. The people come up to you all the time with their problems. Plans, suggestions and decisions are made by the people at the chapter meetings, with the President presiding while his secretary takes the minutes.

Looking back, I feel very fortunate to have received the education that I have. It always has helped me, and it still helps in many ways with the work I do. I have learned to understand my people, and they, in turn, appreciate what I do for them. That is why they have confidence in me. The Fort Defiance community is large, with the chapter area extending at least 15 miles in all directions. I try to cover as much ground and as many subjects as possible in my work. As I said, it is hard, but I enjoy working with the people.

215

During my young years, I also had a real Navajo traditional education. My late father-in-law was a very wise man and a prominent medicine man. He told me many stories pertaining to mythology. I am not a medicine man, but I have learned legends, Navajo history and the teachings of elders. I mentioned previously that the Navajo religion and the white man's Bible stories resemble each other. That is why I attend my church every Sunday with my children, and I respect both religions.

Last winter I had a Night Way Chant performed for me. It is commonly known as the Yei-be-chai dance. I have had other healing ceremonies conducted for me in the past. I have a corn pollen bag, and I use the pollen as an offering and protection for myself and my family. I am not a man of great learning, but what I did acquire in school and at home as a young boy are my teachings now. An intelligent man with the master's degree may offer more, but I do my best to help others who are in need. I have learned from experience to carry my own burdens, too.

I have a permanent home here at Fort Defiance in the Rio Puerco Acre housing. We bought a home which we are paying for on an installment plan. I am president of the Fort Defiance Housing Corporation. I helped plan and begin the housing program for the people who wanted to buy or to rent homes. I have been their president for 10 years.

Right now we are in the process of developing a Navajo savings and loan business at Window Rock. I was elected president of the firm. In the future when people want to save some money it will be the place to make their investments. Then they can apply for loans on new homes, furniture and other necessities. The loan company is needed badly. It will begin as a branch from Phoenix, Arizona. A big firm there will assist us with a good start for a year, and then the Navajos will operate the business themselves. We will have a complete Navajo Board of Directors. It is all in the planning stage now, but it will begin soon. We hope for a better future for our people.

We have a Parents Advisory Council here at Fort Defiance, and I am a member. We promote educational needs and educational programs for the students. Here at the public school I am a truant officer. I visit the parents of students who are on the absentee list for two or more days without excuses, and I talk with them. I encourage the students to go back to school, but not in a scolding manner to hurt their feelings. I use the school vehicle on these missions. One must approach a young person very cautiously, and he or she will listen. The student then considers your kindness and will say that he or she will go back to school.

Now I will talk briefly about the high school students that I am involved with. Many parents are not aware of what their children are doing in school. All they know is that the young people leave in the morning, attend classes and return home in the late afternoon. It has been two years since I really began devoting more time to the students who have problems. I also work with the teachers. They sometimes invite me to speak to their classes about Navajo ways of life. I cannot boast that I know much, but I do what I can to make my speech interesting and educational. The students show their appreciation by listening and getting involved with questions. Many of our students know very little about Indian cultures, and the majority of them these days do not speak the Navajo language. That is because they are brought up in the Anglo ways of life. It is very difficult for them to understand what a person really is talking about because some of the Navajo words have no translations. Also, the boys and girls tell me that their fathers and mothers do not tell them about the Navajo cultures, and I know it is true.

Navajo students like very much to hear about the history of their people and other stories, and I try to tell them things pertaining to mythology which my father-in-law passed on to me. I also relate accounts like when I was a boy in school and it was against regulations for us to talk Navajo. I explain that, when we were caught speaking in our own language, we got severe punishment. We were allowed to speak only English.

216

William "Bill" Cadman—
Fort Defiance, Ariz.

217

Today we have bi-lingual education in some schools. Not many students can speak and write their own language. I think, though, that parents and grandparents are the ones who should teach the young people to speak Navajo. Many are glad to know that their elders are interested in them and what they are. Probably the reason why most older people do not discuss their age-old culture is because they think the youngsters do not care about their own heritage. If a young person knows who he is and speaks his own language then he can say proudly "I am a Navajo." If he cannot do that he may face problems. His parents and grandparents may become strangers because he cannot understand them and they do not understand him. It is really pitiful. "If you are a Navajo let us hear you speak Navajo," is often asked by someone who is testing a person. If he cannot speak Navajo, the questioner will doubt him. That is why it is so important for Navajos to keep their identity.

Many times students have asked me to teach the Navajo language. I only can tell them that one must have many qualifications and credentials to be a teacher. I have no college degree. I only talk to students on what I have learned at home and from other Navajo sources. As I said, I am not a medicine man, but I feel I am a capable and wise Navajo counselor. That is why the people in my community depend on me as their leader.

At Navajo Community College at Tsaile, Arizona, Indian Studies instructors have an illustration of a corn plant. Corn is, or used to be, the main source of food for the Navajos. The illustration has 12 alternating ears of corn—six on one side and six on the other. At the roots it pictures the first four worlds. Different colors represent the foundations of education which are the elements of life. The ears represent the basic educational achievements and their philosophies. The tassels, where a bird sits, show that one has accomplished his goals. One side of the picture represents the Navajo way, the other is the Anglo way. It was not complete, and I helped revise some parts. The poster was being prepared for use in the classrooms by those who teach Navajo culture and philosophy. The Window Rock Board of Education has not yet approved the idea for our school here.

218 The corn plant illustrates the four basic colors which the Navajos use in their religion—white for the east, blue or turquoise for the south, yellow for the west, black for the north. These were the colors of the sacred stones, the sacred mountains, the corn and everything sacred to the Navajos. As I discuss it now, the poster is not quite ready, and it is being studied and other important ideas are being added to emphasize better education in both English and Navajo. We hope it will be used soon. Students will learn a lot from that illustration.

I also speak to the students in Navajo at St. Michaels, Arizona (near Window Rock), when they invite me to their classes. I discuss both Navajo and Catholic religions

Now and then I get a chance to speak to the smaller children. They all sit very quietly and listen. Only once in a while can a speaker have an audience of small children who are interested. With me, they get involved by asking many, many questions. I love to talk to the small fry for that reason.

We often hear unpleasant rumors about our high school students, but I work with those kids, and they give me no problems whatsoever. I know that many of these rumors are untrue. Sure, some teachers do have problems with their students. It is just a matter of respect. We have to learn to cope with them calmly and not upset them with harshness. Otherwise, they will feel rebellious toward us. I learned how to understand young people from my own children. Each has his own characteristics, and each has his ups and downs.

Another thing I like to do is to keep the young people occupied during their summer vacation by planning activities for them. I managed the local youth baseball team for the last 18 years, and I still am interested in that recreation and work. Boys love to play baseball, which makes me very happy. To better the young peoples' environment is part of my job as a community leader. I believe I have a good understanding of young people. Many have come to me for advice, and I try to help them.

Fathers and mothers should help as much as they can. Their children need them. Today, we hear a lot about the corruption of the younger generation, but it is not necessarily true. And, the trouble that we have is partly the parents' fault. If they say, "Our children won't listen to us," that only makes matters worse. If parents will offer a good word now and then, the youngsters will show their appreciation by listening. A child's feelings are very delicate. Fathers and mothers should say "my son, my daughter," and other kind words that the young want to hear. In that way they will know that their parents love them. Parents should show more affection toward their children and not use unpleasant expressions. When elders address or greet a youngster as "my son, my daughter or my child" he or she has an emotional feeling—knowing that there is a wonderful father and a loving mother who want to help and can be counted upon as friends.

219

Ch'ahádiniini' Binálí

MY NAME IS CH'AHÁDINIINI' BINÁLÍ, I am 94 years old (1976). The clan of my father was the Meadow People *(Halstooí).* He was Hopi; they just wandered into our tribe.

My grandfather on my mother's side, whose name was Mr. White, and a brother of his named Mr. Blind, along with their maternal granddaughter, came into our tribe. Not long after, other grandchildren were born. One of them was Mr. Slim, another was Little Yellowman. The youngest, who was my father, was born for the Meadow People clan; so I was born for it also. He was married into the Near the Water clan *(To'ahani),* and from that came the slim relationship of all relatives of the Hopi tribe who became Navajos. I have many relatives on my father's side at Fluted Rock. Anyhow, my real clan is the Towering House People *(Kinyaa'áa nii),* on my mother's side.

This clan came originally from White Shell (Changing) Woman. It was at the base of San Francisco Peaks that it came into being. Under that peak is where Changing Woman arrived from Gobernador Knob, a place which is in New Mexico. Before she came she had twin boys whom she brought along. She took them near San Francisco Peaks to some traditional hogans at that place. There they learned the Blessing Way chant.

Changing Woman then left toward the West where she was supposed to live with the Sun on an island in the middle of the ocean. When she had arrived at San Francisco Peaks she had said to the twins, "My journey has come to an end, and I am going back to where I belong. My children, you have learned all of the Blessing Way chant from me." The two winds would be the air for the twins

220

to help them go to her later. The process would mean the creation of their souls, and then they would become beings.

(The Narrator at this point tells his version of the mythological-legendary history of the Navajo people, developing it to the time of his own childhood. That "history," as prepared through the cooperation of several highly respected and knowledgeable Navajos, has appeared at length and in detail in other publications of the Navajo Community College Press. Then, Mr. Bináli takes up his own life and experiences, as follows—EDITOR's NOTE.)

As soon as I could sit up as a child, I was thrown into the snow. The idea was to make my skin tough, and I would be hard. I understood it when I got older. Soon afterward, I started running at dawn. Those things were required of us by our elders. I went through many "hardening" experiences, like crawling in the snow. I would also go into the water in winter after breaking the ice. Some would say, "I **221** brought back a chunk of ice," but that probably was not true. I tried but failed because it would freeze to my hands. The skin in the crevices of my palms would be like milk as the ice scattered onto the ground, and I would return home with bloody hands. That experience was a really difficult one.

Here is another experience I went through: Some men have said, "When I was really hot and tired, I would crawl into the sweat house where the hot stones and steam were and catch my breath." That was not true, either. Who could catch his breath in there? If a person really was hot and tired before he entered, he would pass out.

Once several of us raced a long way, almost as far as from here at my home to the Valley Store (between Chinle and Many Farms). It was a hot summer day; we had built a fire by the sweat house and put stones in it to heat, with water to pour over them inside the house. I put on moccasins as we got ready to make the long run out and then back. I don't recall how many there were of us. Some were older boys who were barefooted. This was to be really tough. We who wore moccasins kept on running, while others—even the ones who were older—had to sit down along the way because of their bare feet that were sore. We with moccasins continued to the place of destination and then turned back. The others (barefooted) sat down and dug their feet into the sand for a cool spot. We (wearing moccasins) were running back, and I was in the lead. The man who was holding the canvas to the entrance of the sweat house held it up and shouted to me, "In there!" In there I lost consciousness and had to be taken out. The person who was behind me had the same thing

Changing Woman traveled on a rainbow to the west where she would live with the sun on an island in the ocean.

happen to him. The others just passed it up and did not enter the sweat house. It was in a shaded area, in a gully. While others were throwing water on us, we came to—regained our consciousness. That was why I don't believe the ones who said they went into a sweat house "to catch their breath."

As for the rolling in the snow, it certainly was cold; but, after doing it for a while, one got used to it.

I would be chased out soon after dawn to round up the horses, and my parents would tell me, "Don't ride a horse, or you will make it sore; just run them back on foot as fast as possible. Make your backbone tough and strong so that when you get old you will not become all shriveled up. The ones who don't run a lot always shrivel." That was the way the elders used to teach us.

We had instructions about almost everything—like sheep. The older people would say, "Go and herd sheep, so that nobody will say you are not experienced. It will make your moccasins smooth; but you always will have socks, pants and other clothes right up to the top of your head. That is why we say to herd sheep."

I once had 16 head of cattle; then the herd grew to 37, but a poisonous plant killed all of them. For that reason I don't like the plant. It is useless upon our Navajo Reservation. Plants like cactus, however, can be useful, in many ways.

When I was young there were a lot of special teachings for girls. The beings called "women" were not to be made fun of, for when they became older in age they would tell the younger men and women, "If you don't do right, you will become like that certain man or woman. You will start going on the crooked path." One of the instructions given to women was to be careful about men. For instance, if a man were hunting his horses, he might say, "I am

223

The Twins finally killed the monster Ye'iitsoh with their lightning arrows.

looking for my horses," and he would give a description of them to the woman and add, "Since you have herded sheep in different places, have you seen them?" If the woman's reply would be, "I don't know; I have not seen them," suddenly he might charge at her, throw her down on the ground and jump on her—sometimes leading to rape. An incident like that was useless. It was such instructions that were stressed to girls. That was why a male should not charge onto a girl, for the girl could testify later, saying, "He is the one who raped me. No matter how much I fought him—he was the one that did it." With all her bruises, it would be very embarrassing. It would be best for one to be a straight person.

I was told not to steal crops once they were ripened, like little watermelons or cantaloupes; also not to claim somebody else's livestock. Whenever another's livestock got into a person's herd, he was not supposed to keep it. Instead, he was to tell the owner about the lost livestock that was in the herd; either the owner would say that it was his, or it was not. There would be an agreement. Incidents like rape and stealing other people's property were wrong; so "leave it alone" always was preached to me, and that was the way I grew up. I never stole any livestock. I had my own.

224

It is said that the stay at Fort Sumner was for four years. Before that, the Navajos used to go over into the country that is now New Mexico, and some Mexicans came back with the Navajos. There were three of them once, and they were roaming around in Canyon de Chelly. They told the Navajos, "Over in New Mexico, the Mexicans have many horses and sheep. Let's go there, kill some Mexicans, and bring back sheep." It was the Mexicans who raided with the Navajos at first, and they were the ones who gave the Navajos a start in that kind of thing. After it happened a few times, the Navajos were told that they were thieves. Each time they stole from the Mexicans they would be fired upon. They had a saying, "Here come the Coyotes." Fighting always would occur, often at night, when they were sleeping. We would kill many of them. Years went by, and, as they continued to try to kill us off, they never succeeded, for we always overpowered them. At that time a plan was being made for us in Washington, D. C. The Anglos were saying, "Let's trick them on food, for who can resist food?"

Here in Chinle, on a green hilly area, tents were set up. The white men were saying, "You who are hungry—come—and we will give you food. You can make your homes here." All that time they were lying to the Navajos. It was with this trick that our grandfathers and grandmothers were captured and sent to Fort Sumner. Cattle pulled some wagons, with the sheep following behind. Most of the people, from children to old men and women, had to walk if they were able.

Thousands of Navajos were captured and herded to Fort Sumner (Hwééldi), far away in the eastern part of New Mexico. Most of them had to walk the hundreds of miles, but some old people and the very young rode in wagons pulled by oxen, with the sheep following behind.

Back at that time, I know, I had four grandparents, two of whom experienced the Long Walk. Two of my grandfathers and another relative escaped the march to Fort Sumner and hid here at a place called Fish Stream Mesa, where they had climbed with their packs to the top. The area, at a place called Salty Water, was where a stream of water came from Horse Springs, and their water was from that spring. They had three ewes and three nanny goats; also one mare, one studhorse and three saddle horses. That was all. There were no rams or billy goats. They would milk the sheep and goats, and the milk supply never ran out. The men would roam up on Black Mountain and bring back porcupines, wolves and certain plants on which they survived. Three years went by after the herding of the people to Fort Sumner *(Hwééldi).* Two of the men left the moun-

225

*My grandfathers went up onto Black Mountain where
they hunted porcupines, wolves and other animals
and ate certain plants so they could survive.*

226 tain, while the other remained looking after things. Other people
who had managed to stay away from Fort Sumner came and visited
him. They were neighbors from other hogans which were not far
away; so there were three hogans. One grandfather would share with
them the milk of the goats and sheep. The horses had colts; and,
once in a while, during heavy snows, a young colt would be killed
and shared among the three hogans. In that way they all managed to
exist. In the places where it was mountainous they would hunt for
deer, using the saddle horses. Deer meat would be brought back in
the fall. Also antelope.

The people at Fort Sumner were herded together. They were taught about the land. There were fields of red squash and corn. From the cornfields they had food which they knew about, except that insects spoiled a lot of it, and it did not grow well in the salty soil. They did not know about the squash. They were shown something else, too, which they were told was called potatoes. "You will plant these crops," they were told. Onions and carrots also were shown to them. "In the days to come you will plant these right here at Fort Sumner," they. were told. Navajoland was never mentioned as a place where they would be living.

I think the area where each Navajo family planted was about the size of this house. They would put four seeds in each hole in the soil—that was all. The horses that were taken there they still herded. They had only a few sheep. Cattle, given by the government, would be butchered and the meat distributed among the people.

227

Our chiefs kept begging to let the people go. There was one particular leader named Manuelito; he was of the Bitter Water clan. Some said that he was of the Big Water People clan, but that was not true. They said this because it would be something against him. He truly was of the Bitter Water clan, and he became a leader while he was married to one of my grandmothers. Finally, he was told that the Navajos could have their homeland back, or at least part of it.

Some elderly men (medicine men) had learned the Chiricahua-Apache ceremonies while at Fort Sumner; so, at Fort Defiance, they started holding them. Nobody slept during the chants. They were known quite well, like the Chiricahua-Apache know them nowadays.

After returning from Fort Sumner, it was two years before any school was started. The children, all of whom have since passed away, went to school in moccasins, with pants patched at the knees and the seat. Anglos also attended. At first, there was much opposition to the schools, Navajo parents objected, and not many children attended. The number of students did increase, however, until the schools were in full swing, and the people wanted them. As the years went by some jails were built. Hunting for children had to be done because some would run away. The runaways were brought back. Then interest in school began decreasing again. Just anybody, even those who were slow learners or handicapped, were supposed to be placed in school.

Teenagers nowadays have become hard to handle. The situation and ideas to which they are clinging are not right.

I don't know what year the school appeared in Chinle, but I was grown up when it was built, and I had a wife. I guess it must have been 60 years or more; maybe it was almost 75 years ago. Since the return from Fort Sumner 106 or 107 years must have gone by. Once, at Round Rock, Arizona, there was a fight between people who didn't want the schools and some government (Bureau of Indian Affairs) school officials.

The police rode horses among the people after the schools were built, and the students were forced to attend. Even from Fort Defiance they rode out here into the country to put us into school. We would be placed there and our horses brought back home.

The automobile came into existence after the school was built at Chinle and was doing well in enrolling students. The cars at that time had a clicking and kind of rattling sound; they had wooden spokes in the wheels and the tires were small. Sometimes, when they were bumping along on a rough road, the wheels would come apart.

228

Churches came also to our land, to which a lot of the Navajos were converted quickly. The denominations of churches were many. Also, peyote came into use; and, from it, users went the wrong way.

People don't seem to understand anything anymore. What son listens to his father? What grandchild listens to his grandparents? There is no listening. The same goes for the girl—the daughter never listens to the mother or grandmother. It even goes for my family. A son doesn't listen, and our grandchildren never listen to us. All they do is look forward to the day and the time. Once it becomes evening, they take off. They are just barely out the door when they are gone. It is because of the schools. I don't know what is going on. They have certain entertainments like games, dances and other activities that make our kids go crazy—along with the bottle and drugs that make them even crazier. If some of the temptations of today could be destroyed, that would be the only way we could become straight again.

This thing about peyote is not for us. Who is authorized to conduct such a ceremony? In the past it was just the Holy One in whom we believed. Now there is no one who knows anything correctly. Ceremonies are decorated in ways the people want, and some are just too fancy and useless; I have observed them. As for myself, I don't use peyote, and in the days to come I am not going to use it.

This also goes for the churches. They say, "God is looking at you; he is not happy with the things you do, and for not believing him." And also, "On this earth there is no Holy Being," is often heard by others. If the second is true, then what is it you are standing upon? What makes you strong? It is the Holy One who makes you strong; so why say there is no Holy Being on earth—for it is not true! I believe in the Holy One, for I am sure of His existence. A person is born upon this earth. His or her mother's and father's veins and blood were put together to create that boy or girl. There is a Holy One—he is not gone. The white people depend upon the earth the same as we depend upon it; it is the everyday part of their lives, but they are doing all sorts of bad things to it—the very earth that is the living part of us.

229

Ernest Nelson

I HAVE HEARD STORIES of the time the *Diné* (the Navajos or the People) were at Fort Sumner. The People were being chased by the white soldiers like other tribes, but they mainly wanted to get rid of the Navajos. Because they couldn't conscientiously just kill all of them, they were herded like cattle to Fort Sumner (Bosque Redondo or *Hwééldi*) in what is called the Long Walk. While there, the people begged and cried for their homeland. Those who had escaped capture and being sent to the prison camp held ceremonies and prayers for the victims. Somehow those prayers were answered, and the people were released after about four years to return to their homeland. They were told, "Lay down your arrows and promise to fight no more, and we also will lay down our guns." They did this in order to be released. Manuelito was one of the Navajo leaders. I don't remember the white men's names. In Gallup there is a statue of Chief Manuelito.

The ones who escaped the Long Walk, like my grandfather whose name was Spread Mustache, never took their children to Fort Sumner. That was because they had lived in places from which the people had not been taken. The soldiers had not found them.

In the fall of the same year, while the people were moving back, (it was about 1868), my mother was born near Chinle, Arizona, in an area called Rock With White Streak on Top. Left-Handed Woman was my mother's name. Now she is more than 100 years old and helpless. We often visit her. The many people she grew up with, like her sisters, are gone; she is the only survivor.

I don't know much about the early school days in that time. One older brother did go to school, but he passed away on the morning I was born. So, I never saw him. I had three older brothers, but another, who was a year older than I, passed away.

The Navajo police would come around and tell my mother, "We want your children to go to school." One of the policemen was an older brother to my mother. His name was Mr. Waving Hat. Another uncle of mine was a policeman, too. He had ugly hands, and he got his name, Mr. Police With Scorched Hands, from them. A third policeman also was an uncle to me. He was a member of the Black Streak Wood people *(Tsi'naajinii)* and his name was Mr. One Who Hates Him. Another man I knew from Tuba City, Mr. One Who Pulls, also was a policeman.

Whenever my maternal grandmother heard about school starting again in the fall, and that the police would be going around for children, she would take us into the tall mountains and would hide us there. She would pack some food and water for us. Sometimes we would spend three or four days, or until the police would leave the area; then she would take us back. At one time, just when the police were least expected, two came. They were Mr. Waving Hat and Mr. One Who Hates Him. These two took my older brother, Alex, to school on horseback. He was only six years old—just a little boy.

As for myself, I stayed home. At that time, an older man or woman relative would preach to the men, "Start the day early; do not sleep when it gets dawn; who's going to help you? No use to have your head down; be up and around early." Sometimes when it was cold and wintry he or she would say, "Go out; go after the sheep or horses," or "Roll in the snow, for this way you become hard and strong."

Our hair was not taken care of, and it was bushy. Nowadays, the young men have long hair, but it usually is combed down. Ours was all in tangles, with lice in it, which caused sores on our scalps.

The shoes of today were not common then. The slender shoes had just become known. At that time, whenever a horse was killed for meat the skin was used for winter shoes, sewed with yucca fibers.

My main responsibility was tending the sheep and horses. I used to herd sheep down to Rocky Wash and as far away as Distant Corner. I would herd even during the winter. People with no sheep moved to nearby mountains in the summer; so did some of those with sheep because the grazing was better. I would see hogans and summer camps here and there as I herded our sheep.

My older brother was going to a school in Tuba City. Toward the end of the school year my father took a horse and brought my

231

brother home. He was growing taller, and I was getting taller, too. I would go places with him, and he would be talking in English to me—which made me want to learn.

In 1926 there was a Squaw Dance at Cow Springs, and many of the little boys were there. A white man named Mr. Walker, from Tuba City, arrived at the dance. The boys and girls who were of school age were running around. The white man said, "All of these little children should be put in school."

That night, some of the boys and girls ran away. But, since my older brother was in school and he always spoke English to me, I walked up to Mr. Walker and said, "I will go to school." So I left my horse there and went to Tuba City to attend school. It was like running away TO school, just the opposite of what often was done. It was my idea because I wanted to see how it was at school and I wanted to learn.

I arrived in Tuba City, but my older brother by then was going to school in Fort Wingate; so I was without him. I spent about one week there, when some students left for Fort Wingate. Some went to Chaco Canyon; others to the Apache country.

At that time there were no buses like Greyhounds; the transportation we had was two big gray trucks with canvas at the back. I was loaded for Fort Apache. The girls were in one truck, and the boys in the other. When we arrived at Fort Apache, we noted the poor condition of the place. There was no food and no heating system. The houses were made of lumber, with patched roofs. Soldiers had lived in them long ago. The plan had been to use this fort temporarily as a school, but it kept on being used. There were many Navajo school children, both boys and girls.

Apache children were going to school at Whiteriver, separately, but at Fort Apache there were only Navajos. One of the students I attended school with was Howard Gorman. I still see him at Tsaile, Arizona, when conferences with students are held. While going to school in the Apache country I got to know him. Every morning, when the sun rose, he would blow on his bugle. That was the way we were awakened. Then, we would all line up. We were living like soldiers.

School children now change clothes every day, but we had what you would call "uniforms." The pants were brown corduroy. The jackets and caps were also of corduroy. Our underwear was just one whole piece of clothing—"long johns." Then, on top, were our

232

shirts, which were yellow and with no pockets. The jackets did have some pockets. That was how we were dressed. Our shoes were military; the soles were made of thick leather. Our socks were gray. The girls' clothes were all stripes and would hang down from their shoulders. Their shoes were black.

Food was scarce. Breakfast was only a bowl of oatmeal, plus one slice of bread and a glass of milk. At noon it was about the same, except that there were two slices of bread. There were some dairy

233

When Howard Gorman blew his bugle very early every morning we would run and line up like soldiers. We were dressed in a kind of uniform.

cattle—which provided a chore for some boys to do the milking. The man they worked for was Jessie Farmer, an Apache. Meat products were hard to get. Today, there are chicken dinners. At that time, there was no chicken. About the only thing we got was boiled pork rind cut into beans. Half of the time we were hungry.

We used firewood for heating, usually hauled on wagons driven by students. Some of the students went to school from morning until noon; others went from noon until evening. The ones that went to school in the morning hauled wood in the afternoon, while the ones that went to school in the afternoon hauled wood in the morning. We didn't have a power saw. Our wood was sawed by hand.

There was a furnace in the basement where the boys and girls lived. Steam heat was produced, but we still were cold. In that way, I spent my first year at school.

As for schooling, it was mostly learning to read and speak English. I had some friends who helped me read, and I learned many words that way.

In the spring, when school was out, we worked in small fields where hay was grown, along with squash and watermelons. (We received no letters from home. I didn't know whether my parents were happy with my schooling because they never mentioned it. I went to school because I wanted to learn.) Then, after the last day, I stayed there because the officials asked us to work, but it lasted only during June.

234

Because there were no classes we got lonesome. Then, some boys planned to run away. We were not too far from Whiteriver where the Apaches went to school. The "Fourth of July" celebration was soon to start there; but, because we had no transportation, we had to go on foot. At night, Apache dancing was held. On July 2, I had been put to work in the kitchen as a cook. I was the leader of those who planned to run away. So I took some bread, coffee that looked bad (and didn't taste like coffee), along with sugar and a sack of flour which I had hid. There I was, a cook stealing food.

On the night of July 5 we all picked up the food and left. There were Paul Nez, Bob Dejolie, Jackson Menia, Walter Smallcanyon of Navajo Mountain and myself. Together we left Apache country at night. During the winter when some boys would run away from school they would come back and say there were mountain lions and bears. One time, some boys ran away in the winter. One boy was killed by a bear, while another was seriously hurt. A white man came to the rescue and hauled the boys to the hospital. Even though we knew it was dangerous, we left at night. Somewhere close by the Apache sawmill we became lost, so we spent the night under a pine tree. The next day we started again by about midday. Some of the boys who went to school with us were working and living just north of the sawmill. We finally arrived at Blue Canyon, where we spent the night, and the next day I set out alone, on foot, for Shonto. We had left on a Sunday and I returned to Shonto on a Sunday. So I had spent seven days running away from school.

After that, I stayed at home. Not a word was said about me running away or about how dangerous the journey had been. My parents just chased me out to herd the sheep.

During the fall, when children were returning to school, my brother (who had been attending Fort Wingate) was home; so it was decided that I would try to go there. I guess things had been easier and better for the students at Fort Wingate—even the clothes. I had herded sheep wearing the same clothes that I had worn when I had been in school at Tuba City. When we were about to start for Fort Wingate my brother introduced me, saying, "This is my younger brother." But others said, "No—he ran away from Fort Apache." So, instead of being taken to Fort Wingate, I was hauled back to Fort Apache, and there I spent another year. It was still in the same poor condition.

We were taught to saw lumber—how to measure and different ways to saw. Also, we learned pipe laying—how one part connects to the other and the names of various parts. It was about the same **235** for those who worked in the food department (kitchen). They were instructed in how things were made. I never worked in the kitchen again.

I spent another year at Fort Apache, and it was tough because at sunrise Howard Gorman blew on his bugle; then everybody jumped up, hurriedly dressed and ran outside in the cold to line up. We lived in groups with our group leader by our side. We had drills, and they told us not to put our hands in our pockets. Nowadays, the students are taken care of, making sure that they don't catch colds, and they are kept inside more, where it is warm. We were chased outdoors in the cold, and we sure had our share of chills and sickness.

There was a man from Bodaway named Manson whose children, Edward Manson and Alfred Yazzie Manson, were going to school at Fort Apache. In the spring someone from Bodaway came for them to be picked up. Nobody came for those of us who were from Shonto and Tuba City. Then Paul Nez's father, Mr. Tall Deer Springs, who knew me slightly, came to pick up his son. I asked him if I could catch a ride with them, and he agreed. Again I left the school without permission from the leaders. I hid in the car, and they took me to Tuba City; from Tuba City I hitchhiked on to Shonto.

At that time the roads were unpaved from Holbrook to Show Low and down to Whiteriver. There were no paved (or even gravel) roads like most roads are nowadays. They were dirt, and they were high down the center. There were no roads at all around my home. Wagon trails were about all that showed. The roads to Navajo Mountain were poor wagon trails.

Part of the community of Shonto, as it looks from the south.

When I came back home my job again was herding the sheep, while my older brother took care of the cattle. Then, when fall arrived we returned to school.

236   I had two years finished, and once again we went away. My older brother said, "This time let me take him to Fort Wingate." But he was told, "He has to spend three years at Fort Apache before he can go over there (Fort Wingate)." So my brother left for Fort Wingate, while I stayed in Tuba City.

Three boys who went to school at Fort Wingate had an old Model-T Ford. Mr. Walker, the superintendent, had gone to Flagstaff, and the boys said, "Because Mr. Walker did not see you, we'll take you to Fort Wingate." One of the boys was Dick Singer. Another was Mike Malonie, whose older brother was Dan. The third boy was Dee Begay. "We are going back to school at Fort Wingate in a sedan Model-T," they explained. So that morning I got in and left. The load of students going to the Apache country was to be leaving in two days. I was supposed to be with that load, but, instead, I had caught a ride to Fort Wingate with the boys. When I arrived there I saw that the school was pretty good.

They put me in classes right away. I was never told that I did not belong there. I think I was accepted right away because the school was in need of kids. We learned more about how to saw lumber, to make boxes and other things; also, more about how to lay pipe. There were houses that remained from the old-time Army fort that we remodeled on the inside and re-did the floors and the roofs.

The school was just being built. People already had made the boys' dorm, the girls' dorm and the dining room. The building for classrooms was under construction, and the students did various jobs like digging. At the same time, we went to school.

237

Fort Wingate High School in New Mexico.

The football field at Fort Wingate High School, N. M., with dormitories.

It was a good year. Meals were fairly good. Meat was available because the government provided the sheep that were kept in a corral close by. Behind Fort Wingate different kinds of crops were grown for food. Squashes of various types were harvested and stored in a shack, although many were boiled and eaten right away. The boys and girls who were used as cooks worked in the kitchen. They also made bread. To mix the bread they used a machine like a cement mixer. The dorms and the beds we slept in were all right; so were the blankets.

This made three years of schooling for me. After classes were out late in the spring, my older brother returned home because he had completed the highest grade offered. I stayed, along with some other boys, and we were taken to Kansas City where work was going on with sugar beet raising and harvesting. That summer I never went home, but instead worked with those sugar beets. When school was ready to open we were hauled back, and I spent another year at Fort Wingate.

238

I was in the fourth grade. As time went on, whenever I returned home my older brother would help me read and pronounce certain words. I think that was the reason I was progressing because I had only four years of schooling and was in the fourth grade. The next summer the same thing happened. They told me that since I would be in my third year at Fort Wingate, the next summer I could go home because the school would be paid for. But this summer I was to stay again and work on the sugar beets. Many of us stayed. Among them were Curly Tso's young brother, Oliver, and Ernest Walters, who became a councilman from Tonalea. They kept telling us that we would be hauled to Kansas City again, but the days just went by. We could have been working with sugar beets and been paid about $1 a day (I don't know how much an hour). But we never went to Kansas City. Instead, Oliver Tso said, "Let's go back to the Reservation." So I left with him and caught a train from the Fort Wingate depot to Gallup.

The steam engines at that time were different. They ran by burning coal; maybe that's why they were called "fire engines." The speed was similar of that of trains today. Once the train started going fast it would cause a pillar of smoke. At Gallup there was a bus slightly similar to a Greyhound, except for a canvas top and plastic windows on the sides. The bus fee from Gallup to Flagstaff was $2.30 at that time. (Oliver had been given the name Bear Springs

(Shash Bitoo) because he was attending school in Fort Wingate which at one time had been called Bear Springs.) When we arrived in Flagstaff one of Oliver's older brothers, Burt, happened to be there, and we caught a ride back to Kaibito with him. From Kaibito I went to Shonto where my mother was living.

So it was 1929 when I quit school. I probably would have returned, but my family told me to herd sheep. An older brother went to school only until he was 12 years of age because of illness, and he never returned. He died in the springtime at Navajo Mountain. At home they had told me to take care of the sheep and horses; also to work in the cornfields, hoeing and weeding.

I had gone to school for four years, and it seemed like it helped me to find work; I have had no difficulty. For some time I was an interpreter for men who worked on the railroad, no matter how well **239** they spoke English. Occasionally I would interpret a whole day, maybe even two days. New Navajos would be hauled in to work, and, although they looked as though they had some education, they would tell me they didn't understand English—so I had to be their interpreter. That was why I thought schooling had helped me in many ways. When one was really working, one would be sweaty; but I would be paid for the time that I just sat and interpreted. I thought that was good.

Recently, the fine Shonto School was built. But a boarding school in the wash had been before it, started in 1936. It seemed to be unsuccessful because many students would run away. The policemen would not look for them; the workers at the school were the ones who had to search. In 1939 a day school was opened at Navajo Mountain, and it exists today. The Navajo Mountain school was started after the Shonto school. A few children seemed to purposely miss classes at some schools—including the off-Reservation ones. The reason for it was the bottle. Certain kids were drinking alcohol, and it led them the wrong way.

These schools resemble the white man's, with the white man's teachings. But, teaching Navajo culture is good because some children seem to have forgotten the Navajo language. They don't even know all of their relatives or their clans. At Tsaile there is a college where Navajo culture is taught. If schools would be like that college in teaching the Navajo way I think it would be good.

Just north of the Shonto school, land recently was requested for building a Navajo Culture Center, something like the center at

Tsaile. I don't know why, but I said, "I really think a school should be built at the location they are requesting. Jobs would be available for the ones who have graduated. Those who wanted to learn would be able to learn. We should pass the resolution to build a school on this land. Let's have the teachings of Navajo culture, the same as at Navajo Community College at Tsaile."

Both languages are taught, and I think that is good. The Navajo religion is taught also, just as it is in the Navajo and Indian Studies program at Tsaile. I think this should be done in all Navajo schools.

Some tribes of Indians don't know their own languages well. English is what they speak mostly. We Navajos never will become like them, for we will go forward with our own language, as well as with the English. We also will know the white man's teachings and the Navajo teachings of them, the white man's rules and the Navajo rules. That will be good.

240

There has been a school at Tuba City for a long time. I don't know when it was built. Some of our elderly men went there when it started. I have been told that the schools weren't really instructive then. It is said that they were strict on punishment. If one ran away, the punishment (after being brought back) would be to stand outside all day facing the building, without going anywhere—just to stand in one spot. Another punishment was to carry a stick back and forth across a patch of ground for a long time. Still another was to have a barbed wire, attached to a ring-like object, with the other end wrapped around the student's ankle—and he or she had to walk around in circles for maybe up to two days. Dressing boys in girls' clothes was another punishment. They had to do that and go where everyone could see. So dressed, the boys had to eat with the girls in the dining room; and the girls' punishment would be to dress in boys' clothes and be put with the boys to eat. The idea was that by doing this the girls might get embarrassed. It was like that at Fort Wingate and Fort Apache, too.

In the classroom, when one was told to read and did not respond to the instructions, he got a paddling, either with a leather strap or a wooden object. Nowadays, punishment is not like that. It seems that, no matter how small they are, children are bossy, and they have their own ways of doing things. If the rules that we went by in the past were in existence today, I wonder whether the children would be interested in their schooling—whether it would be effective for them! At that time the children were not bossy.

Parents used to be mistreated by the policemen as they gathered the children for school. Also, during the stock reduction period, when some Navajos would not give up their sheep and goats, they were put in jail. Likewise, when children were taken by the police to school, and when the parents protested, those parents were put in jail. Once their kids were in school the father and mother were released. If a family did not bring its children back to school, a policeman would visit and warn the parents to send them or to jail they would go.

Horses were just about the Navajos' only means of travel, for there were practically no automobiles, and the roads were terrible, often just trails. Hardship was felt, but maybe it was the only way to learn and to realize the meaning of education.

Today, it is not like that because practically every weekend students have rides home. It seems like they don't have anything to do. That is why we often see two, three or four school kids hitchhiking on the highways. I don't know what they are looking for. They go to school five days; then, on weekends, they just run around.

Recently, some girls from Navajo Mountain ran away, and, now, after six days, they have not returned. Children like these are missing too much school. I don't know whether they are being taught properly. Maybe that explains the problem.

At the time I was at Fort Wingate, whenever children ran away they were returned and put in jail for seven days. The jail was underneath the main office building. Because of that treatment the children did not run away too much. Runaways from Fort Apache were many, however. Once they were returned they were dressed in girls' clothing and had to walk around separately from the other students. Boys had to eat with the girls too. From these punishments it is clear that the schools were strict in discipline. At that time the boys and girls generally were very well mannered.

From the four years that I attended school it seemed that I gained enough knowledge to be able to learn the singing of ceremonies. If I hadn't gone to school and learned to read I might not have been able to learn that much. Usually, I wrote the chants down on paper as they were sung by a medicine man. There were certain lengths for each song, and each was for a particular ceremony. I would use different kinds of colors of writing pens to help me remember the separate songs and prayers. That was how I learned. It was just like going to school. Thus, from lessons taught in reading and writing I learned the singing of ceremonies.

241

Now, over at Navajo Community College in Tsaile, the young men and women are asking questions about the stories of the past, about the beginnings when we emerged from the various worlds beneath. These students are the ones getting good, strong educations. They take notes about these stories as they are told, and I think by doing this they remember and appreciate more.

The past winter I did not go over to the campus. But I was there last year. I was supposed to have gone again, but I received the letter too late. Howard Gorman of Ganado, a member of the Board of Regents for the College, said, "We missed you."

I think if one is expected to be at a certain place at a certain time a notice should be sent out early. Also, there are telephones in Shonto now; and, if they really wanted my presence at Tsaile, they easily could call. I always am in Shonto.

One form of punishment for running away or for other offenses was to make a boy dress in a girl's clothing and go around where everyone could see—and tease—him. A girl had to wear a boy's outfit.

Thomas Clani

MY HOME IS NEAR THE BASE of Carrizo Mountain, halfway between Teec Nos Pos, Arizona, and Biklabito, New Mexico. I have been a chapter officer for the last 12 years at Teec Nos Pos, and I am involved in many community activities and problems.

I want to tell about my early Navajo education; but, first, I will name my clans. I am of the Bitter Water People *(Tódích'íí'nii)*, born for the Salt People *(Áshįįhí)*. My maternal grandfather was of the Charcoal Streak People *(Naaneesht'ézhí)*, and my paternal grandfather was of the Within His Cover People *(Bit'ahnii)*. My children are of the Red Running Into Water People *(Tachii'nii)*.

The first boarding schools were built at Fort Defiance and Tuba City in Arizona and at Shiprock in New Mexico. Compulsory education was enforced. Navajo policemen went on horseback to the homes where there were school-age children. My father had to enroll me at the Shiprock boarding school. I wanted to go to school, and I was glad he did it, but many of the children had to be taken by force.

In the fall of 1923 my father and I left home in our family wagon. When I got to the school I had to have a physical examination at the hospital before I was accepted. After that, I went to the boys' dormitory. All children who were admitted received government school clothes. The clothing we came to school in was taken home by our parents. All the boys had their hair cut alike; then we had our baths. We were all well groomed, and none of the boys kept their long hair.

The day that classes began we all marched to the school building. Some of the children cried, but others were anxious for classes to start. All of the teachers were Anglo women; there were no male teachers. There was no fooling around in class; everyone had to listen and behave. In those days I think the children learned more. They were timid and frightened at first, probably because the school was new to them and the rules seemed strict. They knew they had to obey or be punished. In the dormitory we had what was called the disciplinarian—not a housemother. He watched us all the time. The boys and girls lived in separate dormitories because the school had rules and regulations not to mix them except during class time; even then we had to sit separately. The boys and girls were detailed to work in different places at school—such as the kitchen, dining room, laundry, farm and various shops.

244 We always were hungry; it seemed that enough food never was served at mealtime. The smaller boys cried a lot, saying they were hungry and lonely. We went to school nine months during the year, without a break, until vacation started in June. That was one happy event. Our parents came in wagons or on horseback with one or two extra horses to travel home on. We all hustled about with excitement as we said our good-bys. During vacation time we helped our parents at home. We herded sheep on the mountain ranges, worked in the cornfields and irrigated the alfalfa fields. In dry farming we hauled water to irrigate the squash and melon patch.

But the summer was too short; September came and we returned to school in our government clothes. When a student was naughty or did something wrong he was punished immediately. The boys' disciplinarian usually kept a strap, and he used it on the boys when they got out of hand—even just slightly. He also used such punishment as marching us back and forth in front of the boys' dorm for at least five hours on Saturday afternoons while we were supposed to be free to play, carrying signs saying, "I am a bad boy." At that time the parents could do nothing about it when they were told these things by the boys.

As I said, compulsory education was enforced. The children were made to learn the hard way, and we did learn. We were afraid of the punishment. We kept our dormitories spotless, and we made our beds. Some of us had to clean the classrooms, too, because there were no custodians to pick up after us. The older boys got odd jobs such as mowing the lawns and weeding the flower gardens to earn a little spending money. They did not get much—maybe 25 cents to buy some candy or soda pop. As you know, all this has changed. The

A section of the Bureau of Indian Affairs school at Teec Nos Pos on the Reservation in Arizona —with Carrizo Mountain in the background.

245

dormitories now have housemothers, and the boys have advisers. The schools have custodians who do the cleaning and take care of the school grounds.

When we wore government-issue clothes no one dared complain; we just wore them. In fact, they were better clothes than some of us had before.

The Navajo Tribal Government was just beginning then. There were only 12 members (called delegates), with a chairman. Their meeting place was at Fort Defiance in Arizona. When there was special business they all would go to Washington, D. C. They discussed education, oil, employment and other important issues concerning the Navajo Tribe.

In those days the people depended greatly on their livestock. Their main transportation was by horseback or wagon. The people went to the trading posts to meet old friends and relatives and to exchange news and events, besides buying things that were needed. There were no clinics or hospitals nearby for sick people; so they had to travel in wagons to the Fort Defiance Hospital or to Shiprock or Ganado. The people used their own healing ceremonies more at that time, too. The ceremonies were conducted very reverently, and the people had faith in their religion, religious and healing ceremonies and native medicines. When a person died there was no funeral with all the works—like an expensive coffin and flowers. The deceased was considered a ghost. Nobody went near the body, except for two people who were immune in the ghost way. Those two buried the dead. When a person died in a hospital the attendants did the burial alone, with no family members. The family abandoned a hogan if a person died in it.

I am glad that I had the chance to get a little education. Thinking back, I believe it was all for the good that the Navajo policemen came around to our homes to get school-age children into the schools. I only graduated from the eighth grade. I am happy that I learned how to read, write and speak English. With this advantage I am able to find good employment, which I am grateful for. Besides learning my A B Cs, I learned how to work with tools. I built my own home which I still live in.

By the people's decision I have been their community leader. I am involved in all community activities and have done my best to help solve problems. I know they rely on me for advice and many of their needs. My interest lies in the betterment of their lives and environment. One of the projects I became particularly interested in was the preschool program. With much enthusiasm the community people constructed a new building where many of our small children now attend preschool. I worked hard, and, with my people backing me, this was all accomplished. My education has helped me with what I do for my people. I often have wished I had more education. I wonder where I would be now; maybe at Window Rock sitting in an office, or somewhere else as a supervisor. Education can be the guideline to gain more knowledge. A person can advance into the opportunities of tomorrow. Obtaining a sound job means a good income for one's family, and that is what we all want.

Traditional Navajo education is good, also. It preserves our culture. Years back the elders did a lot of lecturing to the young people about the right ways to live and the things to do and not to do. The elders were considered wise and experienced. When being counseled about how to be reliable husbands and fathers we boys were told to avoid embarrassment by having our children begging in the neighborhood for food or having them be seen with their toes exposed through their shoes or moccasins. Also, we were taught about conditions in the home and the effects of neglecting livestock and the farm. Strict rules, like exercising and rising very early in the morning, were followed. Sheep herding, horse care, farm work, wood and water hauling and other family chores were part of our daily responsibilities.

Most of our related elders were of the Clump Tree People *(Tsin sikaadnii)*. This area was their original dwelling place, where we live now. Many of the later clan members were medicine men, and they were the elders to whom I give credit for the good life I have lived to this day. I listened to their lectures, and I still live up to their teachings. Now it is my turn to pass those things on to my children and to other young people. The Navajos' traditional education and Anglo education both are very important, and in many ways, they are somewhat alike.

I am loaded with a heavy burden of responsibilities for my people. Many of the young have become accomplished in their chosen careers and are serving the Navajos in various departments or agencies. We are very proud of them, and we want to encourage more young people to do that. The world is progressing rapidly, and the Navajo Nation is doing likewise. The white man's super techniques in science are amazing. We now have faster transportation to get around and take our sick to the hospital. The hospitals have modern equipment; the roads are paved; we have good communication systems, like radio, telephone and television. And we know what is going on in all parts of the world, as well as in our own country.

247

Looking back at the past with an objective view, we can judge our forefathers as humans with very strong resistance. They struggled through many terrible hardships, and they survived so that our Navajo people of today can live and progress. Although only the memories of them, which we must never forget, linger in our minds, we "have it made" today. All the "push button" mechanical devices are doing our work for us. Modern living facilities make us comfortable in our homes. Sometimes we wish that we could bring our forefathers back, so they, too, could enjoy these comforts.

In our chapter meetings we discuss many problems, among them school bus regulations that are enforced because of vandalism on the school grounds, vandalism around the chapter house, etc.

When our community's children come home during the summer vacations we let them practice what they learned during the school year. The boys make stools and benches, and the girls cook their special dishes. We also have summer youth programs in which many young people participate. Some are employment programs which prevent them from being idle and getting into trouble.

We, as elders, want our younger people to become involved in as many programs as they can. This means that they gain experience and more knowledge. Even for me, as I sit here speaking into a recorder, it is a new experience for me, and many will know later what I am saying now.

It is true that our medicine men have many healing ceremonies, and that each specializes in a certain ceremony. Some have knowledge in two or a number of ceremonies. They perform them to serve the people's needs when illness comes into the families.

There are ceremonies like the Blessing Way, the Wind Way, the Flint Way and others. The larger ceremonies, which are more expensive to perform, are the Corral Dance, the Night Way, the Enemy Way and the Squaw Dance. The only way a person really can recover from any illness is to have complete faith in the ceremony that is being conducted in his behalf. The medicine man, too, must perform his ceremony to the best of his ability and knowledge. We hear or see where some medicine men have become careless, even drinking during the act of duty.

248

In our religion we pray to the Great Spirit for the goodness in life. There are other religious organizations on the Reservation now. If we unite and work for the good of our people—and pray—we all can live happy, peaceful and prosperous lives.

Some of us have been questioned and interviewed by representatives from the Navajo Community College at Tsaile, as well as other institutions, about our culture and language; also our religion. I suppose they gather the information to use along with the teaching they do at the College. They also publish it in books by what is called the College Press. We try to contribute what we know about our religion and the legends that go along with it. Some of us, however, are limited in this knowledge.

We also need to counsel our children more. We do not want them to learn the bad ways of living, and we should try various methods to approach them so that they will listen. And we must not give up after the first trial, or they surely will know that we are losers—and then they will have the upper hand. We must control our children. We are aware that most of our young people do not know the culture, religion and language of their own people. That is a very good reason why courses in Indian Studies are offered at the College.

One must not be an imitation white man or something that he really isn't. A Navajo MUST BE A NAVAJO. He must be able to talk to his people and not be a stranger. Someday he might find himself alone among his Navajo-speaking people, and he will need to talk to them without difficulty. On the other hand, he may go out into the Anglo world. With an education it won't be too much of a problem, and he will be able to find his way around. Thus, education and training work both ways in helping to fit into both the Navajo and the Anglo worlds.

A young man who is learning to be a Navajo healer or medicine man is similar to one who is going to school. He learns while the instructor sits in front of him as he gives the lessons orally day after day—sometimes at nights, too. There are no textbooks, paper or pencils. Everything that is learned is by pure memory. The lessons are put into the student's brain. The learning period goes on for four to five years, sometimes much longer—perhaps 12 years. The procedures, legends, songs and prayers have to be memorized exactly, word by word. The uses of herbs and other medicines must be learned properly. The tests are given when the instructor lets his student conduct certain parts of a ceremony alone as he sits and observes. Everywhere he goes to perform his ceremony the learner must tag along to assist him. The lessons become monotonous and very tiresome, and sometimes sleepless nights are spent working. When the younger person passes his final test and completes the course he is like a college graduate. He is on his own as a doctor or medicine man. Success depends on each person's ambition and interest. The service he gives to his people comes first; then the earning of money.

Our great leaders of long ago, after the return from Fort Sumner, (Bosque Redondo or *Hwééldi*) promised to enroll our children in the schools, and today the schools are full. Many of our children have graduated from high schools and other institutions.

We are in great need of Navajo skilled workers. That is one reason why we want our children to go to school. Other than academic work, many also should learn trades. Our Navajo population is increasing rapidly, and our future is at stake. The Navajo Nation depends upon well educated citizens. The challenge for higher education must be met to compete with the outside world. A better environment for our children, and involvement in active programs, is the aim that we must follow. We, as elders and parents, put education as priority for our children. I want to stress this point. Many of our older people had no education, or just a little. For that reason we are faced with many problems. Educating the Navajos is the main purpose of the Navajo Community College, and I am glad to be a part of it and to contribute. It is hard to discuss a subject when you are not prepared for it. For example, when you make a recording such as this, you can say only what comes into your mind;

249

then, when you are out somewhere doing other things, your thoughts go back, and you think of many other things which you should have said.

If all the people walk in the corn pollen path we can live in harmony. The Great Spirit again may bless us with rain. Then the earth will burst out with beautiful flowers and fresh vegetation—as it used to do—to fatten our livestock and to make the Reservation a happier place.

250

To become a medicine man a young Navajo must sit
with his instructor and get oral lessons day after day—
and sometimes at night—for many years.

With peace and harmony our tribal government should function smoothly without unnecessary controversy or misleadings. We also want our tribal leaders and the U. S. government to work together for the best interests of the Navajo people. We, as leaders in our individual communities, set our minds only on what will benefit our people. We spend many sleepless nights when we confront problems. But this is all part of the work that is expected.

Now I want to tell briefly about the history of our people. Thousands of Navajos were released from exile at Fort Sumner (Bosque Redondo) and returned to their homeland more than 100 years ago. I am sure that all Navajos and many Anglos have heard or read about the terrible situation. The College Press has published the facts—as the NAVAJOS tell them—in a book called NAVAJO STORIES OF THE LONG WALK PERIOD.

Our chiefs signed a treaty to fight no more, and they promised to send their children to school. That began a new era. The Navajos settled and built homes; yet many of the medicine men, and others, were reluctant to accept education, and they became hostile.

In 1913 a well known medicine man, who lived at Aneth, Utah, was the leader of a band of hostile Navajos who opposed education, and they almost caused an uprising. Today, no one opposes education. Parents want their children to be educated. Even small children begin at the early age of four in preschool.

The terrible flu epidemic hit the Reservation right after the first World War, and it took many lives. As I have mentioned, there were not enough hospitals, and what hospitals we had often were too far away to take a very sick person who needed help badly.

In 1920 a rumor was spread about a big flood that would strike the Shiprock area. Many people moved up on the high mountains for safety. My family went to the top of Carrizo Mountain. I suppose the rumor reminded them of the flood that occurred ages ago after the *Diné* (Navajo People) had emerged from the lower worlds. They were badly frightened. Those who moved to the mountain top left their wagons at the base of the mountain, all loaded with rocks and tied down. There was no wagon trail to the top; so the people packed the horses with what they needed. It all was silly, but I remember it very well.

It was just a false alarm. We stayed on the top of the mountain for about a month, until my parents were sure there was no flood. As I said, there were few communications—only what the people told one another at the gathering places. All this would have been prevented if we had had radios then. The only source of getting any news was at the trading posts where the people met, or from the man behind the counter—the storekeeper. Times have changed greatly since then.

The Navajos have their own government with headquarters at Window Rock, Arizona. From there, the government extends out to every part of the Reservation. Years ago, before the later administrations, the people had only orators who addressed them at large gathering places, such as squaw dances, Yei-be-chai dances, corral

251

*The "Four-Corners" monument near where Thomas
Clani grew up and has lived. It is the only place in
the nation where four states meet—Arizona, New
Mexico, Colorado and Utah.*

dances and other big "sings." The speakers told the people what they
must do and not do.

At a traditional wedding chosen elders gave long lectures to the
newlyweds. In those days the people did not need a loud speaker
system. The speaker always had a naturally loud voice. There was no
commotion because everyone listened. They respected one another;
even the children were quiet. There were no drunks to cause trouble.

It has not been many years since the Navajo people suffered
from the livestock reduction program. That started when John
Collier was the Indian Commissioner.

The Navajo Tribal Council has 74 councilmen who make our
laws. At the beginning there were only 12 Council delegates. The
general Council meets at Window Rock, but there are chapter houses
in almost all of the chapters, which are political subdivisions. I think
there are 101 chapters now. They are the places where the people
meet and discuss their problems, making recommendations and pro-

posals to the Tribal Council through their elected councilmen. We have Land Board members and Grazing Committee representatives who have heavy responsibilities in working for the people.

The Office of Navajo Economic Opportunity's central office is at Fort Defiance. It has branches in all five agencies of the Reservation, which is divided that way for Bureau of Indian Affairs purposes. The O.N.E.O. operates a variety of programs that are vital to our people. Many Navajos are employed in the tribal administration and government system and also with the O.N.E.O. Thus, the programs provide employment for our people, as well as serving their main purposes. We wonder whether all this would be as it is now if our first great leaders had not made their promise years ago to educate the children.

253

The Anglo people live differently. Most of them prefer to be in the big towns where they have their schools and higher educational institutions. They build their schools according to their population growth. We do not do this. Many of our Navajo children are going to school off the Reservation because the schools on the Reservation are full. We need more schools, but no government seems to build them for us. However, we are working constantly to have better living conditions; and education is important. That is how our children get into the outside world where they can find opportunities and security. At home there is not much opportunity, unless one has a farm and livestock to care for.

I am 74 years old, and I have 10 children. They all received an education. Some have families of their own now, and they have their jobs and homes to look after.

After the livestock reduction, the people were issued grazing permits. The Reservation was divided into so-called districts; and regulations were enforced. One cannot graze his livestock beyond his own district. There is a unit limit to each grazing permit. Livestock immunization and spraying, sheep dipping and an annual livestock count are some of the regulations that are enforced. At the time of stock reduction those who did not have grazing permits and had only a few livestock were promised jobs, and the federal government introduced several work projects on the Reservation. Some Navajos were employed on those projects, but they didn't last long; and many other were recruited as migratory workers and railroad laborers. That was the beginning of wage-earning employment for our people. They had to learn how to earn money and to support their families with it.

254

Thomas Clani, with Mrs. Clani on the left and one of their daughters.

Our population has increased, and we need work projects to reduce the unemployment on the Reservation. The young people who have completed their education need employment. We are aware of, and we are hit hard by, inflation. We know that the cost of living is very high. We cannot look forward to our wool sales and lamb sales anymore because we can't make much profit from them. If we are able to work, we try to find employment. Otherwise, we have to seek other sources of assistance to feed our children.

Again, I will stress education. Our fine community college provides courses for our older children where they can learn good careers. We expect more of our young people to get their higher education there. It is a wonderful opportunity for them. In my young days such an opportunity was unheard of. Only those who possessed money had a chance to get higher education—maybe one out of hundreds. There were no tribal scholarships; so many of us did not even get to high school. We were told the high schools were too full and too far away. Some wanted to continue their education but could not.

The Tribal Council now has a Budget Committee which allocates funds for the young people to proceed with their education. The Education Committee discusses and makes plans and decisions so that our children can have the best educational opportunities possible. We can show our gratitude by encouraging our children to meet the requirements. We appreciate the instructors who have taught our children in the grade and high schools and other institutions because without them many of our boys and girls wouldn't be where they are now. Many have good jobs and nice homes. They take good care of their families because that is among the things they learned in school. As parents, we worked hard to bring them up right. A person always feels that he is obligated and happy to do what he can to help his people.

255

Jones Van Winkle

I AM JONES VAN WINKLE— 61 years old, from Nazlini, Arizona. My clan is the Coyote Pass People *(Mạ'ii deeshgíízhinii)*. It is my mother's family line which originated from the Pueblos—part of the God People clan. My father's clan, Bitter Water *(Todích'íí'nii)* is my paternal tie. The clans are part of the traditions that it is said we live by.

In the fall of 1923 I entered school at Chinle, Arizona, and I attended for eight years. From there I transferred to Fort Wingate in New Mexico.

I will talk about the Navajo teachings of long ago. Today, it seems, there is little training of that type.

As in my own experience, children were taught by menfolk and womenfolk. From the time they began to walk and talk to when they started saying their greetings and on to when they were grown, they listened to their elders' teachings, such as, "This is wrong, do not do it." In the household they were taught that (after being bedded down for the night) when it came early dawn they were to rise and begin their tasks. When a child reached the age of 10, and on to 20 years old, he or she was still a child. Up to about that year they were taught in firm tones, and that was a clasp that held the family together.

The children were taught many things pertaining to taboos. In the old days, before I was born, enemies were expected at all times; and it was not too long ago that the Long Walk was made to Fort Sumner.* This terrible event always was kept in our minds, for it was

---

*The Long Walk and confinement at Fort Sumner–Bosque Redondo or Hwéél-di–in eastern New Mexico extended from 1864 into 1868–Editor's note.

from this experience, as well as from ones before, that the people lived by the strict instructions of the Navajo way.

The teaching of running at early dawn came from the home, especially if one was a young man. In winter he also rolled in the snow or broke the ice of a pond and dived into the water. Another experience had to do with the sweat house. A long run was made; and, after the runner got hot and sweaty, he hurried into the steaming sweathouse. Those things were practiced up until not long ago.

By doing these physical tasks a Navajo became hard and strong. The main reason why he or she experienced them has been expressed this way: "If you are tough and strong you can outrun any enemy. On the other hand, if you are not strong, if you are stupid, or if you sleep past dawn, in the future you will have the feathers of a crow sticking through you. But if you are smart, you will have a brave arrow sticking through you."

257

Advice like that was stressed in the old days.

The persons that one grew up with, like brothers and sisters, were taught in a mature manner—not as in a special way of speaking to a baby or a young relative. Long ago, rules were like this: Someone related to a person, like a sister, was not supposed to put things directly into her hand, even if she said, "Give it here"; instead, it was set down close to her and then she picked it up. The only person who could take things directly from one's hand was the wife.

The relatives on the father's side were embarrassing, because one became somewhat apart from them. Still, greetings were expressed to them, also teasings; and short visits were made, even to the paternal grandparents.

At the longer ceremonial sings a patient was worked on for hours or days; or, it could be just a short ceremony where medicine was taken by mouth. It was once said that when corn pollen was used, it never was put on the head; also one was not supposed to be heated when taking it. Those were the teachings of medicine men— and whatever was not allowed was avoided.

The teachings for a man were stressed because in life he would come across aspects to survive on—like sheep, horses, cattle and other valued possessions, such as money or things that are difficult to come by. If one is fully mature in mind, one is able to make a living with these values. However, one must strive for his goals. It is this which will prevent any poverty. That's why the experience of running and yelling at early dawn is stressed. It is said that yelling will prevent a

258

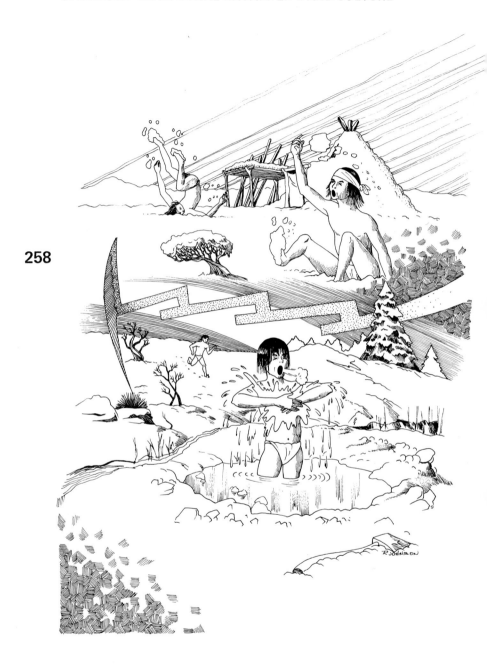

In the winter, boys—and girls—rolled in the snow at dawn, wearing almost no clothes, or they broke the ice of a pond and jumped into the water.

After a long run the men went into the hot sweat house.

person from being speechless in the future. Otherwise, people will make fun of him. The purpose was that, instead of a rough road, his path will be straight. But, today, these things are not taught.

The meaning of the term jealousy also was taught. If one does not crawl in the snow or run at early dawn, right from the doorpath, trouble lies waiting. It may involve prostitution; and it is one thing a person should not live with. It seems like sin is the boss of all things that conquer us. There are happenings like squaw dances, Yei-be-chai ceremonies and other events; and what takes place there can easily bring on jealousy.

Stress used to be made that one was not supposed to pick up that type of attitude. The reason was because, someday, a person would find someone who was precious and would be loved—someone who would not go wrong and whose mind was straight and could make living worthwhile. For that reason we were told, "Get yourself prepared so the two of you can live together. Also, you will be able to rule your children correctly and have right upbringing in the home. So, find someone who will look after your home, your valued possessions, your sacred stones, your livestock."

260

Today, this teaching is overlooked. Instead, boy meets girl, and soon they're living together.

A common preoccupation among the Navajos in former years was looking for a wife. A young man usually was told, "When we start looking for a wife for you, people will know about your background and if it's not good they will say, 'No! The man is not good; we don't want him.' " However, if a young man could master his land, home or whatever—to show goodness—he could be easily accepted; or, as it used to be said, the girl's family would "show appreciation."

These teachings are scarcely mentioned today.

After a person had received all of the teachings, but did not put them to practice, or even pay attention to them, it would be his fault for passing them up—it would be his own thinking that put him in a bad position. This attitude usually led him to meet a prostitute because, once he had met the person, he would cry for her, and his heart would be broken. When this happened he would forget all of his possessions, and, instead, think of the woman. He would be running constantly after her. However, if a man were of a good mind and had a good wife, life would be good, no matter what got in the way. With a strong heart and will, one's wishes would come easy for him.

That is how it is. But, if one doesn't want those good things, he goes to places of gambling or plays the shoe game or other games with his face covered with ashes and his hair bushy with dirt, which is what a wife does not appreciate. The term they used in former years to describe a woman was "the one who observes everything." I know this is true.

Other things were stressed to a son-in-law, too, especially in building a hogan. At the place of his in-laws he had to carry logs on his shoulder while on foot. (The mother-in-law and son-in-law also had a taboo of not seeing each other.) When a hogan was built for the mother-in-law, she carefully put her head in, she looked around, above her and below; then she stepped inside. But, still not certain it was safe, she usually said, "It sure is frightening," while she looked upward. (It is she that one is a son-in-law to. That is why she is not quickly adjusted and why things must be perfect for her—as it was taught long ago.)

There are medicine men who know our many chants. The manner in which they speak to us usually is, "I'm your mother and father." Menfolk should chop wood, build fires or ask questions if they don't understand the medicine men because, somewhere in the future, they might need one. From this, a person can reason that a medicine man, like his mother, always will have bedding for him and always will have food ready; and, like his father, will help him—even if it's from a poor situation—from his toes to the top of his head.

Long ago it was said, "As far as one can shoot an arrow, that much is your land." In plowing, machines were not known; a Navajo cultivated his land by hand, with handmade tools. He received approximately one acre of land after shooting an arrow while lying on his stomach.

In rounding up horses, one was told not to ride them, but to herd them on foot. Also, at early dawn the sheep were taken out to graze, but the Navajo did not eat until it was midday and warm. He could eat again after returning the sheep to the fold.

Sometimes in the past, when a man started raising his own children, if he didn't have food for them, they became hungry and started begging while carrying sacks to different hogans. When his children saw others eat mutton, they would cry and beg for some. At the same time the father would be embarrassed while trying to slap their hands. So, if he was smart and a good worker he would have mutton and food for them at all times. This teaching really was stressed.

262

Many years ago it was said, "As far as an individual Navajo can shoot an arrow while lying on his stomach is the amount of land that he can claim as belonging to him."

The teachings for women were about the same. Each girl was told to run at sunrise so that she would be able to have a husband, one who was good, one who would live a worthy life, one who did things well. Otherwise, if he would just run around, she would be clinging to him and crying. A woman was told, "Here is the corn.

Do some grinding as soon as it is early dawn. Plenty of foods can be prepared from corn. Cook for yourself. Get yourself strong. Learn all household tasks. Learn how to butcher a sheep because—you never know—someday at the place of your in-laws you will be asked to butcher; and, if you don't know how, you will be laughed at by those in-laws. They will be poking each other, laughing because of you."

Another teaching for the woman was that if the young lady took care of herself properly she would be asked for marriage in the future. Grooming of the hair was stressed to keep it nice. Much in choosing a husband pertained to the appearance of the woman. And a saying which described a husband was, "One who is wise and in good physical condition."

Also, in former days, the smell of sheep manure was one of the **263** meanings of life. Today, it's just spray cologne that young people want.

It was in this way that the woman was taught. Preparing food for others was a difficult task for a woman because it took skill to cut up the meat and bones. In the past, mutton sometimes was cut into jerkie because that was part of the diet of long ago. Another source of food for the Navajos used to be plants, like yucca fruit, acorns (a good food if prepared right), boxthorne and berries. All of these plants were food, along with piñon nuts, honey, cooked dry cornmeal and maize. The ways of preparing these plants for food were instructed from generation to generation.

Today we don't eat some of those plants because we don't see them, or we don't know what they are, or we won't bother to gather them. The only food we seem to depend on is the white man's canned stuff.

So, the Navajo way covers the teaching of all things; for instance, like being up early in the mornings to race toward the dawn and learning the uses of white corn, yellow corn and corn pollen. Teachings had the feeling and tone of pleading; and accomplishments were made with good reason because, once a man and a woman started to raise and take care of their own children, they had to be strong and wise in order to do it.

I know of these things myself. The men and women took notice because long ago it was very important to their lives to own livestock, valuable jewelry or buckskin. If a person did not say his prayers there was an expression of sorrow when conversation was

264

In previous generations an older girl learned how to butcher a sheep so that she could do it when necessary, and, if asked to butcher at the home of in-laws, she would not be laughed at.

carried on among the men and womenfolk. A good man should think, "Whatever knowledge I know and have I will pass on to others—my children, my grandchildren or whoever wants to pick it up; and I will not ask for any return. Then they cannot blame me for not teaching them."

If a young man and a young woman listen carefully they will attain understanding and put their lives in the right way. That is one of the best things that can happen—to learn and guide our lives in the right teachings of long ago.

The biggest problem today is that young people don't want to listen.

Entrance to the new community chapter house at Klagetoh, Ariz.

265

Fruit of the yucca plant.

Molly Richardson

IAM 91 YEARS OLD. My clan is the Red Running Into Water People *(Táchii'nii),* born for the Many Goats clan *(Tł'ízí łání),* and I live in the vicinity of Inscription House, Arizona. My story is about the death of Mr. Tádídíní (Mr. Pollen). It took place at the time of the terrible sheep, goat and horse reduction.

I was sitting right in the center back of a hogan when three white men rode up to the doorway. I had been a patient in the Wind-way Chant the night before. My late father was sitting with Mr. Tádídíní on the left side of the hogan; my mother and another lady were on the right side. Leslie May, of the Many Goats clan, had come for a visit that morning; and there were four children in the hogan, too.

One white man—a range rider—came to the doorway, lowered himself to a kneeling position, and said, "Hey, Tádídíní, I know you are here." The white man spoke Navajo fluently.

Mr. Tádídíní replied, "I'm here visiting some of my relatives." He was sitting wrapped in a blanket.

Then the white man said, "We are told that you are sick."

Mr. Tádídíní agreed. The white man walked over to where Mr. Tádídíní was seated. A second white man, who was quite young, now came to the doorway. He blocked the entrance—to stop any of us from running out of the hogan to the nearest neighbor for help. The third white man came inside the hogan, took his coat off and sat down among the family's possessions.

The first man walked over to feel Mr. Pollen's head and shoulders. All of a sudden he forced both of Mr. Tádídíní's arms behind him. Mr. Tádídíní stood up, and the blanket fell to his feet, making

Chapter house at Inscription House community on the Reservation in Arizona.

a struggle very difficult. He had a revolver at his side when the blanket fell, but the gun had its hammer on an empty chamber and was wrapped with a cloth; so it was useless.

267

When Mr. Tádídíní stood up, however, he threw the white man to the ground, and the one guarding the doorway pulled out his own revolver and shot Mr. Tádídíní in the chin. When the range rider got up, Mr. Tádídíní threw him down again, and the door guard shot Mr. Tádídíní another time—in the right side of his chest. He was shot three times before he finally fell.

He stumbled right to the place where I was sitting. In those days the ladies wore big-legged moccasins. My moccasins were covered with blood; so was the sheepskin and the blanket. He had lots of blood coming out from his bullet wounds, and blood poured out of his mouth when he breathed. We had just finished our breakfast when the white men arrived, and the unwashed dishes were still on the floor. Some of them also were splashed with blood. Nothing was taken out of the hogan after the killing.

I could not stand up; so I just had to crawl toward the doorway. The guard wouldn't permit any of us to go out—knowing that if we could get out we would call for help. Mr. May was the only one of us who could speak any English and he talked to the guard. He was the man of the Many Goats clan who had been lying at the left side of the hogan. Then he was allowed to crawl out, and he dragged me with him. Everybody in the hogan was terrified and shocked.

Three men were involved—all white range riders. The one who jumped Mr. Tádídíní was Mr. Peterson, from Kayenta. He spoke the Navajo language very well, and he was able to communicate with the Navajos. They were not part of the police force, but were selected

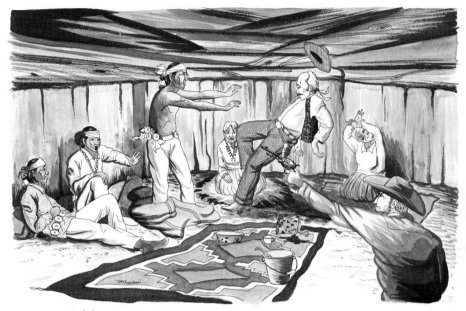

Mr. Tádídíní (Mr. Pollen) got up and knocked the white man to the ground; then the one who was guarding the doorway pulled his revolver and shot Mr. Tádídíní three times.

268 just for this occasion. When we crawled out of the hogan, they started to surround us while putting more bullets in their guns. Mr. Tádídíní was dead. One of the white men turned around to check whether he was breathing.

My father was deaf, and he was the last one out of the hogan. We all left before he did because he had not heard the shots. Most of the other people in the hogan had not really understood all of the tragic events. They were very confused. I seemed to be the only witness who had observed everything.

The men's horses were grazing in the distance, each saddle having a rifle and a revolver. The men continued to guard us very closely for almost an hour after the killing. The sheep got out of the corral, so my sister went to the sheep. She also was being watched closely, and the three men had their fingers on the gun triggers—ready to fire on anybody who tried to escape.

The rider who was guarding us became worried that Mr. Tádídíní's brother, who lived just over the hill, might come at any time. So they finally jumped on their horses and rode away over the hill toward Kaibito and on to Tuba City. Later, the brother of Mr. Tádídíní rode to find the three men, but he was unsuccessful because they were far ahead. People along the way saw the men riding toward Tuba City, but they didn't know of the tragedy at our place.

For a long time Mr. Tádídíní had been hiding out in the Kaibito area because he had refused to send his daughter back to the school in Tuba City after she had run away twice, but he had never come around to our hogan. This husky man was related to us by clan. He had been a policeman. He was a man who could satisfy himself by expressing his feelings.

We knew that someday the matter would come up in court. My father and everybody who was there examined the body closely. Then my father placed a blanket over it. I said, "There are three bullet holes." Some others were not sure of what had happened earlier, so the body was again examined. We found that Mr. Tádídíní **269** had been shot in the chin, in the chest and in the left side of the stomach; my father put the blanket back over the body.

When I first went to Prescott, Arizona, for the hearing we had to ride horses from Kaibito to Fort Defiance and on to Gallup, from where we went in a little old Model-T Ford. The car hauled us to Prescott for the trial. I was one of 10 people taken to the Superior Court in Prescott to testify against the three men involved. The other people were all of the Black Streak Wood clan *(Tsi'naajinii)*. I was the only one who could testify because none of the others seemed to comprehend fully how the killing had happened. Mr. May had been lying in the hogan at the time, but he didn't testify in court because he did not remember all of the facts. We spent 10 days in Prescott, but I was the only one of us who went to court day after day.

The courthouse was very big, and it was crowded with spectators. My interpreter and I were taken there to testify, and I gave a clear picture of the position of the killer, and how Mr. Peterson had held Mr. Tádídíní's arms against his back briefly before the shooting.

One man from our own clan (he was not a witness) raised a statement to the court saying, "I don't approve of my children being fired on; that is why I am here."

The judge told him, "you have no reason to be here."

He replied, "I have a reason to be here. It is not a pleasure for me to come home and find that something terrible has happened. I was out herding the sheep." Finally the court agreed with him because it had been a sad event.

A part of the community of Inscription House,
Ariz., camera facing almost due north.

In the courthouse I was seated with my interpreter. There were
270 three guns in a glass display case in the room. Each time a new
witness took the stand, the attorney would change the position of
the guns. There were many spectators. The man accused of murder
was sitting opposite me, the second range rider (who had grabbed
Mr. Tádídíní) was sitting in front of the spectators and the other man
was seated over toward a corner.

As I said, three revolvers were in the glass display case. I pointed
to each in turn and said, "This is the murder weapon, this useless gun
belonged to Mr. Tádídíní and this gun was not there." When another
witness would take the stand, they would change the positions of the
guns, but I kept saying, "This is the murder weapon." Back at home
when the range rider shot Mr. Tádídíní, I had a close look at his
weapon, and I knew what the gun was like.

After they found the suspect guilty, the court adjourned.

The court asked the brother of Mr. Tádídíní what they should
do with the guilty one. He replied, "He has killed my older brother.
I want the murderer to be executed, and I want to see it."

"The white man who grabbed Mr. Tádídíní should be executed
too," I added.

Outside the courthouse we were sitting under a cottonwood
tree with two lines of policemen guarding us on each side. "Are you

telling the truth—that you want the murderer to be executed?", one policeman asked Mr. Tádídíní's brother.

The brother answered, "Yes, and I want to see it!"

The execution was worse than the murder. It took place far from the courthouse in an area where there was a green lawn. They executed only the man who shot Mr. Tádídíní; not the other range rider.

Afterward, the principal from Tuba City came with a teacher and said, "You people can leave for home in the afternoon. I don't see why you have to stay here. The person who killed Mr. Tádídíní has been executed." He turned around and said to the rest of the people, "This lady won the court case for you. She is not a child."

At that time I had a good memory, but now I am old and some **271** facts escape me. We left that afternoon and went home.

The hogan where this incident took place still can be seen on the road between Inscription House and Kaibito. There were no white people living in the area around us.

I was told by authorities to go to school in the early days, but my mother refused to allow it because I was the only child in the family and was needed to herd the sheep. I have herded all these years until just last year when old age wouldn't permit me to do it anymore. I have taken the sheep to many places for grazing.

The behavior of children at that time was very good. They were taught the arts of living and survival. They also learned to farm, plant, hoe and gather corn and other food. That is how my father took care of things. Nowadays, school children are different, and they seldom are seen working on the farm. We also were taught how to respect the fire for cooking. The only cooking pieces we had were made of pottery, and there were not any of the numerous utensils available now.

We ate a variety of plant seeds, but one food in those days, pigweed, also was the miserable one to gather because it was less than knee high. We had to go around and gather it, and, afterward, it was stored for future use. It is not very available now.

Yes, in many ways life was hard in my youth, but the Navajos lived by their traditional ways and followed their own culture so that we generally were happy and content—close to each other and to Mother Earth.

272

During the trial three revolvers were displayed in a glass case. They would be moved into different positions, and each time I would say, "This is the murder weapon, this useless gun belonged to Mr. Tádídíní and this one was not there."

Lee Kansaswood

MY CLAN IS THE BITTERWATER PEOPLE *(Tódích'ii'nii)*, born for the Red Running Into Water Clan *(Táchii'nii)*.

Before many of the Navajo people were taken to Fort Sumner (Bosque Redondo), over toward the eastern edge of New Mexico, the Navajos had been fighting with other tribes for many years; and there had been a lot of trouble with the Spaniards and Whites in New Mexico. It all added up to the reasons why the Navajos were rounded up and herded for hundreds of miles.

Many of those living in western regions of the Reservation, and some other areas, never went to Fort Sumner. They lived around the San Francisco Peaks and up to or in the Grand Canyon, and other canyons; also on and by Navajo Mountain, as well as along the San Juan River. These things were told to me by my elders.

After being allowed to return to their homeland following the Treaty of 1868, the Navajo people settled down. Among other things, a school was built at Blue Canyon. I do not know how long it lasted there.

In 1902 many people moved from Blue Canyon to Tuba City before or after a school was built there. Some accounts say the Mormons already were there while it was being built. Navajos say they migrated from Utah state and that some settled in Tuba City, while others moved on to Springerville, Snowflake, St. Johns and toward the south in Arizona. I do not know how many stayed in the Tuba City area.

Later, the government bought this land from the Mormons, and Tuba City became an agency. Then the school was built for the Navajos.

Today some Hopis claim the land was given to them by the Mormons, but this is not true. I heard a story from an elderly person who told me that there were two Hopis (man and wife) who left the Oraibi area. The couple started to migrate toward White Pointed Rocks, and when they arrived there they met a Mormon missionary who told them about the beautiful land that was not far from there. He told the couple that the Navajos already were living on the land. The Hopi man and his wife went to that land and made themselves a home.

At the same time, other Hopis were gathering at a place called Moenkopi. First, there were only seven of them. Each was given a piece of land, and, in a few years, many Hopis were living in that region. The elderly people say that the Hopis were not originally around the area and that they migrated from some other place. So, they must not claim that this was their land from the beginning.

The schools had hard times getting the Navajo children to attend. Many parents did not want their children to be away, and the policemen had to go out into the homes and fields to gather young children and take them to school. The children mostly did not like to go. There was no electricity and no real highways in those days. Coal and firewood were the only sources for heat.

There is a story about a man named Mr. Pollen. He lived north of Tuba City up toward Navajo Mountain, in the region of Kaibito and Inscription House. He did not want his daughter to go to school. A superintendent from Tuba City sent three range riders (white men) to Mr. Pollen's place to get his daughter. Mr. Pollen had known that someone might come and take her, but he was not home one morning when the riders arrived at his place. He had gone to the home of Mr. Navajo Mountain that morning. The white men arrived on horseback at this man's place while Mr. Pollen was inside the hogan. One of them went right in, sat by Mr. Pollen and asked what was wrong with him. At the same time, the white man searched to find if the man had any weapon on him and found that he had a pistol in his pocket.

Right then, Mr. Pollen grabbed the white man and threw him against the wall of the hogan. Another white man came inside and saw the fight going on. He pulled his gun and shot Mr. Pollen three times.

The Navajo people living around there reported the incident to Tuba City, Fort Defiance and Window Rock, Arizona. Later, some of them were taken to Prescott, Arizona, to testify at the trial. I do not know what was done about it.

Authorities had a hard time getting the schools started because of the lack of student participation; besides, supplies were short. Almost everything for a school was hard to get in those days.

After World War 1, I went to school in Tuba City. They were offering a military assistance course, and I took it. We had to get up early in the mornings. We had drills and exercises while our hands were about to freeze. They treated us as if we were in the military services; the exercises were tough. Some Hopis attended the classes.

275

"City of Tsegi," Ariz., camera facing from the southwest to the northeast.

While I was at school the students raised their own crops. Also, cows, horses and other farm animals were in the corral. Some were butchered. They had a dairy barn. Most food was produced there, and not much was transported in. Now everything is hauled to the schools.

From 1928 to 1931 some highways were built, and many houses were constructed in Tuba City. Around 1940 to 1950 the school farm at Tuba City had been done away with, and the transporting of goods was begun.

The Tuba City Agency has developed community leaders and better boarding school facilities; and there are public schools, including a junior high school. There also is a Navajo tribal warehouse where people get lumber and home supplies. They have a community center for amusement, as well as tribal welfare offices. Even the jail has been made better and bigger. We have a fine, well educated judge, and more policemen have been hired. The hospital has better facilities, although it is true that the city needs a bigger one. Churches have been built for different religions, too. Long ago, they had one Presbyterian church for the Navajos and one Baptist church for the Hopis.

Today Tuba City is a fairly large community. Some areas of the western region of the Navajo Reservation are becoming crowded. People are moving into Tuba City to get an education for their children and to work in various places like the hospital, courthouse, community center, schools and in the food and clothing stores.

276

The Hopis claimed this was their land in the beginning, and they have argued with the Navajos about it. It never did belong to the Hopi Tribe, however, because, as I recall back about 60 years ago, no Hopis were living there. Navajo elders say that we were living on this land before the Hopis. These old people have died, though.

The Hopis came to the Oraibi region long ago, and they still live in that area. Today, the Hopis claim that Tuba City is part of their homeland, but that is not true. The two tribes are trying their best to settle the dispute, but the government and courts probably are the only ones that can say what must be done.

I have herded sheep in the Tuba City, Page and Bodaway areas; and I never saw any Hopis, except some around Tuba City. If Hopis had been around, we would have known about them by their old home structures or things they would have left behind. I never did see anything like that here, but there are plenty of old Navajo homes and pottery. This shows that Navajos have lived here mostly.

I will now discuss the education I have had. I wanted to go to school; so my parents took me. I was glad at first, but the school was like being in the military service. The students treated me badly sometimes, and the food was not enough to feed everyone.

I learned to speak the white men's language so that I could communicate with them. With the education I received I earned a job with the Bureau of Indian Affairs for 30 years. Now I am getting paid every month from Social Security benefits, and my job, today, is only advising children to go to school. I tell them, "If you become educated, you will have a better way of life." Some uneducated people criticize me about my education. Those critics still have the

When I was a student in Tuba City the school raised and harvested a lot of the food that was needed.

old way of living. The developments of the Anglos are taught to Navajo students. If they learn most of those things they will find it easier to get jobs on the Reservation.

In the past we were raised right with our livestock, but not so many Navajos are doing that today. Education is more important now. Almost everything is taught in English, but the Navajo language also is being taught. If a person does not speak and write in English today, he is behind in most things. There are many job openings for educated Indians; and there are special training centers throughout the Reservation where people can be trained in particular fields. I am willing to help others, and, in turn, I am thankful if they help me. I am pleased by those who get good educations and good jobs. That is the way I feel.

I want to relate another story. When I was taken to school by my parents and got to the dorm, a few white leaders were there. I was introduced to those men. They showed me the big bedroom in the dorm. There were two beds to a bunk. I used to sleep on the ground floor at home, which was the reason why I fell off the bed a few times for several nights, but then I got used to it.

The next day, they took me to a classroom where I began learning the numbers system; then the ABC's—writing animal names and names of articles of clothing; also arithmetic, spelling and reading. I learned music when I was in the fourth grade. Our music teacher was a Sioux Indian, and his name was "Black Hoop." He had all the instruments for us.

The girls learned to play basketball, while the boys had classes in baseball, football, track, wrestling and boxing. We did a lot of boxing during the evenings because they told us there might be another war in the near future. We did much exercising to keep in shape in case we had to fight.

Instructors taught us to raise crops, and to handle horses and cows. They do not teach so much of that in modern schools. In geography class we learned about the lands and their locations. In civics I learned a little about laws, similar to the "law and order" classes of today.

We wore the same type of clothing every day—blue jeans, a blue shirt and black shoes. We'd form a single line going to the dining room. Once there, we prayed before we ate our meal.

There was a carpentry shop, but there weren't enough tools to work with. There were no such things as tractors at the school. We raised a lot of corn which we harvested in the autumn. We used some corn stalks in salads. Hay and grains were stored for the winter. We worked on the ditches in the springtime.

In school if one boy got in a fight with another fellow the administrators would put boxing gloves on us, and we could fight all we wanted. We did much running and wrestling every day. These sports, and others, still exist in modern schools.

278

I left Tuba City and attended Fort Wingate High School in New Mexico for a few years. Then I went to Riverside Indian School in California for a year. That was the Sherman Institute. When I was in the eleventh grade I returned to Fort Wingate, from which I graduated the following year. While I was there, I took a class in carpentry, and the boys learned how to measure and cut lumber. In the past some Navajos had made houses out of logs without cutting the logs into boards. The houses lasted longer that way. Many of our people built their homes of stone. Most of the houses today are made with sawed lumber. They might not last as long as those made of logs.

Some schools today teach students how to take care of livestock. The raising of livestock for those who have grazing permits is legal. Raising livestock without a permit is against the law.

279

In my opinion, I think that people who graduated from school in past years were much more knowledgeable than the graduates of today because they learned more about our land, our culture and the Navajo way of living. I notice that the graduates of today have a better chance of getting jobs, however. I think education is more important for the young generation of today than it used to be because it is very necessary. When education is completed, a young man or woman is in good standing, and many jobs are offered on the Reservation.

So, I say, "Make use of all the knowledge that can be learned in school; it will bring success."

When I attended Fort Wingate I studied carpentry and learned many things.

Howard Bogoutin

MEXICAN WATER, IN ARIZONA, IS MY HOME, and I will tell you what I can remember about traditional Navajo training. It was the custom years ago that parents who wanted to raise their children right gave them long lectures. That was how I was reared. We listened carefully and did what we were told to do. My related elders lectured to us also and helped me to become a man. My father was a good man, and he wanted me to have an education; so he placed me in a mission school at Aneth, Utah, when I was nine years old. I was there only one year. It was a late age for starting to school.

In those days the Navajo people depended much more on their sheep for food and clothing than they do now. They also gathered native food like plant seeds, roots and wild berries. The people did not know much about civilization as it was practiced among the Anglos. They lived in a primitive way. They knew very few white people then. Soon, though, some appeared and built small trading posts from native rock or adobe, but there was not much merchandise—mostly a few food items on the shelves.

When I was a boy my father told me that the sheep were very important, and he taught me how to take good care of them. I took them to the green pasture at the break of day so that they could graze and be fat. In the evening I herded them to the water in a stream. In the late spring we sheared them and sold the wool to the market when the prices were up. Then, in the fall we sold the fat lambs when the market prices were up again. That was how we made our income.

My father also taught me how to work on the farm. We built dry dams, depending only on the rain to fill them, and we used the water to irrigate our farm land. We planted corn, melons, beans and squash.

One day, my father told me I should go back to school. I was a big boy then. I entered the Shiprock Boarding School and stayed for six years. The school officials said I was far over-age; so they put me in a vocational training group. After I had completed my vocational trade school I was hired in the trade that I had learned. Soon I became the foreman of the crew, and then I became the supervisor.

That was how I began to make a living for myself. Even though I did not graduate from high school, I was qualified as a supervisor. Later I married and began to have children. That was when I decided to build a home for my family.

During the time I was working I started buying a few head of sheep on each payday. Soon I had a whole flock. I acquired a large

281

Dry dams were built to catch rain so that we could irrigate our farm and grow things like corn, melons and squash.

piece of land, cleared and cultivated it. With all the work to do at home, I quit my job, and that was how we began our married life.

After I had everything under control at home, I decided to find employment again, but times had changed, and I could not find a job because I lacked a good education. That, however, did not discourage me. I was determined to improve my home and my farm. The sheep had increased to a large number, and my wife and I divided them into four flocks. Three of the herds we gave to our older daughters who were married, and we kept the fourth. My girls take good care of their sheep, just as we have taught them. They all have families and nice homes now. Their husbands support them; so they are completely out of our hands, and we do not worry about them.

282

I have been an independent farmer, raising abundant crops; and I have a good-sized alfalfa field for my horses. At school I had learned to read, write and speak English fluently, which helps me wherever I go. I have been successful, growing my own crops, which we live off of, and I have mutton on my table. I now receive my Social Security benefit, and that helps us.

Just as my parents did, we sell our wool and lambs when the market prices are good. I am glad I learned all these things from my elders. I teach my children all that I have learned, and I encourage them to get more education. I found out myself that only a little education helps some but not much. I use myself as an example when I lecture to my children, and the older ones realize what I am talking about. Success depends upon determination and ambition. We all have our miserable moments, but things that come slowly are for the better. With my dear wife's cooperation we have a good life, comfortable home and a nice family. We are grateful for all this. I have worked hard to accomplish what I have. I have learned to hold no grudge toward anyone. "Love thy neighbor as thyself" is my favorite policy. I get along with everyone. The traders I trade with honor my credit, and I have great respect for them. I pay my bills regularly, and when I need cash they trust me with small loans. I do not cheat or use vulgar expressions. As I said, I have a great interest and pride in my work. I honor and respect my fellow men and my community leaders at Window Rock. They are doing their part to make our government as good as possible.

The small mission school I attended for only a year taught me more than the six years I was at the Shiprock Boarding School. I

Mr. and Mrs. Howard Bogoutin...

...and their residence (looking northwest) in the Mexican Water, Ariz., area.

learned all about being a good Christian—what is wrong and what is good. The little education I had does help wherever I go.

The members of my family always come first in my efforts. I provide them with food, clothing and a happy home. Now I am getting old and my sight is getting poor. I was born in 1890, which makes me 86 years "young" as I record this short life story, but I feel that I am still capable of doing my work around our home and the farm. I often herd the sheep, which are my pride and joy. The people call me No Teeth's Son, but my English name is Howard Bogoutin. The Lord has been good to me, and I live happy and contented. I never have gambled or committed any crime. I live a straight life, so my people have confidence in me. They chose me to be their chapter president, and I served as a reliable leader—one they could depend on. Later, I was elected a Tribal Councilman to represent the chapter. I promoted education as a priority for our area. Now we see that schools have been built for our children, and many improvements and developments have taken place. I believe in a better environment for our people. There is so much that can be done, and the people look up to the leaders to help them.

284

Tillman Hadley

WHEN I WAS BORN, months and years did not mean much to the Navajos; but, from what people found out for me, I was born in 1896 on September 15. That was what they recorded. I once had a Navajo name which I was called by my parents. Later, people began to use an Anglo name, but I don't know how I got the "Tillman." I have been called by that name for many years. About my last name, we had an elderly man for whom my family had great respect and with whom we lived. Laughing Medicine Man was his English name. He was my grandfather. It was from his Navajo name, *Hataałii,* that we were called. At that time the Anglos had difficulty pronouncing Navajo. They would pronounce just part of a word sometimes, or they couldn't say it right; so, they called me Hadley, and that is the way I have been called to this day.

My parents told about my clans. The first one we came from was the Mud Clan *(Hashtł'ishnii);* and, after that, we were called the Big Water People *(Tótsohnii).*

I want to talk about the area called Blue Canyon where there later was a school which I attended, and a trading post was located there. When I was little, menfolk always were the leaders. Laughing Medicine Man was one of them at the time of my school days.

As for the school, when such buildings already had been built at other places, construction finally was started at Blue Canyon. I did not see it being built. I was just a little boy when I was first enrolled. If there was a subject to learn or a reason to go to school, I never did know them. But there were a lot of people around.

Blue Canyon was not a real canyon at that time. The water was down deep in the arroyo. At the time the school was used, there was a crossing, and a lot of cottonwoods grew down in the wash. The place was like that when I was a pupil.

After several weeks of school I became lonesome and wanted to go home. Numerous people lived in the area for about seven miles all around Blue Canyon. That was the region that I came from. Many people planted melons; and I used to go around for some cantaloupes. I would spend at least a day; then, someone always would take me back. The person who did it would have to take along a couple of cantaloupes for me. That was the only way I would return to school.

About a mile from the school was the trading post. It was run by a white man, Mr. Head, with whom our people traded. They gave hides and wool to him in exchange for food and other things, also woven rugs; but, at that time the rugs were made in a poor way. The trader sold those items, and the people got supplies from him. They sometimes blamed one another for buying from the trader. At that time they called him "William."

At the school there was an Anglo who was stocky in build. He had a wife. Mr. Meetham, they called him. In Navajo it was Red Mustache. He was the superintendent, I believe. As for the teachers, there were two women, as I recall. Also there were some Navajo helpers, and there were dormitory aides who were Anglos.

The girls had their own dorm. That same building had a kitchen; and the Anglos had their own boarding rooms, the ones who worked. Just a few feet away the boys had their dorm. The wing of the girls' building that extended toward the west was the kitchen, where the children's meals were prepared. The north section was where the teachers lived. The section from the west and east, as I said before, was the girls' dorm; also, their leaders lived there on the end.

Runaways, both boys and girls, were the worst ones to not obey the rules. We had a jail that was located in the hollow of a rock. It had a pile of dirt around it and wood on top. Pupils were locked in. I never experienced it, though. Others had to stay long enough to cause crying, for crying always could be heard.

The food situation was very poor, but now and then we would have a feast. The Anglos would bring food for us from Flagstaff, which was far away. Wagons were used for transportation, and they moved very slowly. The trader would drive to Flagstaff, and, in a few days, bring his supply of goods back. Altogether, it was a very hard situation; and, in the winter it would snow tremendously.

286

About water, it ran from a rocky place. A hollow had been dug out where the water appeared. It could be lifted from there, and we would bring it back in pails. We washed with that water, and it also was used for cooking. Today there is not water at that spot; it's gone. All that shows is a dark hollow place in the rock.

After some time, the people gradually moved away, and no one used the school area for anything. The building just stood by itself. So an Anglo built a trading post there. We called him Blue Eyes. Richardson was the name, for the whole family. I don't know how many there were. They ran the trading post for I don't know how many years. They built another trading post, where Mr. Richardson died of old age, at the place they call Cameron.

As I said, nobody has lived at Blue Canyon for some time. Many Navajos lived on top of Black Mountain and at other places like Navajo Mountain, Shonto, Oljato and a place which today is called Bodaway. The people had a lot of livestock at that time. Sheep were plentiful. And some people had what amounted to servants—Paiutes whom they acquired, both boys and girls, to herd the sheep.

One year a bad illness struck the people. An Anglo (I think he was a doctor) gave all of us inoculations in our arms. I guess he did have a purpose for doing it. I have a scar on my arm where I received the medication. That happened at Blue Canyon. Others said, "No, we don't want it," because they were frightened. Some sort of flu spread among us.

About that same time the older boys misled us. They told us to smoke. Hard mud was made into pipes; then various dried leaves, and so on, would be used to fill the pipes. We smaller boys didn't like it at first, but that is how we were introduced to smoking.

We packed bows and arrows around. A lot of arrows were carried by the boys. Also sofball was played, where a ball was thrown and a batter had to hit it.

At that time, I guess practically all Navajo men had guns. They looked dangerous. They came around from as far away as Navajo Mountain, wearing war paint, with their saddle stirrups raised high and riding in a warlike fashion. I guess they were having fun. There must have been a lot of horses.

Over in Keams Canyon there was a trading post; and, at that time, there was the one at Blue Canyon. The Mormons lived at Tuba City, and a trading post was there. Also, there was one at By the Water.

287

Some Navajos worked on the railroad in places like Winslow (*Béésh Sinil*) and Flagstaff *(Kin Łání)*. They supported themselves very well because they owned livestock and cornfields back home. The womenfolk had wool, sheepskins and rugs which they sold. Everything was used for self-support. At that time the land was rich and grass was plentiful.

Conditions today are not at all like they were when I was a boy. From my home near an arroyo there used to be a lot of water. After I had gone to school at Blue Canyon, I guess for one or two years, we noticed that our water had seeped into the ground, causing the arroyo to become dry. The water being gone, and with no way to get more, people moved away in different directions. My family went close to an area where there were many acorns. The women and children gathered them. They were stored in sacks, and they were used for food during the winter. They were delicious.

I don't know how people moved to Tuba City at first, for there were no wagon trails. Today, between where the high school is located and the main part of the community is where the school used to be, so they say. I never saw it. Wells were dug into the ground and water was drawn up by hand. There were no pipelines for water. But for the Anglos who lived there, windmills were built right in their front yards. No stream of water flowed by; people's drinking water came from their yards.

In the arroyo that we call Canyon they say that plants grew which the Anglos planted; also hay. At that time there must have been plenty of water because today there are few of those plants. Most of the water today is gone. When I was a boy there were streams which flowed constantly. Here in Tuba City, in the area where the hospital is today, the old hospital had peach and apple trees in abundance around it. In time, the rich land of the Anglos was sold to the government, and the BIA grew plenty of apples. Hauling them was by wagon. The hay was fed to the government's horses.

There was a pond where we used to take baths. The weather sometimes would be very cold. We also would bring back fish after spearing them. The fish, which the Mormons had started in the pond, were big. After we caught them, they were fried for us. Cattle were slaughtered for food because they were provided for us by the government, also sheep. The BIA furnished those things for the school. We had a lot of stew. Horses were pastured in a nearby field. They

288

were used for riding and for pulling wagons. These things all were government property. The field was along the canyon.

The people also grew crops in the fields because there was plenty of water. They harvested the land that they cultivated, but production decreased as the water gradually disappeared. In some places just a very little seeps out now.

Whenever a trip was made to the trading post, we would not return for two days, traveling over the rough trail very slowly with our goods. Maybe one candy bar would be brought back for each person. We sure were happy at those times. When watermelons were brought back we would be especially enthusiastic.

About firewood at Blue Canyon, it came from Black Mesa; but, at Tuba City, there was none. It all had been burned, and it was very hard to come by. Up at Edge of the Rock there was plenty of wood. **289** Mainly it was old dead stuff, but it would be brought in and was used mostly to build fires for the children. At that time steam provided heat in the school dorms. Before that, woodstoves were used; and the food was prepared on them, too. As for lighting at nights, there were only kerosene lamps. There was a barrel for the kerosene.

As for the food, our family had enough to eat, even though it had the looks of being poor. The people could feed themselves fairly well by preparing different kinds of food. Over in Blue Canyon there had been little to eat.

For education, we really could have learned, but I did not notice doing so, mainly because we just played games. Paperwork we did not do because the Navajos did not realize the value of edu-

A part of the northern escarpment of Black Mesa (Mountain) in Arizona, with huge strip-mining equipment showing in the center.

cation for many years. Students who went to school at Blue Canyon mostly have passed on. I believe the average was about 50 during the years that I attended.

A few Hopis were going to school there, and some of the Navajos picked up the Hopi language while with them.

As for reading materials, I don't know what we read; we played much of the time. We could have learned something worthwhile, but, instead, we would steal for boys who were mischievous and who picked on us. We stole things like matches and apples that were stored in the basement. To get the apples we used sticks with nails on the ends to bring them out through the cellar windows. We did not learn that type of thing from the class, but just from one another.

290 I don't recall when the first automobile came into use on the Reservation. An Anglo by the name of Preston had it. It would go by and give off a lot of odor. We would run after it and shout, or we would run beside it as it went back and forth. "Let's give it a name," we said, and *"Chidi"* (automobile) was it. Some dirt roads were available, but mostly there were only horse and wagon trails. Horses were ridden, usually, but a few wagons also were used.

About school again, I attended in Tuba City for a while. I would go to school, and I would be able to be at home, too. At times, I would be absent from school. A young man came around to visit us once. He had been attending school in California, but he had left there and had come to Tuba City. He told us that we were related by clan.

"You are getting out of hand, Nephew," he said. "Mostly, you are getting mischievous. It's not good. Somehow, you should get more education. I was going to school in California. You should go there."

So he advised me. That was around the year 1914. The superintendent's name at my school was Sullivan. He took us down there; and I attended Sherman Indian Institute at Riverside for four years. At that time, young people did not go to school in the same manner that they do today. We were taken care of real carefully, in the fashion of a military school.

A boy or girl really could learn under that method, and I picked up much useful knowledge. After I came back to Tuba City I noticed the environmental differences between the Anglos and the Navajos. Our way of living, our land and our everyday doing just did not look right to me. That's when I thought, "We have not developed to

The first car that was owned by anyone in our part of Arizona (a Mr. Preston) would go by "giving off a lot of odor." We boys would run beside and behind it, yelling and laughing; and we called it "chidi," which means automobile.

where it's easy living for us." The question ran through my mind, "How come in the white man's land all workers really are working? They have everything. The Anglos' living conditions are good. So why is it here that little has been accomplished?"

There was much common sense in having schools for education. I hoped for success and improvement among our people, but things would not move because I was just by myself. No Navajos around Tuba City could speak English when I returned.

I wanted success for us, but things would not seem to go in that direction. That's the reason why I started to stay on the outside. I worked at various jobs, but my mind was only on hope for the future.

At one time I was working for an Anglo man. Once, I led a horse as I rode another back from Cameron. I rode past a house in the evening when working hours were over. As I led the horse by, an Anglo met me. I guess he was the Agency superintendent. He saw me and told me to come over.

"Where are you coming from?" he asked me.

"I live around here," I answered.

"You look different. You don't look like a Navajo," he said. His name was Moore, but I did not know him then.

When I rode my horse, leading another, past a house,
the Agency superintendent who lived there asked me
to stop, and he said, "You look different."

"There's no man like you around here," he said. "By the way,
you speak English, which proves you're not just any man. And
you're young," he added.

"What's your job? Can you work?" he asked.

"I'm a jack-of-all-trades but no master at one," I said. "Anything that is needed I can do. If I'm told to do something, I can do
it," I added.

"You are available. You're just not any man. Come and see me
tomorrow morning," he said.

That I did. I put the horses in the corral at Tohatchi (the water
that smells), which was in the arroyo. I walked home, and the following morning I went to see him.

"Can you work with anything that is run by steam?" he asked
me.

At that time steam was used to work with. No electricity. "Yes,
I can handle it," I told him.

"Well, then, I will now assign you to it," he said. "Watch out
for the little children; there's a furnace, with fire. The heat keeps
the buildings warm; also, this same kind of heat is used for preparing
meals."

I was told this in the springtime. I believe it was 1924. I got the job with the Anglo. I interpreted for him, too. And, in other situations where he had problems, I would help him. I pleased him. The job lasted I guess up to one year.

When the second summer came around I had an uncle who was attending school in Riverside and who returned. He told me, "From the East, there's a white man who is coming this way from Washington, D.C., to talk and to observe how things are run."

He was a government inspector, and he was coming to see my uncle. Then he (my uncle) became ill the day the white man arrived. His back was hurting him so badly that he was in bed. So he advised me, "Nephew, let him come and see you." I asked why the man was coming, and he told me to ask the superintendent. I guess the superintendent I was working for had to be investigated. The next day, while I was taking care of the office, an Anglo walked in. We got to know each other. My uncle, who had hobbled over, told him, "I won't be able to help you because I am ill. Let him—the one sitting over there—assist you. He's like me. You will go around with him."

The Anglo's name was Charles Farris. I left with him. Soon he started questioning me in a joking manner, but I did not know anything about the superintendent's position, except what I had learned doing errands and working for him. I guess that, back in Washington, D.C., someone brought up the point that the superintendent in Tuba City (Moore) was giving land to the Anglos without the consent of the Navajos. That was the reason he came; but, as I said, I did not know anything about it. We left together to a place where my home is now (Cottonwood House), where a group of people lived. There he questioned the people as I interpreted for him.

He said, "This land you are living on, your superintendent has plans for it. Do you know anything about the matter?"

"No, we don't know about it," they answered.

"Some of the land change already has been approved by him, and the papers have been sent in, right here in your area," he explained.

"We don't know about it. Nobody has told us what to do," they said. It was then that I learned the situation was not a good one, especially involving an Anglo who was one's leader (superintendent). But what could be done about it?

Mr. Farris then said, "Over in Zone 'Z' 80 acres of land have been set aside for a mission. Papers were sent out for it."

293

No one knew anything about it. (Today, where the trading post and the laundromat are down this way, there are 80 acres of land which belong to Anglos. Still farther up to where the public school is now an Anglo had moved. He also had an order for 80 acres of land. The water there was plentiful. This same source now is our drinking water for Tuba City.)

Then Mr. Farris returned back East; and, not long afterward, the superintendent left his job. Every once in a while the inspector would return as time went on. We also noticed another Anglo in the area. He had a Navajo partner as his interpreter, a man from Fort Defiance.

After my boss had gone I was left with nothing to do. I guess this second Anglo was to become our new superintendent. He would observe by appearing once in a while. I don't remember how many times he came. Because of the Anglo who had caused all the trouble, and whom I had worked under as interpreter, I guess I also was a suspect. I was not trusted. Still, I provided for myself. The interpreter's name was Harry Shorty. He now has a store at the junction in Fort Defiance. I got to know him pretty well.

The upstairs of the big BIA building was a place where some of the Anglos had their living quarters, and there were extra rooms. The inspector said, "You two may have a room there because it seems like you don't have one."

"That's fine. It will be that way," I said. So we moved together into a small room where there were two beds. There we spent the nights.

He (Harry Shorty) worked for the newly-appointed superintendent. I had an uncle whose name was Big Canyon and who was a police captain in Tuba City. He was a card player (gambler). Over in Cow Springs he lost his revolver in a gambling game. When the superintendent heard about it I was told by him to come to his office. He said, "You will speak to this man about the bad thing he has done." So I said to my uncle in Navajo, "This happened to you. The superintendent is asking questions about it." He replied, "It's true because it's my habit, and I know it is not good." He was told by the superintendent, "You are in this position and you are highly respected. It is a part of the government, and you are working for the government. It is the good way and the right way for you to look after your people; but now bad news is heard about you. That is not right. The government is not pleased with it. Since you caused this to happen, turn in your badge and bring in all your gear."

294

I guess my uncle was thinking about it while sitting there because he said, "All right, my superintendent, all right. I once held the position of a respected person. It's true I made a mistake, but what I'm going to say to you I want you to know. This badge that I held once, the one that is highly respected and the one I am turning in, don't ever give it to an unknown person. The man sitting there, he's my nephew. Give him the opportunity to wear it because he's a man that we know."

It was not long before I was given the honor, and I became a policeman. It was the Anglo who gave me the job. I continued to stay with Harry Shorty. It was the newly-appointed superintendent's idea. I would talk to Harry of anything that was on my mind about our people, my hopes for them and everything. Several months after that he said to me, "Cousin, I was closely questioned by the superintendent to know where you stand, your thinking. 'Get it out of him and report back to me,' the superintendent said. That was a few months ago. So I thought about it and talked to you; then I talked to him again. 'He's the type that is honest and clean,' I advised him. I am going to leave now to go back to Fort Defiance, back to my own homeland."

Being a policeman, I did not have much work to do. It was a man's job, but the punishing of people was not my responsibility. The superintendent told me, however, "We are in need of people like you. Now I will assign the position to you." He added, "This big part of the Navajo Reservation I cannot handle alone, for I have a lot of other work. You will do your job in keeping order in whatever way you want to do it. I will hear about it."

He advised me that way, and I started thinking about it before I paid him a visit.

"How can I travel, for I'm on foot?" I asked him.

"Why don't you first try it out?" he answered. So I saddled a horse that he got for me, and I started working from here.

There are people who are leaders, some who are medicine men who know the good way ceremonies, some who have property like sheep and some who are councilmen. Whenever I went among those people I gathered information and reported to the superintendent. One day he said, "I want you to go to Prescott with an Anglo. We purchased two cars there, which are waiting. You two will bring them back." So the two of us traveled to Prescott and drove the cars back for the Agency's work.

He again said, "In Flagstaff, at Babbitt's garage, I left a car." He had not had an auto at the Agency, even though he worked for the government. Instead, an old car that was patched up with not much more than wheels and a lot of bolts was what I guessed he meant was at Babbitt's. A new one had been purchased for him, and he had left the old car in Flagstaff. When he told me that, I caught a ride into Flagstaff where I inquired about it, but the garage men advised me there was no car parked there. Then one of the workers said, "There's one over there in the far corner; it must be the one."

He was right. It was just plain, with no top; only the windshield was up, with the sides all open.

It was snowing and cold; so I bought a knitted cap and coat, and I started back in that old car. Along the way, the snow stopped and rain began to pour down; and, behind me from the west, the wind was blowing. I was a sight, wet and cold, with mud and water splashing all over me from the dirt road. By evening I arrived in Tuba City, and I drove right up to his house and walked in, mud and all.

"Where did you get the mud?" he asked.

"You are the one who told me to go," I said.

"That's the way it is. Whenever one is sent on an errand, things begin to happen," he replied. "All right, now you can travel around in it."

His was the new car. I started fixing up the old one, and new tires were put on. That's what I drove around in my work.

I started working from Oljato. All the old men were talked to, from Black Mountain toward Dennehotso and up north, between the mountains. These men were to be organized to choose a headman, and this particular person would be able to communicate with the superintendent regarding the people's wishes and plans. He would be something like a Councilman today. The area also included Bodaway and Gray Mountain. At that time Leupp and Keams Canyon were in another district. I reported back to the superintendent, "It's like this now. The people will gather together; they will come to certain meeting places." So he and I traveled around, and the people gathered in great numbers—the older men, that is. He talked to them and said, "That's how it is; this is what I plan to do. It is the best way."

Later, I said to him, "I still learn a lot from these men. They have their own ways of living; they have rules."

He said to me, "There are younger men who have attended school, what about them?" So a returned-student organization was

Keam's Canyon, Ariz., from the southwest to the northeast.

Entrance to the Hopi Indian Agency at Keam's Canyon, Ariz.

297

our next aim. Some of them had come from off-reservation schools, and we started picking them out. They were all for the idea, and plans for the future were made.

Shiprock, Fort Defiance and Leupp were other places where returned-student organizations began to grow. It all was very interesting. They would gather together and talk about conditions, problems and possible solutions. They acted something like the Council members that we have today. All were men.

Also, along about 1922, was the time over in Shiprock when oil was first discovered. It was said that the Navajos would own it, and, because of that situation, the Navajo Tribal Council later came into being. From here the Council representative was the man I talked about before—the one who was an uncle of mine. At that time, once a year, meetings were held starting in July. They did not get together at other times.

The members (and other people) attended the meetings. I was elected vice president. I served, I guess, for two years. Lee Bradley, who passed away not long ago, was the one that I held office with. Many plans were made. In Washington, an administration had been newly elected, and it was said that a lot of work of Indian affairs was going to be erased and a new plan would be made. That was when everything became a mess, and the Navajos were upset about it. The Anglo who was named head of the Bureau of Indian Affairs, as well as whoever was in charge of the Reservation, along with others who were holding office in Washington, made proper documents for it, and the old plan was done away with. That was the word that we received in Tuba City.

There were Anglos from the outside who had observed and studied the Navajo culture and people, and they said, "The changes will not be good for the Navajos."

If a person doesn't know anything about a happening, or if it is pushed through without his or her knowledge, that man or woman naturally is suspicious. So, the change occurred in Washington, and there were many complaints about the poor understanding of Indians in general and of Navajos in particular.

Tom Ration

I AM FROM THE CROWNPOINT, NEW MEXICO, AREA of the Reservation, and I have lived here for most of my life. I was born in 1901 at Smith Lake, N.M., just north of the Hosta Buttes. My clan is the Towering House People *(Kinyaa'áa nii)* on my mother's side, and I was born for the Water Flows Together People clan *(Tó'aheedliinii)* on my father's side.

The Towering House clan came from near a natural feature called Towering House. My parents told me I was born not far from that place, just south of it. Long ago it was traditional custom to return to one's birthplace now and then and roll in the earth there. Today, though, almost no one practices that because many babies are born in hospitals, making it impossible. Imagine a person rolling around in the obstetrical ward! They would think that he was crazy.

My mother married my father in Tohatchi, N.M., where he had lived. My father's name was Water Flows Together With Eye Glasses. When I was four years old my parents and I often went to visit my aunt at Willow Extended Red near Tohatchi. Her husband's name was Hard Ground Man. She was my father's sister. I remember the large irrigated farmlands at Willow Extended Red because there was plenty of water there; and the people raised abundant crops.

We lived at Willow Extended Red for quite a while. At that time, Smith Lake was on public land. Navajos migrated freely in any direction they chose. Families made temporary shelters wherever they found good grazing areas which had water for their sheep.

Looking back to the first Navajo government, it is amazing to see how we have progressed; and we can give the credit to our Navajo leaders who made it possible. I remember when there were no dis-

299

trict lines in our area. It was all open range, and we made our settlements wherever we chose. We could live in one place a short time and then move to another area with our livestock. Now we have boundaries and permanent home sites. We have grazing regulations by which we must abide. In the good old days no one called us trespassers. It was anybody's land.

Suddenly, however, early in this century lines were drawn and enforced on the New Mexico public lands. It was called the checkerboard area because some land belonged to white ranchers, some to the Navajo Tribe and some still was public land. Each Navajo land user had a permit. Those permits were documents signed by Woodrow Wilson, the President of the United States. All the natural resources found on a particular piece of land were claimed by the one who had the permit for that piece of land. No one could take it away. All trespassers who violated the law could be prosecuted. As a result, we have had many disputes about the land we live on in the checkerboard area, among ourselves and with the Anglos, also with those who live within the true Reservation.

300

There were times, in those days, when a Navajo sheep grower had two or three large herds of sheep. In the open country, we could see sheep grazing on a mile-wide area. That was something really beautiful, and I wish we could see something like it again.

Those days are gone, however. As I have said, it was once entirely public land and things were different.

The sheep price was low. A single animal was worth $2.50, and a horse could be bought for only $9. Today, a good quarter horse costs more than $1,000 and we have to pay $30 to $40 for one sheep. If the price had been that high long ago just think how wealthy sheep raisers would have been. In my thinking, I believe the prices are higher because people have more money to spend now than they did long ago. The price of land was about $1 an acre. Now that acre sometimes is $1,000. Once an Anglo man named Blue Eyes bought a huge piece of land near Crownpoint for that low price. He could have afforded to buy more, but he was stopped. Another rich Anglo named McGaffy purchased the whole timber range on Zuni Mountain at a very low price.

About our food in those days, at Tohatchi, where we lived, the people had large cornfields. In the fall, they had "husking bees" where many gathered to help one another. Piles of corn lay in the fields. The men, with oak clubs or poles would thrash the corn be-

*Tohatchi Mountain in the Chuska range in
New Mexico, facing toward the northwest.*

tween the folds of army tarpaulins to remove the kernels from the cobs.

Food usually was scarce; so the women went out to gather plant seeds, roots, berries and fruits of the yucca and cactus. They prepared these foods for immediate needs, and some were stored for winter use. Among the native foods were gamot, jellied rolled yucca fruit, pit steam-cooked fresh corn, ground steamed dried corn, dodder plant, grass seeds and a beverage—mormon tea.

A family had to take care of its cornfield so that a good crop would be produced. Weeding was very important, and it was a hard task hoeing in the hot sun. When there was a piñon nut crop anywhere the people went there to pick the small nuts. They are very good, especially after they have been roasted. The women also would grind the nuts and make piñon nut spread. It was a very rich food. Grass seeds were ground into flour and made into delicious cakes. Mutton with creamed gamot also was very good. I have mentioned corn foods which we loved and which we don't see so often on the table today. We ate all these native foods, which was another reason why we have stayed so strong. Good wholesome food gave us energy and prolonged our lives. There were no artificial flavors nor chemical elements added to those foods; and, since such things have been used so much, people have begun to have more ulcers, appendicitis, diabetes, cancer and other sicknesses.

Our great-great-grandfathers and grandmothers lived on those foods alone. They gathered gamot and parched it in hot ashes. Then it was stored for winter use. It was very good with mutton stew. Blue corn patties dunked in mutton stew were delicious, too. What a dish! Later, when the Navajos began to produce more sheep and horses, they had more mutton to eat, and the women had more wool to work with for making clothing and weaving rugs. That was when the Navajo economy began to improve and living conditions changed for the better.

Talking about our herds, in 1911 or '12 sheep dipping was first introduced on the Reservation. Government officials explained to us that it was good for the animals, and at school we were taught how to dip them.

302

The Navajos still eat the corn which they love, but not as frequently. They usually plant it on dry farmlands, depending only on the rain to provide them with their crops. An Anglo farmer fertilizes the soil before he starts planting to make it rich for abundant crops. The seedlings are treated like potatoes, which makes the plants grow larger and produce more ears of corn. Many Anglo farms are irrigated, as is some Navajo land. Anglos also have many mechanically-operated implements; so some have miles and miles of farmland.

Well drilling operations began on Navajo lands fairly recently. Because of that, some of us now have good drinking water. Long ago we depended on the rain. We got water from where the rain collected—in water holes found on large rock surfaces, from the old ponds, natural springs and small streams. No one heard about sanitation then. These days, the wells in operation are covered and some are treated. However, take a good look at me. I drank water from the ponds with the sheep and horses, and doing it never has harmed me.

Not too many years ago, before the Navajo Tribe began to drill water wells on the Reservation, the Navajo sheep raisers and cattle raisers suffered much loss at times because there was no water available for their stock. So the government introduced a work project. It was called the Soil Conservation Project. Officials, with Navajo labor, built many dry dams and depended on the rain to fill them. Some were successful, and these supplied water for stock and for households. As I said, sanitation was unheard of. Navajos drank what water they could find and it did not seem to harm them. Officials would say now that the water was unclean or filthy. An old pond where the dogs and other animals drank and took dips was our water hole. However, it was a traditional custom to make the sign X by the water hole before we filled our water bags or containers to make sure the water was safe to drink. We practiced the custom whenever we fetched drinking water. Today, Public Health Service people go among the Navajos giving them immunizations of all kinds to prevent sickness. They also tell us we cannot drink water from old ponds or open wells. The tribal water department is busy drilling wells for the people where water is greatly needed. We have windmills in many areas where we can get good drinking water for ourselves and for our stock. Some places are fortunate, with artesian wells where the people have running water installed in their homes through Public Health assistance. For that we are very grateful. Our tribal leaders are concerned about the people; so they want to help them. We have many programs and enterprises on the Reservation where our people can get assistance and employment.

303

In the years 1909 through 1913 the people in the Crownpoint area began to be given land-use plots in New Mexico. It took four years to establish a family on its own land for use. As I explained before, a large section of New Mexico became known as the "checkerboard" area. However, my family did not get a land plot because we had not stayed in New Mexico all the time. We had moved back and forth from Arizona to Tohatchi.

My father had worked at Fort Defiance, Arizona, where the construction of stone buildings was going on. He was a good stone mason.

At that time, a brawny, tall white man was superintendent of the Fort Defiance Boarding School. He always wore a black hat, as I remember him. When my father began to work there I entered the school, and I stayed until my father was laid off. The work he had been doing was completed. The following year, 1909-1910, I went to school in Tohatchi.

My father then began to haul lumber on a wagon for a lumber company to Fort Defiance, Tohatchi and other places. His helpers were Mose Yazhi, Mose Tsoh, a man called Prairie Dog Fat and Ban Di Do. They had a freight wagon with a four-horse team. The lumber was brought into Gallup by train and was distributed by the freight wagon. Not much later, my father bought a nice new wagon which we were very proud of.

The Catholic Church at Naschitti, N. M.

304   I helped my father with the freight many times, even in bad weather. It was too cold to just sit and drive; so we walked briskly along the side of the wagon to keep warm. Such work was part of our way of life.

In those days there were few wagons. The common form of transportation was horseback. We didn't use regular saddles, but we had crude home-made ones which belonged to whoever made them or got them by trade. There were several hitching posts in front of each store where the people could tie their horses while they shopped or visited. A few years later, more wagons appeared. There were no automobiles on the Reservation at the time—not that I saw, anyway. Some white men came in ox-pulled wagon trains with their own supplies.

About our ways of life, Navajo children are very precious to their parents, and we want the best for them. I have the same feeling toward all young people, however, no matter who they are. I do not want them to destroy themselves. Life is too short to be taken for granted, or misused, especially while people are young. They have so much to live for.

When I was a boy there was no such thing as an idle day, partly because my father and mother had a large flock of sheep. Times were hard; so we all did our share of the work around our home. I brought in the horses BEFORE SUNRISE; after that, I herded sheep all day. I carried a tortilla, with a piece of mutton folded in it, for a snack. At sundown, after the sheep had been put into the fold, my father made me wrestle with a tree to develop strong muscles. He would say, "Train yourself to be ready for any sudden attack by a bully." A strongly developed body was very important, and that was why we yelled while we raced. We took snow baths in the winter, and we did strenuous exercises very early every morning. Those things helped us have strong lungs, good voices and clear, sound minds. I ran—fast—each morning until I was over 20 years old. And, even now, when I take a notion to have a snow bath, I still do it. When younger, I was sort of an athletic person. I liked to do gymnastics, and sometimes I acted like a Navajo Tarzan swinging on the trees. Anyone can see what I am like at 75 years of age. I still have strong resistance to illness, and I see well. Some men I know who are much younger than I are stooped, and their hair is much whiter than mine. I have a cousin, eight years younger, whose hair is pure white, and he looks aged. Many people have asked how I keep looking so young. I reply, "My early exercises account for it."

305

A person doesn't see many tall, brawnily-built men and women these days—as Navajos often were a generation or more ago. Now, men and women often are short and fat or large-bellied. They are lazy, and they have more to eat. The people of long ago worked hard, with less food; and they died of old age if they were not killed in battle or otherwise. They were slim and tall, and I believe they were like that because of the kind of food they ate and the exercise they got. Some died from sickness and other causes, but that number was not too high. As I said, that was the way I grew up, and it is why I kept my health so long.

As a student, I was bright, and I learned fast. I now realize that knowing how to read, write and speak English has helped me a lot. I also had the traditional Navajo education at home.

During the warm weather, my father made me rise at dawn to bring in the horses and to run races or wrestle with a tree stump,

The elementary school at Naschitti, N. M.

making it fall over. That was hard exercise, especially if it was a pretty good-sized stump. Almost all the elders made their children do those exercises for their own good.

Our clothes were not very fancy. My mother saved all the empty flour sacks and made crude-looking shirts and pants from them. No one could afford luxuries. The trading post didn't have many such items on its shelves, anyway. It was not like today's supermarkets and clothing stores. Now, one often sees tiny babies bundled up beautifully. It makes me wish I were just now born.

Anyway, our wardrobes consisted of flour-sack trousers and blouses. Each had huge printed flowers, or a bird or a bunch of wheat as a design, and we were proud of those clothes. Probably there would turn out to be a bird on the side or seat of our trousers, or a flower or a sheaf of wheat on the back of a shirt. All these were hand-sewn, of course.

The girls also used to have the old-time regular Navajo education at home. At an early age they were taught how to work with raw wool. A little girl would sit by her mother and pluck on the wool, making it fluffy, and she would try to remove dirt particles before her mother carded it. A few years later she would be doing the carding and spinning. She would dye the wool in her selected colors, and she would prepare her loom. Her grandmother might have bequeathed tools to her, or she might have new ones made by her father. She would begin to weave first by helping her mother, and soon she would have her own rug to make.

The girls also were taught to prepare native foods on the open fireplace. The elders preferred them. Commercial foods seldom were seen. Native things were more nutritious, I think, and the eater would not get hungry for some time. A girl learned to prepare various kinds of cornbread, either with dried corn or fresh corn. She ground the corn and prepared mush, gruel, dumplings and cakes.

Her daily chores began at dawn, when she started to help her mother with the morning meal and cleaning the hogan. She also ran races, like the boys, and was made to take snow baths.

I got my first paid job when my father was a foreman on the railroad construction crew near Thoreau, New Mexico. The Navajos worked as laborers. There were no machine-operated shovels or tractors; the men worked hard with picks, hand shovels and other tools. There were earth scoops pulled by big horses which put the dirt in a bank for the tracks. I was hired as a water boy. I must have been nine or 10 years old then. I carried drinking water to all of the crew. My salary was 50 cents a day. The laborer's salary was $1.50 a day. That was a very low rate compared to the minimum wage scale today. One would say, "That's peanuts," if one were paid only that much now. Of course, the cost of living is much higher. I suppose that is because people make more money now, as figures go, and they are expected to pay a lot more for everything. In those days living was cheap; so it all comes out to about the same thing.

Most trading posts were very isolated, and it took two or three days to get supplies and return home. Today, we travel faster to get to various markets, and there is much more to be bought. There are meats of all kinds, fruits, breads, candies, assorted clothes, tools and many, many more things—and it is nice if a family has funds to buy them.

307

When I began to earn that first money it was hard work. Today, most people earn much more than that per hour, and many still are not satisfied. I used to feel great when I got 50 cents, and I kept on working to get more. It went a long way. I remember when a five-pound bag of sugar was only 10 cents, and a 25-pound sack of flour was only 25 cents. Cotton material (calico) was 10 cents a yard. But usually those things were scarce. When a supply came to the trading post it did not last long.

Going back to my younger years, I remember that there was a government boarding school at Tohatchi, and I had a first cousin (my father's nephew) who went to school there. His name was Rex Becenti. One day Rex carried me on his back to school and had me enrolled. I was still a small boy, and he did it on his own without permission from my parents.

After my father found out about me, he decided not to do anything to change what had happened. My parents thought seriously about the whole situation, and decided that it was best for me to get an education—especially since I already was enrolled.

My cousin and I were allowed to go home on holidays and certain weekends. We walked because it was not too far. There were no buses to ride, anyway. When we compare those days with the present, school children now are very fortunate to have buses for their transportation. They should appreciate all this and take advantage of the opportunity to learn and be educated. That has been my opinion for a long time. When I went to school we did not have the facilities that go with modern classrooms. We struggled along with

When I still was a young boy my cousin,
Rex Becenti, carried me on his back several
miles to school and enrolled me.

the little that was offered us. Yet, I have no regrets. I am glad to have learned how to read, write and speak English fairly well. I have learned to utilize what I was taught and to support my family.

Some of us never had eaten white man's food until we entered school. Meals were strange and what was served tasted peculiar, but we learned to like it. Our only complaint was that we hardly ever had enough to eat. Sometimes we went to bed very hungry.

I attended Tohatchi Boarding School for a few more years. Then my parents decided to move back to Smith Lake, but I stayed at the school until vacation, when my father came for me. At that time the Crownpoint school was being planned, and construction began later.

The first superintendent, appointed before the school was started, was a short white man named F. S. Stalker. He was a good man and understood the problems of the Navajo people. When I first saw him he was on horseback. Mr. Stalker and another white man, a Mr. Goodnight, were always riding horses together. They were looking for a good site to build the school. When the location finally was decided, seven white tents were pitched at the new location. My father said, "Son, there is going to be a new school nearer to our home. We are going to enroll you there." I was the youngest of my family at home.

One of my classmates at Crownpoint was Jacob C. Morgan, who was to become Tribal Chairman years later. He lived at Dalton Pass. Another schoolmate was Haskie Wood. In Navajo they called him "Whirling Scholar." He spoke good English and was an interpreter for "Little Superintendent" (Mr. Stalker). They traveled together in a black buggy. Those two boys had been in school ahead of me, but when I entered I was placed in their class. Soon J. C. Morgan and some other students were transferred to Carlisle Indian School in the East, somewhere in the state of Pennsylvania. I was not one of the selected students. I remained at Crownpoint for only four years, during which I was promoted to the next grade every year, from primary through the fifth. When I entered the sixth grade I was transferred to the Santa Fe Indian School. That was in 1912.

During that time there was an Army post at Fort Wingate, N.M. It was the last year the Army was stationed there. I had an older relative named Jeff King who had been a scout for the post.

We are told that Navajo life is different from that of other tribes, which may be so. But there are many people who live in ways similar to ours. That goes for different nationalities, too. Of course, today, many prefer to follow the Anglo way of life, and their living conditions have much improved. However, building a hogan for a Navajo family may be a problem. The members have to want to live in it, and we cannot make them like it. Some prefer hogans, though. We are moving with modern progress, but there are some Navajos who still do not like to sleep on a bed or eat canned food. We also have some good and wise elders among us who share their wisdom with the young people. Our people still depend to some extent on their sheep as a source of food and income. For some families caring for their sheep comes first in priorities. Many of them also keep their Blessing Way songs for the sheep and horses, as well as soft goods and hard goods songs. When they are away from home some still chant their traveling songs and the sacred mountain songs. These songs and prayers are part of their everyday life. Blessings are fulfilled for them through these chants when they are sung in reverence.

310

There was a place called Beautiful Mountain, also in New Mexico, where some Navajos rebelled against sending their children to school. Compulsory education was being enforced by the government, and government officials sent a troop of cavalry to apprehend the rebellious Navajos who had retreated to the top of Beautiful Mountain. A person sometimes thinks back and remembers such incidents and wonders about them. That is the way I am.

In 1913, I was moved to the Albuquerque Indian School. In those days there were no high school grades. Education for Indians went only through the eighth grade. While at the Albuquerque school I heard of only two schools in the same area. There was the Manual Public School where most of the Chicano students went, and another public school where there were mostly Anglos.

I attended the Albuquerque Indian School for two years. When I had completed the eighth grade I was told that I had graduated and was on my own; so I went home. World War I had broken out by that time, in 1914.

At the boarding school we had had plenty of exercise. We played baseball, football and basketball, all of which required lots of energy and developed strong bodies. I now advise young people to get involved in such activities because they will help keep them from being lazy.

The Teec Nos Pos trading post in Arizona.

I also had some vocational training in carpentry work. I learned **311** how to use measurements and how to estimate the amount of lumber needed to build certain sizes of houses. We used our training to build better homes for our families in which they now are living. You don't see many new round-type hogans anymore, although some Navajos still live in them. Round hogans are built now mostly for ceremonial purposes.

About Anglo and Navajo education, I feel that both are essential and are to be studied side by side. Our children should learn both cultures. We value the teachings that our great-grandfathers taught us from generation to generation, and we must not forget them. Men of wisdom have said, "If one knows the legends he will be blessed with goodness." That describes me.

Educational progress has moved forward tremendously. The Navajos now have a college close to the center of the Navajo Nation. We have many high schools on the Reservation; and the schools have buses to transport the children to and from their homes. What more could we ask for?

Long before my time, people traveled on foot. After that, horses became their main transportation. Today, one hardly ever sees anybody running on foot and not many on horseback. They ride in cars and trucks and get to their destinations quickly.

That is why I say that I wish I were a boy again. It is wonderful to know how to speak, write and read English—even if not real well. With that knowledge, wherever a Navajo goes he has an advantage and confidence and a sense of direction. However, to not know English can leave a person ignorant and helplessly alone in strange places. Many Navajos have had that experience.

So, education is a priority. It provides all kinds of opportunities for us. Thinking back, I know that I did wrong when I ran away once from the Crownpoint Boarding School. I do not know why I did that foolish thing. Maybe I was bored or hungry. Navajo children today cannot complain, however. The schools provide all kinds of activities, and our children are well occupied in their spare time. There are few dull moments. I feel that there is nothing to stop us now, so we should move forward into the world of opportunities. A person's future depends on education; so I tell young people not to be dropouts.

In our days, there were hardly any extra activities. Young people laugh at us when we say we went to school. Maybe we don't look as though we know anything. They laugh at their elders, saying, "They are stupid or dumb." But our wise elders have pride, dignity and self-respect, which is more than some younger people have. That is why one never should laugh at another person, old or young. Everyone first should take a good look at himself. That is all part of Navajo traditional education.

When the railroad was being built many Navajos worked as laborers on it. They were in great demand, and they came from faraway places like Black Mountain and other points. Some worked at the lumber mill, too. My father was a foreman for the timber cutters in the forest, and I helped him. The locomotive was small, with five or six freight cars. Logs were put on the train and taken to the mill for processing, and then the lumber was returned for distribution to various locations where houses or new schools were under construction.

Years back, when I was young, there was a railroad station at Thoreau, N.M. The tracks went to the east. There was once a small sawmill on Zuni Mountain which later became the large McGaffy mill. The Navajos called it by different names such as Speckled Iron, Bear House and First Storage Bin. A very wealthy Anglo man named McGaffy owned the mill. He bought the whole timberland of the Zuni Mountain, and many Navajos worked in the forest and at the mill.

In 1919 the first railroad was built to the McGaffy mill. The lumber was shipped from the mill to various railroad stations and then delivered to farther points by wagon freight where government schools and other buildings were being constructed.

A Mexican man named Little Prairie Dog was the manager of a small store which was connected to the railroad station. He lived at

San Mateo, N.M., and he was a well-to-do man with some livestock and a large ranch. He had three partners who were co-owners of his business. When the Navajos drowned out the fat prairie dogs they gave him all the little ones. He had quite a bunch which he raised as pets. So the Navajos gave him the name Little Prairie Dog, which also became the name of the place. There was no dam then at what is now Bluewater Lake. The water flowed freely all the time, and there were large farmlands along the river. The people filled their own irrigation ditches from the stream. Nearby was a crusher pit where rocks were crushed for the railroad. Some Navajos were employed at that place. One who worked there for some time got the name Rock Crusher Man. Given names were decided upon by how the person looked, what he had, what he did, what he said, where he lived, etc. Those, then, became their names and also their children's names. Some were names like Silversmith and His Son, the last part pronounced in English as Begaye.

313

I was a young man then, and my father worked at the McGaffy mill. He was a foreman for the lumberjacks of the cutting crew. They used large mules to drag logs to the mill where they were processed into lumber. At that time we lived at Thoreau, and I remember how I used to hitch rides in the empty freight cars to McGaffy to be with my father. At that time there were only four buildings at Thoreau.

Today, the Navajo tribe has its own huge sawmill at Navajo, N.M. There is a shipping station where the processed lumber is sold and shipped. Previously, an old sawmill had been used. It is plain that the Navajos in the lumber business all are doing their share of work. As you can see, our people have made a lot of progress.

The Crownpoint school was just beginning to grow. The roads were bad and sometimes too rugged to travel on. There was only one Santa Fe railroad track from Albuquerque to California. The locomotive was small with a tall smokestack. It would come through toward the east. Then, many days later, it would come back on its way to the West Coast. I remember how the Navajos gathered at the tiny railroad station to watch it at what is now Manuelito, N.M. It was described as "Fire That Goes on Wheels," or "Iron That Runs." They knew about when the train would stop there, and they would come to see it. The locomotive was beautiful and something to admire.

Today, Gallup is amazing. It is like the sparks that appear when someone hits a fire with a poker. You can see lights everywhere at night. When I first saw that town there were less than 30 buildings. I remember a small grocery store like a trading post where there now stands a big food supermarket. The storekeeper was an Anglo whom the Navajos called "Sheep Pelt." (I do not recall his real name.)

Now, about our history and legends: Navajo elders are asked about the origin of the hogan—how it was made, and why the door always faces the east. These questions seldom are answered correctly, and I briefly will tell you why. It may be that some Navajos are afraid to give out such confidential information. They value its holiness.

Long ago, at the emergence place, it was said that Talking God performed a "No Sleep" ceremony, or vigil. At that "sing" the people could not find anyone to do the bathing of patients. Talking God gathered sand from where the ground was black, blue, red and white. He made a picture in a round, pan-like shape, with the colored sand used to design it. It became the ceremonial basket. The finishing outlet was arranged toward the east. It was very beautiful. Later, again at Huerfano Mountain (the emergence spot), the first Blessing Way was held at a place called Mating of the Corn. Here, again, the question was asked about who was to do the bathing, how and in what way it should be done. Talking God was told to go exactly to the emergence area, to the hogan there, and get what he had hidden in the far side of the hogan. He ran and brought it back. It was copied and the design has been kept. Today the ceremonial basket, with that design, is used for ceremonial baths. It was granted to the people for use in the Blessing Way "sings." Its outlet faces the east. Thus, the doorway of the hogan faces the east, too. We must remember, also, that all good things enter with the dawn from the east.

Talking God and his follower, Hogan God or Calling God, were People of the Dawn. It was said that they came at the break of day with valued possessions. That is why we were told to rise with the dawn to meet these gods so that they could present us with worthy goods. Our parents would say to us, "Wake up. What are you sleeping for? Take the ashes out. Clean around outside. We do not want trash around the hogan." It was said and done so that the Dawn People would not see any trash. They would know they were welcomed at our place and would say, "There is no wealth here. Let's go in and give them some." (Trash meant there was wealth.) Where a place was dirty and trashy they would ignore it and say, "Too much wealth here. Let's go to another place." The lesson is that a person was expected to keep clean and be an "early bird to catch the worm."

Navajos would gather at the railroad station in Manuelito, N. M., to see the train pull in. They called it "Fire That Goes on Wheels," or "Iron That Runs."

Also, the people used to offer their thanks at dawn by sprinkling cornmeal toward the east to thank the Good Spirit for the night's rest and to greet another pleasant day. The men offered white cornmeal at dawn and in the evening. The women offered yellow cornmeal each time. At noon corn pollen was offered to the sun because the sun preferred pollen. The offerings were made for good health and prosperity.

About the hogans, long ago there were two ceremonial types. One was a "dugout" hogan and the other was the round hogan. The hogan was made round in the way Talking God made the round basket. The main beam logs were placed with their growing ends clockwise to the east; the next one to the south, clockwise; the west, clockwise, and the north the same. During the blessing of a new hogan white cornmeal was anointed on all main beams clockwise— east, south, west and north.

Our history begins with the underworlds, where the dark world was known as the first world; the second was the blue world; next was the yellow third world, and the fourth was the white world that sparkled. Each level had its prayer sticks painted the appropriate color. The last (the sparkled or crystal world) is where we live now.

Prayer sticks were granted to us by the Holy People who inhabited the world then. They were for us to use.

All the legendary stories have their significance, and it is wonderful to be able to understand them. I know that many Navajos do not have the correct idea about them because they had not heard the stories before. I always have wished that someday I could have a chance to tell my stories to big groups of young people. Now I have the opportunity—even to have the stories printed; and it makes me very happy, but I regret that the stories are not complete. An elder who tells stories usually prepares himself for at least two or three days and nights to tell one complete story. That is about how long it takes to tell whole legends in song. For instance, the story of One-Who-Wins-You would take that length of time from its beginning to the conclusion. Telling about the Cliff Dwellers or the Ancient Ones takes a lot of time, also. Another reason why I shorten my stories is because they are valuable to me, and the payment I receive for telling them barely covers the value. If someone pays the real price for a complete story, then I can say I will tell it with all the usually withheld information included. There are accounts of various kinds about the ancient ruins, like Pueblo Bonito or Pintado, Mesa Verde and Canyon de Chelly. Some stories go 'way back to California and the ocean, even to a small mountainous island, where One-Who-Wins-You was born.

Now I will tell you a real story, briefly. The location was Chaco Canyon. There was this man named One-Who-Wins-You. He was like a wizard with all gambling games. He won everything from his opponents. I do not know what he did to have such remarkable luck. Maybe it was made possible by mere instinct. He was born as a twin, but no one has told us exactly who he really was. As for myself, I think he might have been an ancient Anglo of some kind. I judge it could be because of what he said one time. The people from whom he has won practically were his slaves. They all worked very hard. They carried limestone on their backs from a rock quarry to Chaco Canyon. There, the rocks were masoned into blocks to make stone houses which had many rooms, of which we now can see only the ruins. Today, many archaeologists dig in our ruins for ancient relics. Their findings tell us that people lived there ages ago. But their research still does not really tell who the Ancient Ones were. One-Who-Wins-You lived above the Canyon. Below his home was where the slaves built the houses. The people who did the building were called the Cliff Dwellers. (There is a lot of detail to the story, but I will give only the main points.) Someone dreamed that the wizard would be a loser not too far in the future. He had a brother who was his identical twin. The only way to tell them apart was that his brother was an honest man. He lived at Bird Knoll. The people all said, "Let his own twin be his next opponent. That will change his luck, you will see." It is said that twins are extraordinary beings. In this case I will tell you the part where his brother personally encountered him.

In those days the Holy People communicated closer with each other and knew more of what was happening. Who were the Cliff Dwellers? That I do not know. However, the legend I am now telling happened during the time when all the people, no matter what descent they were, mixed themselves in sex relationships. It was told that these mixed tribes inhabited Chaco Canyon, a place used as a sort of retreat. From the activities that occurred there, new tribes were added and other races were born. But, as I said, One-Who-Wins-You might have been an Anglo man, or at least someone who was different. It was told that a real brother could win from his own brother only after having had sex relations with his sister-in-law. That was what happened when the gambling wizard's brother came to his home. The visiting brother was advised by the people not to greet his wizard brother as "My dear brother." He was not supposed to shake his hand, either. The only greeting expression was to be, "My opponent," and then to immediately sing a song from the Prostitute Way. After that the gambler would say, "Let's play a game and see who wins." The wizard knew he always won; so they started with the shinny game. One game after another the gambling wizard lost. The last was the tree-breaking game. The only possessions One-Who-Wins-You had left were his wife and children. "We will bet our wives and children," he said.

The two trees were at the far end of the race track. They got set, and the race was on. About halfway, One-Who-Wins-You shot a witch missile at his brother's feet, but he missed. That was how he had won all the races from his opponents before. However, his twin brother caught the missile and tossed it back to the wizard's feet. By that time the honest twin was ahead. Before he got to the finish line Horned Toad was running beside him. Horned Toad told the twin that of the two trees ahead one was a cane reed tree and the other was a hard oak tree. Horned Toad pointed out the oak. Usually

317

the one who broke the tree lost. The twin was struggling with the oak when One-Who-Wins-You got to his tree and broke it without a struggle. We all know the hard oak cannot be broken; so we know that the gambling wizard lost everything he had, even his wife, children and home.

His honest twin brother had redeemed all the people, with their belongings, as well as their children and wives. Everyone was happy. One-Who-Wins-You was downhearted. He told his brother to take good care of his family, and he began to speak to the people, but they ignored him. "Send him away," they shouted. "Put him on a strong swift Black Arrow and shoot him up yonder into space," they shouted.

318 Ages ago the Holy People used holy arrows. The gambling wizard was placed on the arrow. Before he left, he yelled, "Even if you send me far into space I will return. I will see you, and I will be above you. Wait and see." (The words he spoke were prophetic about today's airplanes, and they help me to believe that he must have been a white man.)

One-Who-Wins-You also said to the people, "In the future there will be round objects which the people will play games with to win. They will be a reminder of me." We know that today many pieces of game equipment are round—like baseballs, volleyballs, basketballs and golfballs. People play with them to win. They all are part of the white man's games that have been introduced to us. Thus, there are many round objects which remind us of the gambling wizard who became a loser. Whatever is round belongs to him. He also said that the lightning flash would be his power, and also the wind. He added, "When I return, everything that is round will roll beneath you with the wind. We will travel on the rolling rainbow arc." Today, that is all very obvious. We travel on the highways with yellow and white stripes. A highway reminds us of the rainbow as it curves. The round objects under us are the wheels of whatever we travel in—such as trucks, automobiles, trains, bicycles and other things; and we travel with the wind. The lightning, I also know, has to do with electric current. People have lights in their homes and business places, along with all kinds of electrical devices. We have electricity everywhere today. Taking these things together, One-Who-Wins-You must have been a white man. We Navajos also call the radio "Wind that Talks." It is a white man's invention. That is all I will tell about the gambling wizard.

The Toadlena, N. M., BIA school, from the north.

Another traditional custom our elders followed was that when a **319** child was born a man of wisdom was chosen to consecrate the infant. The man was there with the relatives during the delivery. It was a very special occasion. When born, the infant was given the sap juice of the inner white bark of the piñon tree to extract all the foreign substances from its stomach. Corn pollen, diluted with water, was fed to the baby. Right at high noon the father took the infant to an especially nice place where the man of wisdom offered a blessing prayer for a long time. A prayer might go like this:

Today we are blessed with this beautiful baby.
May his feet be to the east,
His right hand to the south,
His head to the west,
His left hand to the north.
May he walk and dwell on Mother Earth peacefully.
May he be blessed with good health.
May he be blessed with assorted soft valued goods.
May he be blessed with precious variegated stones.
May he be blessed with fat sheep in variation.
May he be blessed with good swift horses in variation.
May he be blessed with many respectful relatives and
    friends.
I have asked all these blessings with reverence and holiness.
My mother is the earth; the sky, the sun and the moon
    together are my father.
I am the essence of life which is old age.
I am the source of happiness in beauty—
All is peaceful. All is in beauty,
All is in harmony, all is in happiness. Amen.

With such a blessing the child would grow up healthy and strong. Later, he would have all the good things he had been blessed with as a baby. These blessings are not practiced now.

I have told you about the blessing of a new-born child. It is said that at that time his future life was set for him. If he abided by the goodness of life he was surely bound to live long. It was—and still is—an obviously true fact, if you think about it. If a person reaches old age, he knows whether he has had a fruitful life. He also knows that it soon will close where the lifeline ends. Those who have complicated lives usually do not live long. Somewhere along the way their lifeline breaks. Sometimes lives are troubled by sickness. We may recover with modern medicines or with our own healing ceremonies. But, if all fails, the lifeline breaks, and it makes no difference that life is precious and holy. We can't take it for granted.

About religion, our people in the past always took it seriously. Today, that has changed, I regret to say. Our people used to pray after they enjoyed a meal, whether it was just bread and coffee or a real feast. A person would pick up the fire poker and push all the charcoal back into the fire after it had served its purpose, and then give a prayer of thanks. A prayer might go like this, "May I live in prosperity, in beauty, in happiness." These prayers were spoken with great reverence. I could tell you many more things, but what I have said are examples.

All kinds of stories were told by our elders. In fact, some Navajo myth-stories and some white men's Bible stories are similar in ways. I say this because I have read the Holy Bible, and I know. Visiting missionaries that have come among us have told us, too. The David and Goliath story is an example. This I want you to think about.

Long ago, the main weapons the white man had were the spear and the sword. When there was a conflict those weapons were used. It was said that in one army there was a giant who wore a thick armor which weapons could not penetrate; and he killed many people. The battles were fought on foot. There were no vehicles of any kind. A boy named David was a sheepherder, and he did not have any armor or a regular weapon. The only thing he had for his protection and his sheep's protection was a bola. The Lord gave him strength. David arrived very early at the battle ground near the River Jordan, and he prayed. The Lord blessed the stones that David was going to use. The giant led the soldiers. He was huge and stood with his hands on his hips. He thrust his spear into the ground. David got a stone, put it in the thong (bola) and swung it. The first stone missed, but the second hit the giant on the forehead, and he fell to the ground—dead.

In our story Enemy Slayer, or Monster Slayer, also killed a giant named *Yé'iitsoh* close to Mount Taylor and Grants, N.M., at a place called Red Mountain, near the lava beds. His first lightning arrow did not kill the giant, but, when he threw his knife, it hit *Yé'iitsoh*, who fell to the ground, dead. He also slew many other monsters.

Another story that is similar is about when the People were threatened by the flood after Coyote stole the offspring of the Water Creature just as the People were emerging to the upper world. The Bible story of Noah and his ark is about how most of the earth's inhabitants were destroyed by the water. The people laughed at Noah when he was building his huge ark, but the flood did come. Noah saved all kinds of the animals in twos, male and female, and also the birds and all other living things. **321**

That is how I mean the stories are almost alike—David killing the giant with a bola, Enemy Slayer killing the giant with a thrown knife, and both warriors missing their first shots, David with a bola and Monster Slayer with an arrow. Stories like those are very precious to our people and we need to preserve them. That is why our leaders should consider the stories worthy of being printed and preserved; and I am glad it is being done.

I am very concerned about the matter, and I often wish that more could be accomplished to restore our culture and religion. We want only the best for our people.

I realize that many Navajos know little about our religion and legends, and that is why I am telling you all these things.

On the subject of drinking, a person who does not drink might look at one who often is drunk and wonder how that person became an alcoholic. Drinking among our people is one of the biggest problems they face. We have heard many stories about Coyote who got involved in numerous mischievous actions. I will tell you about when he became intoxicated, and I want Navajos to think about it. It is said that Coyote was the first person who suggested that anyone get drunk. In those days it was called "spitting the medicine into the mouth of another." The people used all the plants that were poisonous, like poison ivy, sow thistle, big thumb, vine plant, jimson weed and others that make people go loco. Coyote, long ago, advised the people who had such plants to bring them to a suggested location called Mancos Creek. The people came with all the plants and put them together in a large container to be boiled. After the mixture had cooled, it was poured into an animal-skin water bag, with a gourd ladle beside it. Then the people waited for Coyote who was late in arriving. By the way, his other name was First Scolder. When he finally arrived he said, "I thought you all would be celebrating by now. What were you waiting for?" They replied, "You were the one who suggested this; so we waited. You may have the first dip." Coyote quickly grabbed the dipper and filled it. He gulped it all down too fast. Some dripped from his mouth. Not long afterward his eyes crossed, he began to stagger and his mouth foamed. He said, "I am about to scream." He was drunk. He jabbered senselessly and did scream. The people stared at him and said, "He has gone crazy." Give him a neutralizer.

322

There was another animal called White Tail who thought of a cure. He yelled, "Don't just look at him. Do something."

"He will pass out soon," said someone.

"What is the neutralizer?" asked another.

White Tail answered, "Grind some sacred stones into a fine powder and add cool, clear water."

The people quickly did it and poured the fluid down Coyote's throat. The sacred stones were white shell, turquoise, abalone shell and canal coal. Coyote soon became himself again. Thereafter, that neutralizer was used whenever someone became loco from poisonous plants. Many young people do not know about these things. As I said before, many of them go loco with alcohol and do not understand how to control it. The evil habit has corrupted our people, resulting in much suffering and heartache.

Coyote was a sly person who thus started the people on the drinking habit. Now we have the sickness called alcoholism which has spread widely among Indians (and almost all other people), both young and old. The horrible habit can destroy a person's physical being and dignity and make him an unwanted and dangerous person. I hope that our young people will concentrate on this problem very carefully. Someday they will remember what I have explained to them and say, "Grandfather told us about this at Navajo Community College, and it was printed in a book." It will make me very happy that the students have listened. Then, again, their children will say, "My parents taught me these things," and those parents also will

Soon after Coyote began to drink the powerful liquor his mouth foamed, and he was drunk. He screamed and jabbered senselessly while the people stared at him and said, "He is crazy..."

be proud and happy. I know because I have had the experience my- **323** self. My parents taught and lectured me. How else could I be telling these stories and offering this advice?

I reformed myself from drinking in 1936 while I was still young, and I never have touched the stuff to this day. My elders lectured me sternly about it, and I listened and decided to lay off. In other words, I followed their teachings. Today's generation needs to know, also, that wine and liquor destroy. Without them a person will have a happier life, and a clear mind will help him or her to learn more. If a person drinks, it confuses the mind and makes a "scatterbrain." A good sound-minded person is more successful and can achieve his goals.

Drinking alcoholic beverages also is very dangerous, especially in the winter. One might "pass out" and freeze to death. Driving while intoxicated is a real killer, not only for the driver, but for others with him or her and for innocent victims in another car. Many do not realize that all this is extremely serious. It is said that drinking makes one forget problems, but, actually, it just adds more problems. Some say that one can drink for pleasure, but we see poor, sick, drinking people, some of whom hardly have had a decent meal for days. We can see that they probably will not reach the old age stage; and we wonder where the pleasure is.

I do not smoke or chew tobacco, either. The doctors advise us that those things are harmful, and that is another reason why I have lived this long.

Coming back to the subject of ceremonies, many stories are affiliated with them. There are different branches to most ceremonies, and each has its own stories. For instance, the Blessing Way is divided into the Chief Blessing Way, the Valued Possession Blessing Way and a Blessing Way for Increasing Livestock, which includes wildlife. (The last one is used only when especially requested.)

We live by keeping the holiness of these beautiful songs. We, who have a sincere knowledge of various ceremonies, offer our services to the people who need us. Some medicine men have great respect for our ceremonies. Others do it only for the money and do not really care to help the people. I am quite aware of the statement often heard, "Nothing is holy now." We who still have faith in our religion know that EVERYTHING is holy. How else can we be alive. The air we breathe is holy, the natural spring is holy, childbirth is holy. My statements all go back to the traditional training by our elders.

I think sadly of all the important ceremonies our forefathers knew and how some are now extinct. How many more will become unknown when those who have the knowledge are gone and no one has learned them? We elders are aware that this is happening, and we are thinking about what we ought to be doing about the problem. As I said, there are many branches in our healing ceremonies; and only three medicine men are left who know the Male Beauty Way Chant which connects with the Mountain Top Way. There is a man named Larry Encino from Cañoncito, N.M., who is of the Salt People, a

324

man named Old Cowboy (his English name is Mike Wilson) and myself, Tom Ration. We are the only ones living who have this knowledge.

Navajos love to attend the beautiful exhibition of the Corral
Dance, and, again, there are only five medicine men left with knowledge of it. Do you see my point? I have been pleading with the
Navajo leaders, but they do not seem to be concerned very much
about all this. There should be a better program to preserve our
heritage. We hear many words, but we see only a little action. I am
certain some way could be found to meet our need to preserve
these parts of our culture—that is, in addition to what already is
being done by Navajo Community College and other places.

As I have said, it is frightening to think about people being
helpless without our healing ceremonies. The two most used ceremonies are the Enemy Way and the Night Way Chants. Others are
the Male and Female Shooting Way, Navajo Wind Way Chant, Mountain Top Way and the Diagnostician Rituals. How long will we have
these ceremonies? The skills are vanishing with the older medicine
men. Even the Blessing Way, which is the most common, may vanish,
too. The situation, as it stands now, is that only a few conduct this
ceremony with reverence. We can see for ourselves that the few Night
Way Chant medicine men have heavy schedules of requests for
ceremonies. This shows the crisis we face.

I have many stories and songs which were taught to me by my
elders, but hardly anyone has asked me to re-tell them until just
recently. Now I am recording some of the material.

The sacred songs have done wonders for our people by increasing the population to a great number.

Many years back, the elders told stories about how the horse
was created. the Navajos once were afraid of horses and sheep. In
the stories about the monster era there were hoofed animals called
the Twelve Antelopes who trampled people to death. That was why
the Navajos were afraid of all hoofed animals at first.

But the Holy Divinity created the sheep and the horse, and they
were granted to the people to use. At first, the animals roamed the
mountain ranges, such as the La Platas. That is when the horse and
sheep songs first were sung, and the animals appeared before the
singers like tame ones, and they became domestic. These songs are
all in the Blessing Way. Before long, the animals were used for food,
clothing, income and transportation.

325

In the past the Navajos raced horses. The people took their horses to large gathering places like Squaw or Yei-be-chai dances where they had those activities. Everyone enjoyed watching because it was good entertainment, and the more prosperous Navajos bet worthwhile goods.

Let me tell another story, one about the first fire poker. It was made from a branch of a tree that was pointing to the east. That poker, or igniter, was made down in the underworld. It is told how, long ago, the people ate raw food. There was no fire to cook it, and when they ate raw meat the blood trickled down from their mouths. It also has been said that when they ate raw meat they developed a strong sense of smell.

One day Big Fly said to the people, "We will soon discover a firemaking thing." He told someone to get two smooth flint rocks. He rubbed the two rocks together vigorously, and sparks flew from them. Then he asked for some cedar bark. He rubbed pieces together until the bark became soft, and then he put a little pile of it on the ground. Again, he rubbed the flint stones real close to the soft, dry bark. The fire sparks flew into the bark which began to smoke. He blew upon it, and that was how fire first was made. The first fire was sacred. After that, the tinder box and the fire drill were invented. For the drill, a yucca plant's long stalk, very flammable when dry, was used. That method of igniting was called "fire struck with a drill." In our legends it generally was used in a fire ceremony, along with a firedrilling song.

Nowadays, prior to performing this ritual, all remains of a fire that had been started with ordinary matches is removed from the fireplace before starting the fire ceremony which has been greatly in use.

Other ceremonies also are used for healing, besides those I named before. They include the Ghost Way chant. Some chants involve the fire ceremony. Other chants commonly used are the Snake Way, the Beauty Way, the Upward Reaching Way, the Ant Way and others.

At a fire ceremony store-bought matches are NOT used to ignite the fire; the tinder box method generally is used. The ceremony usually lasts four days. The ashes are removed daily and taken to all four cardinal directions—to the east one day, the south the next day, and so on. The firewood used in the ceremony is a special kind. We do not burn big logs or chopped wood. First, we break the

326

dried twigs of junipers from beneath the green living ones. A large bundle is gathered for that purpose daily for four days. As I said, we follow what the Holy People did ages ago. We have respect for our healing ceremonies, and most of us have no intention to misuse them. But there have been some reckless persons who have done wrong by their foolishness.

The stories we tell were recited by our elders from generation to generation, on down the line. They were not kept in written books.

The stories I have told for many years are educational, especially for Navajos today. People should think very carefully about what I have said and see if it means anything to them. Whether the words I have spoken are interesting or boring, I believe I have revealed some information which other consultants or elders never have told. I have done it so that Navajos will be able to know more of their culture, and then I hope they realize how important I consider the Navajo Nation's growth and development. Telling long legends is very tiresome to all concerned. It becomes monotonous and makes a listener restless and sometimes sleepy. I know that if I should give an entire story at one time anyone listening would be fast asleep before I got one-third of the way through it; and, if people took recesses, they would forget some parts of the story I had told them. All legends include songs that cannot be left out of them. So, if done absolutely right, it takes several days and nights without a rest. That was the way my elders told their stories to me, but now listeners like to rest during the day.

About our own traditional culture, those of us who have gone through hardships use our experiences when teaching the young people. We have struggled to live and it has been well worth it. We relate background so that our young people will realize how fortunate they are. If we compare the white man's culture and the Indian's culture, we find some similarities. I know this because I compared what I learned in school to my traditional education at home. One problem is that the majority of school children today have little or no knowledge about their native Indian culture. However, some are now beginning to ask questions. Years ago, the elders were very good at telling stories to the children. Now, many of these people are gone. Also, almost all of the original Navajo scholars are gone. Probably, those who remain have told stories similar to mine.

327

As I have said before, our young people now should learn their native culture along with the white man's culture. That is very important. Navajo elders of my age level understand it because people are getting fewer who still know the various ceremonies, the two most valued of which are very holy to us. They are the Enemy Way and the Night Way. There are medicine men who still have great respect for these ceremonies and who conduct them with their utmost sincerity and reverence. Long ago, when I was a young lad, I remember a grandfather named Cut-Hair-Bangs-Man who performed the Night Way Chant perfectly. He took great pride and care in seeing that nothing went wrong during this sing or chant. I also had a paternal grandfather named His-Money-Man who had great knowledge of the ceremony called "Bring Down the Eagles." I do not believe there is another person who could perform such a sacred ritual and always get results. He sang powerful chants and used impressive prayers to lure the huge eagles down to the ground. There was a great demand for the eagle feathers which were used in many of our ceremonies. Another important part of the eagle is the gall. It is vital medicine used as a remedy against the witch cult. When a person has this in his possession, he is not harmed by frenzy or other harmful witchcrafts.

328

Next, I will tell about the origin of silversmithing as I heard it. There was a Chicano who used Mexican silver to make jewelry, and he taught the art to some Navajos around his area. One of the outstanding silversmiths on the Navajo Reservation has been Ambrose Roanhorse who was just a boy when he learned the art. The early silversmiths made horse bits for their bridles and large conchos for their belts, as well as silver buttons to decorate the bridles. In the early days turquoise was not common. The stones were hard to get; so only a few pieces of jewelry were made with turquoise. Later, it became fairly plentiful, and Navajo silversmiths began to use it in large quantities. I became a silversmith when I was about 23 years old, in the 1920s. Today, my children have become silversmiths because I have taught them. They are self-supporting and can take good care of their families. It can be a fine money-making art and business.

Skills like that were what we learned from our elders. I remember them saying, "Learn how to be a silversmith so we can have concho buttons on our bridles." Many Navajos have become silversmiths; and all Indian stores carry a lot of Indian-made jewelry. But,

My grandfather knew a sacred ritual and powerful chants which he sang and used, with prayers, to lure huge eagles down to earth. There was a great demand for eagle feathers.

I became a silversmith when I was 23 years old (in the early 20s); and today several of my children have become silversmiths because I taught them. They are able to take good care of their families.

330

instead of the Indians making good profits, they help to make the white traders rich. This has happened because we have forgotten the songs of the soft goods and of the sacred stones. We are deprived of the riches by our own carelessness. This also goes for the sheep and horses. It was said long ago that when a person sings the proper songs with reverence he is gifted with goodness and blessed with horses and sheep.

About sandpaintings, those which we see hung as pictures are not completed, nor are they the right ones. All the ceremonies the Holy People did long ago are called "Chants in the Holy Way." Also, in all the ceremonies which include sandpaintings not one design ever is repeated exactly. The figures, lines, colors and sizes always differ, at least a little bit. Medicine men who have this wonderful knowledge have spent a long time, have memorized all the details and know exactly what to put into, and not put into, the sandpaintings. The pictures are right in their minds. They instruct assistants exactly how to make the figures, colors and sizes, as designs appear in their minds and how the paintings are supposed to be made. Medicine men have names for everything pictured, and each sandpainting has a name. I could tell you more about this subject, but it would take a lot of time.

At my age I often think about how conditions were in the past. One can see a wide difference in comparing the past with today. When elders are asked to tell about their history or childhood days, their eyes glisten with tears. All of the Navajos' sufferings to survive have made it possible for our children to learn. We older Navajos envy today's children and wish we were young again, able to grab at all the opportunities that are before the younger people.

There was a great leader not long ago who was known very well throughout the Navajo Nation. Even as a young man he was a real chief. I knew him when he became the Tribal Chairman. He was Henry Chee Dodge. The people in our area named him White-Boy-Who-Plans. Mr. Dodge helped his people a lot. Other Tribal Chairmen were Sam Ahkeah, J. C. Morgan and others who followed them. Today, the Tribal Chairman, Peter MacDonald, also is a great leader. **331**

We elect our Tribal Council members according to certain standards. Then we know if (or at least hope) that they are really capable of helping the people who rely on their honesty and immediate attention when situations and problems arise.

About higher learning, our leaders planned and worked very hard to start and maintain Navajo Community College for the young people from all tribes and nationalities so that they could obtain a higher education here on the Reservation. We do not want our elders to be disappointed. Students can show their appreciation by their efforts and determination to make it a fine college. Our present leaders expect even better leadership in the future; and students' scholastic achievements will give them that ability. Our leaders want more graduated from the College so that they will know their efforts are not wasted. This should be kept in mind. The College opened at Many Farms, Arizona, in 1969; and it later moved to a beautiful big new campus at Tsaile, also in Arizona and near the center of the Reservation.

Many grade and high schools on the Reservation now realize that their native heritage is very important to all Indian students, and they include Indian studies in their programs. Navajo Community College offers many such courses, too. What does Navajo Community College mean? My definition is that it is a place for higher learning, where our young people can advance their education in more professional ways. The principles and knowledge that our

Mesa Elementary School at Shiprock, N.M., as it is today.

young men and women learn there certainly will benefit them and their children whom they also will teach.

The College is a good school for higher education, and Navajo elders have wanted the "Indian Studies" program to be the core of the College. It is up to the individual student, though, to learn.

I am not well acquainted with the College, and I do not know much about what courses are taught. But I do know that students go there on their own because they want to learn more that will help them in the future. Many have scholarships, or their tuition and expenses are paid. I would advise them to think seriously as to why they are in College, and I admire their ambition to get a higher education. I hope they all will accomplish their goals.

It is good that the College has Navajo and other Indian Studies as part of its curriculum. That is what the Navajo elders want the young people to learn—who they are (and then never change).

Many Indian consultants are invited to the campus to speak about their particular cultures. They tell accounts of Indian history, character, etc.; and we do not want the students to forget them. They must be re-told to their children. We must cherish this information for our own protection and for our loved ones. We should say, "More power to what we know." The stories can be repeated over and over. If we elders keep them to ourselves, in about 15 or 20 years we will not have them. They will be gone. There will not be any songs or prayers because the legends go together with them. One cannot exist without the other. We must be grateful that we have these stories now, and we must not allow them to vanish. The Holy People granted the ceremonies to the Navajos to be cherished and used. So, consultants go to Navajo Community College's classes to tell of all these things.

The reason many young people today lack a proper knowledge of Indian culture and religion is because they are brought up in

*A scene at Shiprock, N. M., showing part of the high
school (in background) and administration building.*

homes where the parents themselves prefer the Anglo culture and
where the children are put in school and get Anglo learning at a
very early age. Today we live in a white man's world.

The Navajo people have greatly improved their living conditions
in recent years. Only a small proportion still live in hogans, and they
mostly are in remote areas. However, far too many still live poorly.
I hope all of them will have good homes soon. On the other hand,
there are some who prefer to live in the traditional ways.

Our forefathers struggled for survival so that we could enjoy
what we have now. I should think the least a Navajo can do is to be
grateful to his ancestors and remember what they stood for. We
should look back and see how they suffered and how today we are
so comfortable, with all kinds of wonderful opportunities knocking
on our doors. We should be ready to accept them, and the future
should be thought about.

We have hospitals now where the doctors use modern equipment to diagnose all kinds of ailments, and where there are medicines
for helping the sick to recover. For a very long time, however,
Navajos were born at home in hogans (or elsewhere), and they survived. There are Navajo medicinal herbs which are very effective. We
who are Navajo doctors or healers (medicine men) know all the various plants and herbs used for food and medicines. There are seeds
and roots, various wild berries and fruits, as well as nuts. Some are
eaten fresh, while others are dried and stored for winter use. Our
elders of long ago stored their foods in hidden caves or in dugout
pits which were concealed carefully.

Concerning automobiles, when they first came to the Reservation, Mr. Stalker had one. When he came "putt, putt" down the
road, the boys all ran alongside yelling with excitement. It was new
and strange—on wheels, with a motor.

I had a related elder named Paul Charley who was the first Navajo around Crownpoint who owned a car. He was a wealthy Navajo sheep raiser. He had more than 2,000 head of sheep and many good horses. He operated a huge ranch, and he lived in a large house.

In those days we used kerosene to light our homes and the school. There was no electricity until later. Finally, we heard that electricity was being installed at Crownpoint. That was about 1914. We were all gathered in a large assembly room. Men had put in the electrical fixtures and were all set to turn on the lights. A band was playing. It was a very special occasion. We were all told to look at the ceiling. Someone started the generator, and the bulbs slowly lit, one after the other with a very dim light. Everyone yelled and clapped hands with excitement. It was the first electricity at Crownpoint, and I saw it. It was a white man with an incredibly scientific mind who invented the use of electricity. A short time later, the light bulbs and the power improved and were much brighter.

334

Next, a telephone was installed at the school. The teacher let us listen to someone talking at the other end, which was strange and unbelievable. The sound was weak, and we barely could hear it. We were told that it came from Albuquerque. Of course, that, too, improved every year. Those early telephones were operated by batteries. Today, telephones are found almost everywhere.

When it comes to these wonderful things, the white man works hard and accomplishes what he wants; and he gets what he wants with his earnings. Today some of us have learned to do that; and, yet, other Navajos are failures.

Time marches on, and lives change with progress. The white man's scientific techniques have produced many tremendous develop-

Foliage of Mormon tea plant.

ments. As traditionalists, little do we know what the future holds and what is at stake concerning our culture and values. The modern machine age has made life easy—in fact, too easy, for us. We depend too much on mechanical contraptions to do most of our work. Then we sit at home comfortably and get fat. We do not use our muscles much these days. Some Navajos are too weak and irresponsible to carry on their proper tasks. Those of us who barely had an education wish we could have learned more. Today one can put a small child in school, and, before long, he will begin to speak English. In earlier days, it took children a longer time. Why was it that way? Can it be because today's child has more intelligence? Or is he or she just getting a better start? Or was it because long ago children were slower in learning? Or was it the teachers' fault? Anyway, I am glad that I am able to speak English and Navajo.

335

I have lived a long time, and I am grateful to the Good Spirit. I often have considered what benefits I got from all that my parents taught me, such as exercising at dawn which immunized me to extremely cold weather. Altogether, my early life and training gave me a long and happy and healthy existence.

Now that I have talked at great length, I hope that Navajo young people and others will remember what I have said, especially my pleading to refrain from drinking alcoholic beverages. They will live longer if they don't smoke or drink. Protection prayers will guide them on their journeys through life. A person who has self-respect and a well-adjusted and stimulated mind is likely to succeed. He pays attention to elders like me and keeps their teachings in his head.

I pray that I have taught my readers something that they have wanted to know.